Thomas Cranmer

Thomas Cranmer's place in English history is firmly established, yet the complexities of his character have remained obscure and he continues to be one of the most problematic figures of the Tudor period. Susan Wabuda's biography sheds fresh light not only on the private Cranmer, but also on the qualities that enabled him to master a shifting political landscape and to build a new English Church.

Athletic by nature, Cranmer enjoyed hunting and he was a keen collector of books. He was blessed with several lifelong friendships and twice risked his career by marrying the women he loved. A skilled debater and a deft politician, Cranmer sought to balance his long-term plans for the Church against the immediate demands of survival at court. Obedient at all times, yet never entirely trustworthy, he had to reconcile the will of his God with the will of the monarch he served.

For too long, Cranmer's legacy has overshadowed the life of the man himself, but this new biography enriches and extends our understanding of both. Accessible and informative, it will be essential reading for students and scholars of the English Reformation and the Tudor age.

Susan Wabuda is Associate Professor of History at Fordham University, New York, USA. Her previous works include *Preaching During the English Reformation* and she is currently writing a new comprehensive study of Hugh Latimer.

ROUTLEDGE HISTORICAL BIOGRAPHIES

Series Editor: Robert Pearce

Routledge Historical Biographies provide engaging, readable and academically credible biographies written from an explicitly historical perspective. These concise and accessible accounts will bring important historical figures to life for students and general readers alike.

In the same series:
Bismarck by Edgar Feuchtwanger (second edition 2014)
Calvin by Michael A. Mullett
Oliver Cromwell by Martyn Bennett
Edward IV by Hannes Kleineke
Elizabeth I by Judith M. Richards
Emmeline Pankhurst by Paula Bartley
Franco by Antonio Cazorla-Sanchez
Gladstone by Michael Partridge
Henry V by John Matusiak
Henry VI by David Grummitt
Henry VII by Sean Cunningham
Henry VIII by Lucy Wooding (second edition 2015)
Hitler by Michael Lynch
John F. Kennedy by Peter J. Ling
John Maynard Keynes, by Vincent Barnett
Lenin by Christopher Read
Louis XIV by Richard Wilkinson
Martin Luther by Michael A. Mullet (second edition 2014)
Martin Luther King Jr. by Peter J. Ling (second edition 2015)
Mao by Michael Lynch (second edition 2017)
Marx by Vincent Barnett
Mary Queen of Scots by Retha M. Warnicke
Mary Tudor by Judith M. Richards
Mussolini by Peter Neville (second edition 2014)
Nehru by Benjamin Zachariah
Neville Chamberlain by Nick Smart
Oliver Cromwell by Martyn Bennett
Queen Victoria by Paula Bartley
Richard III by David Hipshon
Stalin by Christopher Read
Thatcher by Graham Goodlad
Trotsky by Ian Thatcher
Thomas Cranmer by Susan Wabuda

Forthcoming:
Churchill by Robert Pearce
Gandhi by Benjamin Zachariah
Khrushchev by Alexander Titov
Wolsey by Glenn Richardson

Thomas Cranmer

Susan Wabuda

Routledge
Taylor & Francis Group

LONDON AND NEW YORK

DA
317.8
.C8
W33
2017

First published 2017
by Routledge
2 Park Square, Milton Park, Abingdon, Oxon OX14 4RN

and by Routledge
711 Third Avenue, New York, NY 10017

*Routledge is an imprint of the Taylor & Francis Group,
an informa business*

British Library Cataloguing in Publication Data
A catalogue record for this book is available from the British
Library

Library of Congress Cataloging in Publication Data
Names: Wabuda, Susan, author.
Title: Thomas Cranmer / Susan Wabuda.
Description: Abingdon, Oxon ; New York, NY : Routledge, [2017] | Series:
Routledge historical biographies | Includes bibliographical references and index.
Identifiers: LCCN 2017002797| ISBN 9780415500777 (hardback : alk. paper) |
ISBN 9780415500784 (pbk. : alk. paper) | ISBN 9781315563633 (ebook : alk.
paper)
Subjects: LCSH: Cranmer, Thomas, 1489–1556. | Great Britain—
History—Tudors, 1485–1603—Biography. | Great Britain—Politics and
government—1509–1547. | Great Britain—Church history—16th century. |
Statesmen—Great Britain—Biography. | Bishops—England—Biography.
Classification: LCC DA317.8.C8 W33 2017 | DDC 283.092 [B]—dc23
LC record available at https://lccn.loc.gov/2017002797

ISBN: 978-0-415-50077-7 (hbk)
ISBN: 978-0-415-50078-4 (pbk)
ISBN: 978-1-315-56363-3 (ebk)

Typeset in Sabon LT Std
by diacriTech, Chennai

Printed and bound in Great Britain by
TJ International Ltd, Padstow, Cornwall

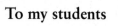

To my students

Contents

Acknowledgements   viii
Abbreviations   x
Genealogical tables   xiv
Chronology   xx

1 Introduction   1

2 Early life, 1489–1526   13

3 The king's 'great matter', 1527–1533   39

4 The new archbishop, 1533–1535   66

5 Thomas Cromwell ascendant, 1535–1537   98

6 Invincible Henry, 1538–1540   132

7 The Privy Council, 1540–1547   156

8 Edward VI and the *Book of Common*
  Prayer, 1547–1552   186

9 Oxford, 1553–1556   218

10 Thomas Cranmer's legacy for the English Church   242

Suggestions for further reading   249
Index   252

Acknowledgements

Over the years that I have studied Archbishop Thomas Cranmer and his place in the Reformation in England, I have incurred many debts. I am grateful to the following research institutions and to their helpful staffs:

Borthwick Institute of Historical Research, University of York
British Library (BL)
Cambridge University Library (CUL)
Folger Shakespeare Library, Washington, D.C.
Lambeth Palace Library (LPL)
The National Archives, London (Public Record Office) (TNA:PRO)
The Parker Library at Corpus Christi College, Cambridge

Fordham University released me from the classroom so that I could take up a Short-Term Fellowship at the Folger Shakespeare Library in the early months of 2013. I also was granted a Faculty Fellowship for the Fall 2014 semester and another leave at the end of 2015 so that I could bring this book to completion.

A selected portion of material intended for this book was presented as a paper before the Montreal British History Seminar and McGill's Centre for Research on Religion in March 2014. I am grateful to Bob and Ann Tittler, Torrance Kirby, and the participants of the Seminar for their helpful suggestions. I also wish to acknowledge Professor Mark Ormrod and the Archbishops' Registers of the Diocese of York 1225–1646 Project.

Special thanks for their wise advice go to Professors Jane Dawson, Judith M. Richards, and Lucy Wooding. For their encouragement over many years, I wish to thank Susan Brigden; Peter Newman Brooks; Euan Cameron; Anne Dillon; Eamon Duffy; Lori Anne Ferrell; Thomas S. Freeman; Bartlett and Faye Gage; Paul Hammer; Alasdair Hawkyard; Norman L. Jones; John Ryle Kezel; Peter Lake; Saskia Limbach; Scott C. Lucas; Joseph M. McShane, S.J.; Hilary Mantel; Peter Marshall; Ebru Turan; Andrew D. Pettegree; Alec Ryrie; David Starkey; John Vidmar, O.P.; Russell Wabuda; Stephen D. White; and David Whitford. I also wish to thank Albert Ryle Kezel for introducing me to the story of St. Barlaam of Antioch. I am also grateful for the helpful comments by the two anonymous readers of the manuscript of this book.

I also wish to remember many late friends and colleagues whose invaluable discussions helped to develop my thinking about Cranmer and the Reformation: Patrick Collinson, A. G. Dickens, G. R. Elton, Joan Henderson, E. W. Ives, Thomas F. Mayer, Eugene F. Rice, Conrad and Elizabeth Russell, R. W. Scribner, and Rosmarie Sunderland. Most especially, I am indebted to the late Maria Dowling for the references she gave me over the years when we discussed Cranmer's career. Readers will notice that I have departed substantially from some of the points made by Professor Collinson in his essay 'Thomas Cranmer and the Truth' in his collection *From Cranmer to Sancroft* (2007). I have departed as well from Diarmaid MacCulloch's *Thomas Cranmer: a Life* (1996).

The errors and omissions that will remain in my book are mine alone.

List of abbreviations

APC	*Acts of the Privy Council*, ed. J. R. Dasent, second series, vol. 1 (1542–1547), (London, 1890); vol. 2 (1547–1550), (London, 1890); vol. 3 (1550–1550), (London, 1891).
BIHR	Borthwick Institute of Historical Research, University of York
BL	British Library
CCCC	Corpus Christi College, Cambridge
Churchman and Scholar	*Thomas Cranmer: Churchman and Scholar*, eds. P. Ayris and D. Selwyn (Woodbridge, 1993).
Cranmer, *Lord's Supper*	*Writings and Disputations Relative to the Lord's Supper*, ed. J. E. Cox, Parker Society (Cambridge, 1844).
Cranmer, *Miscellaneous*	*Miscellaneous Letters and Writings*, ed. J. E. Cox, Parker Society (Cambridge, 1844).
Cranmer's Register	The Register of Archbishop Thomas Cranmer of Canterbury, LPL
CS	Camden Society
Duffy, *Altars*	E. Duffy, *The Stripping of the Altars: Traditional Religion in England c. 1400–c. 1580* (New Haven, 1992).
EHR	*English Historical Review*
FOR	*Faculty Office Registers 1534–1549*, ed. D. S. Chambers (Oxford, 1966).

Foxe 1563	John Foxe, *Actes and Monuments* (London: John Daye, 1563, *RSTC* 11222).
Foxe 1570	John Foxe, *Actes and Monuments (The Ecclesiasticall History)* (London: John Daye, 1570, *RSTC* 11223).
Foxe, *AM*	John Foxe, *Acts and Monuments*, ed. George Townsend, 8 vols. (London, 1843–1849).
Gardiner, *Letters*	*The Letters of Stephen Gardiner*, ed. James Arthur Muller (Cambridge, 1933).
Grace Book B I and *Grace Book B II*	*Grace Book B Part I and Part II: Containing the Proctors' Accounts of the University of Cambridge,* ed. M. Bateson, 2 vols. (Cambridge, 1903, 1905).
Grace Book Γ	*Grace Book Γ: Containing the Records of the University of Cambridge for the years 1501–1542,* ed. W. G. Searle (Cambridge, 1908).
HJ	*Historical Journal*
Ives, *Anne Boleyn*	E. Ives, *The Life and Death of Anne Boleyn 'The Most Happy'* (Oxford, 2005).
JEH	*Journal of Ecclesiastical History*
Lamb	J. Lamb, ed., *A Collection of Letters, Statutes, and other Documents from the MS Library of Corpus Christi College Cambridge* (London, 1838).
LAO	Lincolnshire Archives Office
'Life'	An anonymous biography of Cranmer, printed in *Narratives of the Days of the Reformation*, ed. J. G. Nichols (Camden Society, vol. 77, 1859), pp. 218–233.

LP	*Letters and Papers, Foreign and Domestic, of the Reign of Henry VIII*, eds. J. S. Brewer *et al.*, 21 vols. in 33 parts (London, 1862–1910).
LPL	Lambeth Palace Library
MacCulloch, *Cranmer*	D. MacCulloch, *Thomas Cranmer: A Life* (New Haven, 1996).
More, *Correspondence*	*The Correspondence of Sir Thomas More*, ed. E. F. Rogers (Princeton, 1947).
Morice	Ralph Morice's account of Cranmer's career, printed in *Narratives of the Days of the Reformation*, 234–72.
ODNB	*Oxford Dictionary of National Biography*
OL	*Original Letters Relative to the English Reformation*, ed. H. Robinson, 2 vols., PS (Cambridge, 1846–1847).
Parker	Matthew Parker, *De antiquitate Britannicae ecclesiae et priuilegiis ecclesiae Cantuariensis* (London: John Daye, 1572, *RSTC* 19292).
Pole's Register	The Register of Reginald Cardinal Pole, Archbishop of Canterbury, LPL
PS	Parker Society
Ridley, *Cranmer*	J. Ridley, *Thomas Cranmer* (Oxford, 1962).
RSTC	*The Short-Title Catalogue of Books Printed in England, Scotland, and Ireland … 1475–1640*, W. Pollard and G. R. Redgrave, comps., rev. K. F. Pantzer *et al.*, 3 vols. (London, 1976–1991).
Scarisbrick, *Henry VIII*	J. J. Scarisbrick, *Henry VIII* (Berkeley, 1968).
SCH	*Studies in Church History*
SCJ	*Sixteenth Century Journal*

TNA:PRO	The National Archives (Public Record Office), Kew, London
TRP	*Tudor Royal Proclamation*, ed. P. L. Hughes and J. F. Larkin, 3 vols. (London, 1964).
VCH	*Victoria County History*
Wilkins, *Concilia*	D. Wilkins, *Concilia Magna Britanniae et Hibernia*, vol. 3 (London, 1737).
Wriothesley, *Chronicle*	Charles Wriothesley, *A Chronicle of England During the Reigns of the Tudors*, ed. W. D. Hamilton, 2 vols. CS, new series, vol. 11 (1875) and vol. 20 (1877), referred to as vol. 1 and vol. 2.

Genealogical tables

THE CRANMER and HATFIELD GENEALOGIES

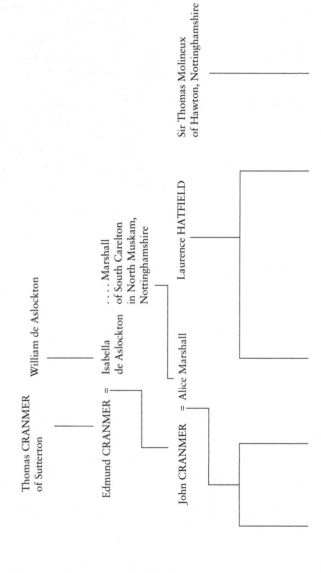

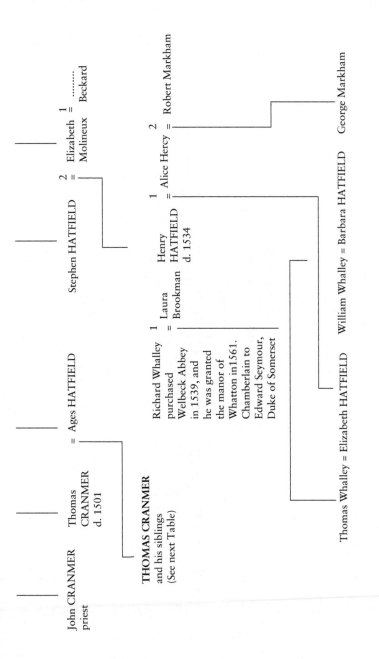

THE CRANMERS AND THEIR DESCENDENTS

THOMAS CRANMER = AGNES HATFIELD
d.1501

Joan =1 JOHN 2= Margaret | THOMAS | 2= Margaret EDMUND ALICE DOROTHY = Harold AGNES = Edmund | JANE =1 John | EMMOTT
Fretcheville CRANMER Fitzwilliam Joan =1 CRANMER Preu CRANMER num Roselh Cartwright Henry Monnings
.... b. 2 July 1489 = 2 Edward alive in d. 1554 2= Bingham
d. 21 March 1556 Whitchurch 1554
= 3 Bartholomew three MARGARET
Scott sons

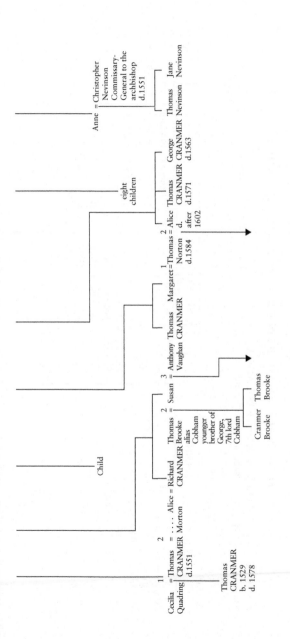

EUROPE'S RULING FAMILIES IN THE EARLY SIXTEENTH CENTURY

HABSBURG
Maximilian
Holy Roman
Emperor
d. 1519
= Mary
of
Burgundy
d. 1482

TRASTÁMARA
Isabella
queen
of
Castile
d. 1504
= Ferdinand
king of
Aragon
d. 1516
TRASTÁMARA

TUDOR
Henry VII = Elizabeth
king of   of York
England   d. 1503
d. 1509

Margaret
of Austria
d. 1530

Philip
of Burgundy
'the
Handsome
d. 1506
=

Juana
of Castile
d. 1555

Katherine
of Aragon
d. 1536
1 =
2 =

Arthur
d. 1502

Henry VIII
king of
England
d. 1547
2 = Anne
Boleyn
d.1536

STUART
James VI
king of
Scotland
1 =

Margaret
d. 1541
2 = Archibald
Douglas
earl of
Angus
d. 1557

Mary 'the
French
queen'
d. 1533
1 =

2 =

VALOIS
Louis XII
king of
France
d. 1515

Charles
Brandon
duke of
Suffolk
d. 1545

James V
kings of
Scotland
d. 1542
= Mary
of
Guise
d. 1560

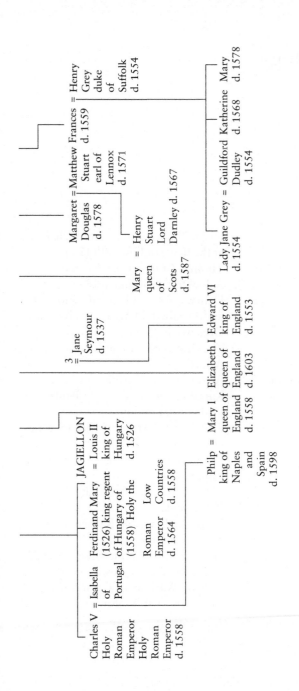

Charles V = Isabella
Holy   of
Roman   Portugal
Emperor
Holy
Roman
Emperor
d. 1558

JAGIELLON

Ferdinand Mary = Louis II
(1526)   king regent king of
of Hungary of   Hungary
(1558) Holy the   d. 1526
Roman   Low
Emperor Countries
d. 1564 d. 1558

3
= Jane
Seymour
d. 1537

Margaret = Matthew Frances = Henry
Douglas   Stuart   d. 1559   Grey
d. 1578   earl of   duke
          Lennox   of
          d. 1571   Suffolk
                              d. 1554

Philp = Mary I   Elizabeth I Edward VI
king of queen of queen of   king of
Naples   England   England   England
and   d. 1558   d. 1603   d. 1553
Spain
d. 1598

Mary = Henry
queen   Stuart
of   Lord
Scots   Darnley d. 1567
d. 1587

Lady Jane Grey = Guildford Katherine Mary
d. 1554   Dudley   d. 1568   d. 1578
                 d. 1554

Chronology

1485 August 22	Henry Tudor's victory over Richard III at the Battle of Bosworth Field.
1489 July 2	Thomas Cranmer was born in Aslockton, Nottinghamshire.
1491 June 28	Henry, the second son of Henry VII and Elizabeth of York, was born at Greenwich.
1501 May 27	The death of Cranmer's father in Aslockton.
1501 November 14	Arthur, Prince of Wales, married Katherine of Aragon in St Paul's Cathedral, London.
1502 April 2	The death of Arthur, Prince of Wales, at Ludlow.
1503	Cranmer's mother Agnes sent him to Cambridge.
1509 April 21	The death of Henry VII at Richmond.
1509 June 11	Henry VIII married Katherine of Aragon at Greenwich.
1509 June 24	Henry and Katherine were crowned in Westminster Abbey by Archbishop William Warham of Canterbury.
c. 1510	Cranmer's first brief marriage.

1511 August–1514 January	The humanist Desiderius Erasmus of Rotterdam made his second and longest visit to the University of Cambridge, where he occasionally lectured.
1511	Cranmer proceeded to the Bachelor's degree in Arts.
1515 March 24	Cranmer was admitted to the subdiaconate at York.
1515 April 7 Easter	Cranmer was made deacon in York Minster.
1515 June 2	Cranmer was ordained priest at the conventual church of the Dominican friars in York.
1515 summer	Cranmer proceeded to the Master's degree in Arts at Cambridge. He may have entered a fellowship at Jesus College around the same time.
1517 October 31	In Wittenberg, Martin Luther called for theological debates on points of doctrine.
1518	Cranmer's brother Edmund was ordained to the priesthood in York.
1520 June 15	Pope Leo X issued his bull *Exsurge domine* against Luther.
1520	Cranmer was elected University Preacher.
1521 January	Leo excommunicated Luther.
1521 May 12	Thomas Cardinal Wolsey burned Luther's books at Paul's Cross in London.
1521 May 25	The Holy Roman Emperor Charles V issued the Edict of Worms against Luther.
1521	Cranmer proceeded to the Bachelor's degree in Theology at Cambridge.
1526	Cranmer received his Doctorate in Theology.
1526 August	The Battle of Mohács.

1527 May	As papal legate, Wolsey convened an inquisition to examine the validity of the king's marriage to Katherine.
1527 May	The Sack of Rome.
1528 autumn	Cranmer was introduced to Thomas Cromwell for the first time.
1529 April	At the meeting of the Imperial Diet at Speyer, Lutheran princes and cities made their famous 'Protestation' in defending Luther.
1529 midsummer	The special legatine court was convened briefly at Blackfriars to consider the king's marriage, but it did not render a judgement.
1529 August	At Waltham, Cranmer suggested to Edward Fox and Stephen Gardiner that theologians should debate the doctrinal questions concerning the validity of Henry's marriage to Katherine.
1529 October	Wolsey was deprived of his offices, and Sir Thomas More became Lord Chancellor.
1529 November–December	As archdeacon of Taunton, Cranmer attended Convocation as the 'Reformation Parliament' began its sessions.
1530 January	Cranmer was sent to Rome, where he became Penitentiary for England. He returned to England at the end of the year.
1531 February	The defensive alliance of the League of Schmalkalden of Lutheran princes and cities was begun.
1531 August 19	Thomas Bilney was burnt near Norwich.
1531 October 11	Huldrych Zwingli was killed in the Battle of Kappel.

1532	Cranmer was sent as ambassador to Charles V's Court. In Nuremberg that summer, he married Margaret Preu, the niece of Andreas Osiander.
1532 May 15	More resigned the office of Lord Chancellor.
1532 August 22	The death of Archbishop Warham. At the end of the year, Cranmer was recalled to England.
1533 January	Cranmer arrived in London. Henry and Anne Boleyn's marriage was solemnized privately.
1533 March 30	At the Palace of Westminster, Cranmer was consecrated as the sixty-eighth archbishop of Canterbury.
1533 May 23	At Dunstable, Cranmer passed sentence that Henry had never been lawfully married to Katherine.
1533 June 1	Cranmer crowned Anne Boleyn in Westminster Abbey.
1533 July 4	John Frith was burnt at Smithfield.
1533 September 6	Anne gave birth to Elizabeth at Greenwich.
1533 December 3	Cranmer was enthroned at Canterbury.
1534 April 20	The execution of Elizabeth Barton, the 'Nun of Kent' and her associates at Tyburn.
1535 June 22	Bishop John Fisher was executed.
1535 July 6	Sir Thomas More was executed.
1536 January 7	The death of Katherine of Aragon at Kimbolton Castle.
1536 May 19	The execution of Anne Boleyn on the Green in the Tower of London.
1536 May 30	Henry married Jane Seymour.
1536–1537	The Northern Risings.
1537 October 12	The birth of Prince Edward.

1537 October 24	The death of Queen Jane.
1540 July 28	The execution of Thomas Cromwell on Tower Green. On the same day, Henry VIII married Katherine Howard at Oatlands Palace, Surrey.
1540 July 30	At Smithfield, Robert Barnes, Thomas Garrard, and William Jerome were burnt for heresy, while Thomas Abell, Edward Powell, and Richard Fetherstone were executed for treason.
1542 February 13	The execution of Katherine Howard on Tower Green.
1543 May	The King's Book was issued.
1543 July 12	Henry VIII married Katherine Parr.
1543	The 'Prebendaries' Plot' against Cranmer.
1545	The Council of Trent began.
1547 January 28	Henry VIII died at Whitehall.
1547	The first *Book of Homilies* was issued.
1549 June 9 Whitsunday	The first *Book of Common Prayer* was released. The Prayer Book risings followed immediately in Devon, Cornwall, and East Anglia.
1552 November 1	The second *Book of Common Prayer* was issued.
1553	The *Forty-Two Articles* were released.
1553 July 6	The death of Edward VI at Greenwich. His cousin, Lady Jane Grey, was proclaimed queen, but within a fortnight Mary led a successful coup against her.
1553 August 3	Queen Mary entered London in triumph.
1553 September 14	Cranmer was sent to the Tower.

1553 October 27	In Geneva, Michael Servetus was burnt by Calvin.
1555 October 16	Latimer and Ridley were burnt in Oxford.
1555 November 13	The death of Bishop Stephen Gardiner.
1556 March 21	Cranmer was burnt in Oxford.
1556 March 25	Reginald Cardinal Pole received the pallium as archbishop of Canterbury.
1558 November 17	The deaths of Mary and Cardinal Pole occurred on the same day Elizabeth became queen.
1559 December 17	Matthew Parker was consecrated archbishop of Canterbury.

1 Introduction

'O Lord which dost teach us that all our doings without charity are nothing worth: send thy Holy Ghost, and pour into our hearts that most excellent gift of charity, the very bond of peace and all virtues, without the which, whosoever liveth is counted dead before thee: Grant this for thy only son Jesus Christ's sake.'[1]

The present book is an introduction to the life and career of Thomas Cranmer (1489–1556), the sixty-eighth archbishop of Canterbury.[2] Although his *Book of Common Prayer* defined habits of worship for generations of English-speaking people, Cranmer is the most challenging of all the major figures of Tudor England to understand. His career was complicated and his decisions for the reform of the English Church were filled with contradictions that were hard to follow at the time and defy easy explanations even now.

Cranmer struggled against sustained opposition, not just from powerful people who remained satisfied with the Catholic Church in England as it was before he became archbishop of Canterbury in 1533, but he also faced resistance from his greatest benefactor, King Henry VIII (1491–1547). Only during the brief reign of Henry's son, Edward VI (1537–1553), could Cranmer align the English Church directly with the theology of continental leaders of Protestantism, including Martin Bucer (1491–1551) and Peter Martyr Vermigli of Strasbourg (1499–1562); Heinrich Bullinger of Zurich (1504–1575); and John Calvin of Geneva (1509–1564). The greatest of all of Cranmer's goals was to encourage the Protestant Churches to reconcile their doctrinal disagreements at meetings which he told Calvin should be a counterweight against the Council of Trent. But although Cranmer was successful, for the most part, in implementing reforms in Edward's Church, he did not have enough time to bring his full plans to fruition. He could not satisfy those who wanted a more complete reformation of the English Church. Cranmer was interrupted in 1553 when Henry's elder daughter Mary (1516–1558) took the throne after her young brother's untimely death.

By Acts of Parliament, Mary restored the Catholic Church in England. Cranmer was arrested and questioned. He was condemned as a traitor. After many months of imprisonment at Oxford, he was tried for heresy and convicted. He was a reluctant martyr and he made several recantations which threatened his legacy for the English Church. At Oxford on 21 March 1556, Archbishop Thomas Cranmer was brought to a stake and as he was burned, he made a heroic gesture of his faith. He was succeeded at Canterbury by Reginald Cardinal Pole (1500–1558). Had Mary and Pole lived longer, they would have completed their reversal of the reforms of Henry's and Edward's reigns and they would have done their utmost to reinvigorate Catholicism in England. In Mary's reign, Cranmer's archiepiscopate was reviled as a grievous mistake, and in time his memory would have been expunged.

But both Mary and Pole died within hours of each other on 17 November 1558. Elizabeth (1533–1603), the new queen, was Cranmer's god-daughter. A substantial portion of his vision for the English Church was reinstated during her reign, though probably less than what he would have achieved had he been permitted to complete the reformation he began.

Cranmer's story is important because his achievements transformed England culturally and politically in his lifetime and beyond. In a series of wrenching breaks with the past, he launched a distinctive national Church that was Protestant. He wanted England to have political independence from the papacy, but his greatest ambition, the motivating factor that dominated his career, was to save souls. He believed that salvation could be achieved by faith alone, which came through the spoken and written Word as a manifestation of the love God expressed towards humankind in the life and sacrifice of his son Jesus Christ. Cranmer raised four important pillars for the English Church: an English Bible (1539–1540); a *Book of Homilies* (1547) that taught faith and obedience; the *Book of Common Prayer* (1549, 1552); and the *Forty-Two Articles* (1552–1553) that defined essential tenets. They were his greatest achievements for the Church of England.

Cranmer's life has been difficult to understand not only because of the tumultuous reversals of the Tudor succession, but because great cultural gulfs divide his time from the present day. The importance of the Church as part of the British Establishment has receded since the 1960s. The *Book of Common Prayer* went through a controversial revision in 1928, and alternatives have replaced it since 1980 in many English parishes. Christianity is not definitive for many people in today's multicultural societies.

Some major figures of the sixteenth century, like William Shakespeare (1564–1616), have left few records for their lives beyond their printed works. In contrast, the array of sources that relate to Cranmer's career is unusually large and complex. Portions of his working papers survive, and they are exhaustive in their attention to detail on various questions of doctrine, most especially on the Eucharist.[3] His archiepiscopal Register, which recorded the business of the province and diocese of Canterbury, is in Lambeth Palace Library. Cranmer's correspondence was extensive. Scores of his letters survive in manuscript, and selections of them have been printed in modern editions.[4] An investigation he conducted in Kent in 1543 produced a thick bundle of documents that is kept in the Parker Library of Corpus Christi College, Cambridge.[5] Government documents for the reigns of the Tudors are in the State Papers collection of The National Archives (formerly known as the Public Record Office) and they are also in the Cotton and Royal collections of manuscripts in the British Library. Some of the most important have been in print since the early nineteenth century, but only now, through digitization, are many of the manuscripts associated with Cranmer's career becoming available to anyone who wishes to consult them through the Internet.

The printing press was the new medium in the sixteenth century, and Cranmer wrote or commissioned a large number of books in addition to those that have already been mentioned. Colleagues across Europe dedicated their books to him. Several printers were amongst his closest friends. At the time of his arrest in 1553 Cranmer possessed one of the finest libraries in Europe of more than seven hundred books and manuscripts.[6]

Cranmer's life and execution have been studied at length since John Foxe (1517–1587) began in 1556 his initial version of what ultimately became his vast ecclesiastical history, the *Actes and Monuments*, commonly known as Foxe's *Book of Martyrs*. In the reign of Elizabeth, Foxe received information from Cranmer's secretary Ralph Morice, as well as a 'Life' written by a member of the archbishop's household whose name we do not know.[7] The seventeenth-century antiquarian John Strype (1643–1737) compiled a flawed but influential biography of Cranmer.[8] At the beginning of the twentieth century, A. F. Pollard (1869–1948) presented Cranmer as a figure of the Establishment, and five decades later Jasper Ridley (1920–2004) examined his career with a more critical eye. Diarmaid MacCulloch's (b. 1951) magisterial, award-winning *Thomas Cranmer: A Life* appeared in 1996.[9]

Every generation asks its own questions about the past, and in the last three decades historians have furthered our understanding of Tudor England and the English Church. The present book will provide an introduction to Cranmer's life, but it will also advance original points of interest. My book is a fresh study that makes substantial departures from all previous accounts of Cranmer's career, including MacCulloch's biography. I give new attention to members of his family, like his brother Edmund (*c.* 1496–*c.* 1557), who helped to build the successes that the archbishop enjoyed. Cranmer was helped but also overshadowed by his friend and rival, Thomas Cromwell (*c.* 1485–1540), who, as the king's vicegerent, exercised power over the entire English Church on a scale that exceeded anything that Henry allowed to Cranmer. This book will also suggest that while Stephen Gardiner (*c.* 1495–1555), bishop of Winchester, was one of Cranmer's most important opponents late in their careers, the archbishop's early nemesis was the bishop of London, John Stokesley (1475–1539). Cranmer's greatest enemies aside from Stokesley and Gardiner were the popes of the time as well as the great Habsburg dynast Charles V (1500–1558), Holy Roman Emperor.

Cranmer's spiritual development has posed difficult problems for his biographers, and they have not always been able to agree on its stages. One of the purposes of this brief study is to provide a nuanced time frame for the theological shifts in the archbishop's thinking. This will, I hope, contribute to our understanding of the Church that Cranmer sought to build.

For *Thomas Cranmer* I have found source material that sheds new light on previously obscure portions of his life. The transitions that took place in his opinions had profound consequences for the English Church. We know now for the first time that Cranmer was ordained to the priesthood in 1515. Although he may have been conventionally devout at the beginning, as a theologian at Cambridge, he came under the influence of the writings of the humanist scholars Jacques Lefèvre (*c.* 1455–1536) and Desiderius Erasmus (*c.* 1467–1536). Through their studies in Greek and by using critical analysis, they aspired to understand the epistles of St Paul (d. *c.* 67) as the apostle meant them to be understood. They summoned their readers to the wellspring of the Gospel, and invited them to make deep explorations into the meanings of Scripture that would bring about spiritual renewal from within. Historians still do not completely agree on the best term that should be used to describe the earliest generation of scholars who were persuaded that Scripture defined faith, devotion, and practice, those who responded to Erasmus's and Lefèvre's call to biblicism. Although the word 'evangelicalism' has been imported from eighteenth-century studies and applied to the sixteenth, the term is not completely satisfactory. Evangelicalism as it is used in this book should not be confused with the fundamentalism of the present day.[10] At about the same time that Martin Luther (1483–1546) emerged in 1517 to disturb the stability of the western Church, Cranmer accepted the standards of biblicism that Erasmus and Lefèvre endorsed. However, Cranmer probably did not embrace Lutheran ideas until 1532, when Henry sent him as an ambassador to Nuremberg.

The contributions to Christian thought that Luther made over his long life were so prodigious that most of them cannot be taken up in this present book, but two features of his thinking will be essential to our understanding of Cranmer: the tenet of justification by faith alone, and Luther's insights about the

Eucharist. 'Justification' is another word for the salvation of the soul. Luther (like Lefèvre before him) emphasized a strand of thinking that he developed from the epistles of St Paul in the New Testament of the Bible. Luther measured the traditions of the Church against Scripture, and he wished to discard any practices that he thought were distractions from the meaning of Christ's sacrifice. Luther argued that Christians are justified or saved only by their faith, and that their very faith was itself a gift from God. The tenet of justification by faith alone challenged the teaching of the late medieval Church, which had built an entire economy of salvation on the pillars of faith and good works. Many varieties of good works in the late medieval Church were accredited with powers of salvation. Relieving the poor, supporting monks and nuns, building chantry chapels, or above all, providing for Masses, could help to move a soul after death out of the prison of purgatory into the unending bliss of heaven. People could promote the health of their own souls through good works, and they could also work for the salvation of the souls of departed members of their families or their friends by praying for them and by supplying Masses in their memory. Luther's criticism of the existing doctrine of works and his insistence that good works did not help the dead suffering in purgatory was an essential break in western thought. Luther believed that works were a sign of faith, and not in themselves the means to salvation. From 1532, Cranmer seems to have agreed with Luther about justification by faith alone.

Amongst the many controversies that Luther unleashed, none were more bitter than disagreements concerning the Eucharist. Luther challenged the tenet of transubstantiation. In the thirteenth century, St Thomas Aquinas (1225–1274) applied the logic of Aristotle (d. 322 BC) to the Mass. At the words of consecration, the bread and wine were transmuted, through the miracle of God, into the very same body and blood of Christ that had hung upon the Cross. The 'accidents' (or the appearance) of the bread and wine stayed the same, but the 'reality' of what they were changed at the consecration. Aquinas's explanation was almost exclusively accepted in the western Church until Luther objected that the Mass could not be a sacrifice. He argued that Jesus's sacrifice of himself on the cross was completely sufficient for the salvation of humankind. Luther argued that claims that the Mass could save souls were ill-founded and mistaken. Only faith in Christ's sacrifice saved.

Paradoxically, although Luther disparaged the tenet of transubstantiation, he and the Roman Catholic Church both taught that the presence of Christ in the Eucharist was 'real': in the sense that the actual body of Jesus Christ, born of the Virgin Mary, and the blood he shed when he was crucified, were present in the consecrated bread and wine. The Church taught that the 'accidents' of the appearance of the bread and wine, after consecration, hid their true nature as the Body and Blood of Christ. The transformation of the bread and wine through the miraculous intervention of God into the Body and Blood was complete, in the teachings of the Roman Catholic Church. In contrast, Luther believed that the Body and Blood were present together with the bread and the wine. Although he did not use this term himself, some theologians have referred to Luther's opinion as 'consubstantiation'.[11]

Once Luther succeeded in challenging the papacy, serious disagreements broke out amongst his colleagues especially concerning the nature of the presence of Christ in the Eucharist. They were deeply divided over the question of the 'reality' of Christ in the consecrated bread and wine. Huldrych Zwingli (1484–1531) of Zürich believed in justification by faith alone, but he disagreed with Luther, for he argued that the presence of Christ in the Eucharist was purely 'spiritual' in nature. The Lord's Supper was a memorial of Christ's death, in keeping with the words of instruction Jesus spoke to his disciples on the night he was betrayed. The bread and wine remained bread and wine. Christ was present in the Lord's Supper, spiritually but not physically or 'corporally'. Both Luther and Zwingli gained numerous followers in the 1520s. Resistance at the Imperial Diet of Speyer in 1529 to the Habsburgs' plans repress reform eventually established the term 'Protestant'. But disagreements concerning the meaning of the presence of Christ in the Eucharist divided Protestants, and threatened the survival of Protestantism in the face of the Emperor Charles's implacable opposition. After Zwingli died in battle in 1531, he was succeeded at Zürich by Bullinger, who was interested in developing unity amongst Protestant leaders. Calvin in Geneva aligned with Bullinger. Bucer of Strasbourg spent most of his career building agreements across doctrinal lines. But the breach between the Lutherans and the leaders of what came to be known as Swiss or 'Reformed' Protestantism never truly healed.

Cranmer was obsessively interested in the Eucharist, and his opinions changed over time. They have been explored for us by Peter Newman Brooks, who has established that in his early years as archbishop, Cranmer believed as the Lutherans did: he rejected the tenet of transubstantiation, but he believed in the real presence. Then from the late 1540s, led by Nicholas Ridley (*c*. 1502–1555), Cranmer gradually accepted the opinion that the presence of Christ in the Lord's Supper was 'true' or spiritual in nature. The eventual transformation of his opinions had profound implications for the 1549 and the 1552 editions of the *Book of Common Prayer*. The miraculous aspect of the Lord's Supper was not the act that consecrated the bread and wine, but rather, God's intervention for the souls of those who receive them. Christ was spiritually present with the men and women who received the bread and wine worthily with faith.

In terms of his character, Cranmer was adventurous and bold, yet at the same time he was genuinely self-effacing. When he became archbishop, Henry VIII gave him a new heraldic device that replaced the cranes of his father's coat of arms with pelicans, a symbol of Christian sacrifice. Cranmer possessed a rare sensibility that allowed him to respect and accommodate opinions that were different than his own. But we cannot call him tolerant in the sense that we now use the term. He was a relentless opponent of those who refused to obey the king, and he hounded members of the religious orders, especially the mendicant friars, who wished to honour their vows of obedience to the papacy. Historians now think that the vast majority of English people did not wish to leave the Catholic Church and they resented Cranmer's impositions.

Because large portions of the Church's medieval administrative structure were retained, despite Cranmer's reforms, competing claims between conformists and various strands of nonconformity began to emerge in the English Church even while Cranmer was archbishop. They were not fully reconciled during his lifetime, nor later in the sixteenth century, and some of them have never been absolutely overcome.[12] I have tried to avoid terms like 'the Anglican Church' that would be anachronistic for the sixteenth century. Cranmer wanted to establish a Protestant Church in England which would define its doctrine in concert with other Protestant leaders. At their most mature, Cranmer's aspirations for the English Church can be described as fitting into the Reformed Protestant tradition. Although he established a national Church for England, it is less certain that he intended to create what some authorities have termed an 'Anglican way'. The 'moderation' for which Cranmer tends to be known might be better understood as his desire to create a 'broad Church' that was capable of accommodating a spectrum of opinion as part of a coherent whole, under obedience to its king as the Supreme Head of the English Church.

Cranmer was neither a loyal son of the papacy nor a friend to those members of the 'radical' Reformation, like the Anabaptists, who raised uncomfortable questions about the humanity and divinity of Christ that far exceeded the kinds of questions Luther and Zwingli posed. Anabaptists were attacked by all sides: the Roman Church, the Lutherans, and the Swiss all executed Anabaptists as heretics. To cite one important instance, in Geneva, Calvin endorsed the burning of the polymath Michael Servetus (*c.* 1511–1553).

In the rigorous process of severing England's communion with Rome and implementing the king's supremacy over the English Church, many people were executed. Cranmer shared in the responsibility for their deaths. Heresy was a capital crime under English law, and for most of Cranmer's life, it was illegal to deny the real presence in the sacrament of the altar. From the fourteenth century, the Church and the English government were united in their efforts to suppress the Lollard heresy associated with the followers of the Oxford theologian John Wycliffe (d. 1384). Cranmer's predecessor Archbishop William Warham (*c.* 1450–1532) energetically pursued Lollards and Lutherans. Executions had always been a type of theatrical spectacle. Now they were harnessed by the Tudor regime for its own purposes. The theatre of the public scaffold was used to promote the legitimacy and orthodoxy of the

English Church and its leaders. John Frith (ex. 1533), Elizabeth Barton (ex. 1534), and John Lambert (ex. 1538) were amongst those executed with Cranmer's approval and assistance during Henry's reign for having defied the king's authority. However, even under Edward, when Cranmer had more latitude to implement the policies he desired, Anabaptists – like Joan Bocher, who was burnt in 1550 – continued to be executed.

Cranmer has a unique status amongst the figures that appeared in the pages of the *Actes and Monuments*. Foxe noted as he examined the writings of Stephen Gardiner that Cranmer was involved in the trials of Lambert and several others, but he ultimately adopted the same opinions for which they had died. Foxe was therefore conflicted when he considered whether or not Cranmer deserved to be considered a martyr. In prison, under extreme duress, Cranmer retracted the opinions he had worked so hard to establish for the English Church because he hoped that his life might be spared. After his execution, his recantations were printed to discredit him and Protestantism. He was a reluctant martyr. But at the last moment, Cranmer retracted his retractions just before being taken to the stake. His last and most famous gesture, the one by which his life has come to be known, was made at his execution, when he held his right hand in the flames as an act of repentance to punish himself for having signed his recantations. This was his last message to posterity. His gesture has been widely acknowledged as a sign of his outstanding courage, his faithfulness to God and his belief in Protestant teachings. But decades later, Foxe continued to be troubled that Cranmer could be party to the persecution of men like Frith and Lambert while later embracing the same beliefs for which they had died.

This brief book cannot solve all of the problems that Cranmer's life presents, nor can it rescue his reputation from every detractor. For most of his life, Cranmer knew how deeply he was hated. Just as Virginia Woolf wished that we could follow Shakespeare along the Strand and pluck him by the sleeve to ask him what he meant by *Hamlet*,[13] Cranmer's biographers from the very first have struggled to make sense of the conflicting aspects of his career and legacy. The intention of this present book is to provide readers with a guide to the life and achievements of one of the most problematic figures who ever presided over the English Church.

Notes

1 The collect for Quinquagesima Sunday in Lent, written by Thomas Cranmer, for the second prayer book: *The boke of common praier, and administracion of the sacramentes, and other rites and ceremonies in the Churche of Englande* (London: Richard Grafton, August 1552, *RSTC* 16285), 27v–28r.

2 Matthew Parker (1504–1575), seventieth archbishop of Canterbury, counted his predecessors in a preface to *De antiquitate Britannicae ecclesiae et priuilegiis ecclesiae Cantuariensis* (London: John Daye, 1572, *RSTC* 19292), in the table preceding p. 1. His account of Cranmer's life: pp. 381–405.

3 BL, Royal MS 7. B. XI and MS 7. B. XII; also CCCC MS 102; and LPL, MS 1108.

4 Cranmer's letterbook: BL, Harleian Manuscript 6148. Many of his letters have been printed in Cranmer, *Miscellaneous*.

5 CCCC, MS 128.

6 D. Selwyn, *The Library of Thomas Cranmer*, Oxford Bibliographical Society, third series, 1 (1996).

7 Ralph Morice, 'Declaration' of the 'lyf and bryngyng upp, of the most Reverent Father in God, Thomas Cranmer, late archbishop of Canterbury': CCCC, MS 128, 405–36, printed in *Narratives of the Days of the Reformation*, ed. J. Gough Nichols, Camden Society, first series, 77 (238–40). The 'Life': BL, Harley MS 417, from 90, and printed in *Narratives*, 218–33. MacCulloch suggested in *Cranmer*, appendix I, that the 'Life' was written by Stephen Nevinson, the cousin of the archbishop's commissary.

8 John Strype, *Memorials of the Most Reverend Father in God, Thomas Cranmer, Sometime Lord Archbishop of Canterbury* (London, 1694).

9 A. F. Pollard, *Thomas Cranmer and the English Reformation, 1489–1556* (London, 1906); Jasper Ridley, *Thomas Cranmer* (Oxford, 1962); Diarmaid MacCulloch, *Thomas Cranmer: A Life* (New Haven, 1996).

10 Peter Marshall, *Religious Identities in Henry VIII's England*, (Aldershot, 2006), 7; Ashley Null, 'Thomas Cranmer and Tudor Evangelicalism', in *The Advent of Evangelicalism: Exploring Historical Continuities*, eds. Michael A. G. Haykin and Kenneth J. Steward (Nashville, 2008), 221–51 and the same author's *Thomas Cranmer's Doctrine of Repentance: Renewing the Power to Love* (Oxford, 2000).

11 B. A. Gerrish, 'The Reformation and the Eucharist', in *Thinking with the Church: Essays in Historical Theology* (Cambridge, 2010), 229–58.

12 John Bossy, *The English Catholic Community 1570–1850* (Oxford, 1976); Patrick Collinson, *The Elizabethan Puritan Movement* (London, 1967), 29–44; Peter Lake, *Moderate Puritans and the Elizabethan Church* (Cambridge, 1982), 16–24; Alexandra Walsham, *Church Papists: Catholicism, Conformity, and Confessional Polemic in Early Modern England* (Woodbridge, 1993).
13 Virginia Woolf's desire to meet Shakespeare along the Strand was expressed in her essay, 'The Strange Elizabethans', in *The Second Common Reader* (London, 1932, rpt. 1986), 9–23.

2   Early life, 1489–1526

'Almighty ever-living God, which for the more confirmation of the faith, didst suffer thy holy apostle Thomas, to be doubtful in thy son's resurrection: grant us so perfectly, and without all doubt to believe in thy Son Jesus Christ: that our faith in thy sight never be reproved: hear us O Lord, through the same Jesus Christ to whom with thee and the holy ghost be all honour and glory, now and forever, Amen.'[1]

Aslockton

Thomas Cranmer was born at Aslockton in Nottinghamshire on 2 July 1489, the eve of the feast of the translation of St Thomas the Apostle.[2] Cranmer may have been indebted for his name to the Doubting Thomas who had to touch Jesus' wounds before he would be convinced that Christ had risen, but he also owed his name to his own father, Thomas Cranmer (d. 1501), a gentleman whose family was reputed to have come into England with William the Conqueror (d. 1087).

The family settled in Lincolnshire where they lived in a 'mansion house' called 'Cranmer Hall'. Its windows bore the original Cranmer coat of arms of a chevron between three cranes. An early spelling of the name was 'Craynmeyr', and the cranes may have been a canting reference to Lincolnshire's watery fens. Stained glass with the same arms was once visible in the parish church of Sutterton, a fen village near Boston, leading later generations to assume that Cranmer Hall was nearby. After the Cranmers had been settled in Lincolnshire for many generations, a new branch of the family was created in Nottinghamshire when Edmund Cranmer, the archbishop's great-grandfather, married Isabella, the heiress daughter of William de Aslockton. Neither Cranmer Hall nor the house where Cranmer was born survived beyond the sixteenth century.

Cranmer's Norman heritage defined his family as belonging to the gentry in the midlands where the counties of Lincoln, Nottingham and Leicester meet. The Cranmers shared their sense of heritage with the Molineux, Newmarche, Bingham, and Crecy families, and with the more prosperous Markhams of Cotham, with whom, over the generations, they mingled and married. The Cranmers were also aligned with the austere religious order of the White Canons Regular of Prémontré, who had arrived in Lincolnshire from northern France within a century of William's invasion. Welbeck Abbey, about twenty-five miles to the north-west from Aslockton, was the only house of the White Canons in Nottinghamshire. Welbeck Abbey was the patron of the parish church (dedicated to St John of Beverley) that the Cranmers attended in Aslockton's neighbouring village of Whatton.

Recent events may have played a part in shaping the Cranmers' understanding of their background. Following the defeat of Richard III (1452–1485) by Henry Tudor (1457–1509) on the strength of an invasion Henry mounted from France, the Cranmer family's association with the Norman Conquest probably enhanced their social status. Ralph Morice (*c*. 1522–1570), Cranmer's secretary, told of a time during the reign of Henry VIII that Cranmer held a banquet at Lambeth Palace to honour 'a gentleman being a Norman born', who accompanied a French ambassador to England and who said his name was the same as the archbishop's. After dinner they compared their coats of arms. Although the possibility seemed unlikely even to the devoted Morice, Cranmer and his visitor decided that their arms were so similar that there were hardly any differences between them. Thus they were encouraged to believe that they were indeed distantly related. To their mutual satisfaction, this discovery increased each man's prestige. Glamorous references to a heroic past shaped the identities of many gentlemen's families, and Cranmer's references to his Norman origins indicated that by virtue of his inheritance, he was qualified to hold authority over others.[3]

The Cranmers as a family held certain expectations which were reflected in Cranmer's own perception of himself. The connections that they enjoyed may have meant that he did not think of himself as belonging to Nottinghamshire or Lincolnshire (or perhaps even England) in the same way that Nicholas Ridley defined himself as a Northumberland man, or that Hugh Latimer (*c.* 1494–1555) thought of the county of Leicester as his home. The Cranmer coat of arms distinguished his family above their nearest neighbours, the Craforths, Dawsons, Gilbys, and Wrights, who tilled the same soil and left their bones in Whatton's churchyard.[4]

Despite their heroic Norman past, the position that the Cranmers actually occupied in Nottinghamshire at the end of the fifteenth century was precarious. Aslockton and Whatton were isolated hamlets twelve miles in any direction from the nearest market towns of Nottingham, Southwell, Newark, Grantham, and Melton Mowbray. Recent generations of Cranmers had not produced any officials of note: no sheriffs, no justices of the peace, and no shire knights to attend Parliament. They enjoyed fewer advantages than did the Markhams, whose lands in the counties of Lincoln and Nottingham were much more extensive.[5] Sir John Markham the elder raised his sword for Henry VII at the Battle of Stoke Field in 1487, and he was able to marry his son to an heiress of royal descent, a Neville kinswoman of the Lady Margaret Beaufort, the mother of the king. In contrast, Cranmer's father managed to place only one of his daughters in a religious order. Alice Cranmer, as a Cistercian nun at Stixwould in Lincolnshire, represented her family's gentle status, but only barely.[6]

Cranmer's mother was Agnes, the daughter of Laurence Hatfield of Willoughby on the Wolds, a village to the south of Aslockton down the old Roman road of the Fosse Way. The Hatfields too were an old, well-established family, and Agnes's father was a gentleman 'of like degree' with Thomas Cranmer. Like the Cranmers also, the Hatfields were sunk in local obscurity. The archbishop knew the history of a persistent 'unquietness' in Nottinghamshire that stretched back a half-century or more before he was born. The Hatfields were disturbed by land disputes that involved the Secular Canons of the Collegiate Church of Blessed Mary the Virgin in Southwell. Writing to Thomas Cromwell in 1534, Cranmer explained that his Hatfield grandfather had been caught up in disagreements so bitter that they led to 'great occasion of manslaughter' more than once. Although what befell Laurence Hatfield remains obscure, Cranmer indicated that a violent past continued to weigh heavily on his family.[7] As archbishop, Cranmer worked steadily to increase his family's security.

Cranmer was a younger son amongst nine surviving children. As part of their upbringing, his father taught his sons how to shoot and to ride some 'rough horses'. He also let them hunt and hawk, which in the late fifteenth century were prerequisites of good birth. Cranmer's elder brother John (named for their uncle, a priest) was their father's heir.

According to Morice, Cranmer's father also 'set him to school with a marvelous severe and cruel schoolmaster' whose name has never been established, although all of his biographers have wished to know more about this man. The author of the 'Life' recounted that Cranmer first 'learned his grammar of a rude parish clerk'. It seems reasonable to suggest that Cranmer began his lessons in Latin grammar from a local curate. The vicar of their parish of Whatton during his youth was Thomas Wilkinson, the eventual abbot of Welbeck Abbey. Wilkinson was non-resident, and he left parish matters in the hands of curates. William Norton and his assistant George Ehson served the parish in 1501.[8]

Then, if by being 'set' to school, Morice meant that Cranmer was sent away from home, he could have gone to any of the market towns that ringed Aslockton. The best possibility was Southwell, for at the end of the fifteenth century all of Nottinghamshire's schools were under the jurisdiction of the secular canons of Southwell's chapter. Cranmer was extremely familiar with the school at Southwell. In autumn 1533, only six months after he became archbishop, he wrote to his brother-in-law Harold Rosell to recommend that his son Thomas be sent to Southwell. But then he heard of an outbreak of sickness so serious that 'they die there'. So he arranged for the boy to be sent elsewhere.[9]

Another possibility for Cranmer's early education was Grantham's venerable grammar school. Its most famous student, a century-and-a-half later, was Isaac Newton (1642–1727). Many of Cranmer's lifelong friends came from Lincolnshire: William Benson, *alias* Boston (d. 1549, the future abbot and dean of Westminster Abbey); Thomas Goodrich (1494–1554, the future bishop of Ely and lord chancellor); Henry Rands *alias* Holbeach (d. 1551, a Benedictine monk, later bishop of Lincoln) and John Whitwell (d. 1561, ultimately Cranmer's chaplain). Later we will observe the roles they played in Cranmer's career. Goodrich's family held property to the north of Boston in East Kirkby and Bolingbrook. When Goodrich was elected to the bishopric of Ely in 1534, Whitwell spoke to his character in a deposition that was recorded in Cranmer's archiepiscopal Register. Whitwell and Goodrich had been friends from the age of seven. They were 'of old familiar acquaintance and have been at school together' first in the country and then later at Cambridge.[10] Although they were about five years younger than Cranmer, it is not impossible that all three were schoolmates in Lincolnshire, before they were at Cambridge at the same time.

What is noteworthy about Cranmer's unhappy experience at school was the near universality of his experience and the effects that he said that it had on the rest of his life. Students who could not remember their declensions were forced to learn them. Many young boys endured beatings as they were introduced to the rudiments of Latin grammar. Severe punishment was one of the defining features of the history of education then, and well afterwards. Most sons of ambitious parents suffered the same terrors at their schools as did Cranmer. So his references to his 'marvelous severe and cruel schoolmaster' was at once typical, and yet quite extraordinary, for Cranmer was able to articulate, better than most, what the effects of punishment had had upon him and his schoolmates. As a result of the ill treatment he had received as a child, Cranmer believed that he had lost forever his natural memory and the 'audacity' that had been his. Rather, he had been 'mutilated and wounded' by injuries that his classmates had all suffered. His schoolmaster so 'appalled, dulled and daunted the tender and fine wits' of his students, that most of them hated learning and good literature as a result (and here Cranmer may have echoed Erasmus's warning in the *Paraclesis* against heavy-handed schoolmasters). Cranmer believed himself to have been permanently damaged. The losses that he and the others had suffered were incalculable. He told Morice on many occasions that he could 'never recover' the natural abilities that had been annihilated by his teacher's 'tyranny', a loss he mourned because he treasured the independence of his mind and his ability to think things through clearly for himself. The implication behind his story was that he valued making his own decisions based on what he concluded was correct. He believed that he might have achieved much more throughout his life had he not lost what he understood were the keenest of his abilities. Moreover, he believed that others were likely to have been damaged by the same methods. Cranmer won Morice's sympathy for the suffering he endured as a child, and he excused himself on the numerous (and perhaps unavoidable) occasions when he disappointed his friends, or fell short in his responsibilities towards others.

Many of his biographers have been tempted to see a theme here in Cranmer's relations to those in authority over him, and especially to Henry VIII. There were paradoxical sides to Cranmer's character that Morice himself pointed out: that although the archbishop 'feared not to ride the roughest horse that came into his stable', in other regards he was cautious to an astonishing degree. To many he appeared 'subtle', which was a criticism in the sixteenth century, for it meant he was both hard to understand and calculating. In the privacy of his household, amongst his family and his friends, the archbishop could be open. Yet, as we will observe in this and later chapters, the face he turned to the world was deliberately unrevealing. Cranmer had many secrets.

In 1501, his father succumbed to a fatal malady. He may have been ill for a long time, but his death arrived while he was in the prime of life and his children were still young. He lingered long enough for Wilkinson to be summoned to his deathbed to witness his will on the day he died, 27 May 1501. The bequests he made 'pro salute animae meae' (for the health of my soul) were surprisingly modest for a man of his standing. He left one mark (or thirteen shillings and four pence) towards the fabric of Aslockton's chapel, and a new bell to the church in Whatton.[11] His body was interred in Whatton's church under a limestone slab carved with a rough likeness and his coat of arms.[12] In the eighteenth century, the story was told that whenever Cranmer returned to his birthplace, he was fond of sitting out-of-doors in the evening to listen to the 'tuneable bells' of Whatton,[13] a charming tale that hints of an attachment to his father's memory, but that has no basis in the facts as Cranmer's earliest biographers knew them. His father, as

Cranmer remembered him later, had done what he could to start him in life.

At the time of his father's death, Cranmer was not yet twelve years old and his younger brother Edmund may have been six or seven. Now suddenly the Cranmers were even less secure. Perhaps his father had wished to prepare them for uncertain futures, which would help to explain the rough horses and the brutal school-master. John received the bulk of the estate as the heir. Out of the income of his tenements and lands in Whatton, their father left Thomas the slender annuity of twenty shillings, and the same sum to Edmund: the full amount was to go in survivorship to the other should one of them die. Small as they were, their annuities may have been a perpetual drain on their brother's resources. In the late 1530s, when John Leland (*c*. 1503–1552) went riding through Nottinghamshire as part of his itinerary through the realm, he was surprised by Aslockton's meagreness. There was no parish church. The house where Cranmer was born was so insignificant that it was beneath notice. John's son Thomas (d. 1551) was now the local head of the family, and the Cranmers' land was worth scarcely forty marks, or a little more than thirty pounds a year.[14]

The rest of Cranmer's education he owed not to his father, but to his mother. Following her husband's death, Agnes Cranmer decided to keep Thomas at the same grammar school for the next two years. Then, although the expense involved must have been considerable, she sent him, and later Edmund, to the University of Cambridge.

Cranmer as an undergraduate

Thomas Cranmer was fourteen years old when he arrived in Cambridge in 1503, the youngest age under the university's stat-utes that a student could matriculate. Similarly, Latimer was four-teen when he was sent to Cambridge in 1507 and both Robert Barnes (*c*. 1495–1540) and Thomas Bilney (*c*. 1495–1531) also arrived at the university before they could shave. At fourteen, Cranmer may have shown signs of early promise, for most boys who entered university were a year or two older.[15] Cranmer had relatives at Cambridge, and they included his 'near kinsman', Dr Christopher Tamworth, a fellow of God's House, the college dedicated to the study of grammar.

As the author of the 'Life' recorded, until he was twenty-two, Cranmer was required to devote himself to the study of logic and 'philosophy moral and natural', and he was tested against the 'dark riddles' of the great scholastic authors, including Duns Scotus (d. 1308), Hugh of St. Victor (d. 1141), and Nicholas Dorbell (d. 1475). Most especially, he became immersed in the writings of Peter Lombard (d. 1160) Thomas Aquinas (d. 1274), and most especially Augustine (d. 430). Some of Cambridge's traditions in the study of grammar and logic had been influenced by trends that had come from the University of Paris as long ago as the eleventh century, and they were founded on the study of the *Summa Theologica* by Aquinas and Lombard's *Sentences*. Scholasticism applied a fourfold methodology that examined texts by means of their literal, allegorical (or figurative), tropological (or moral), and analogical (or prophetic) senses. The foundation of Cranmer's intellectual training, like that of all his contemporaries, owed much to the scholastics.[16]

But allusions to 'dark riddles' imply that Cambridge was still in thrall to a woefully old-fashioned curriculum in Arts, and that Cranmer as a student too often had to wrestle with abridged texts that had been removed from their historical contexts and then contorted under the demands of medieval dialectic. That was not the case, even though not all of the instruction he received was useful. Many years later, Cranmer remembered that he had had to attend the lectures of 'an ignorant reader' who used petty excuses to skip the chapters he could not understand.[17]

Rather, Cranmer arrived at Cambridge at an exhilarating time, when the new intellectual currents of Renaissance humanism in language and literature that had been rising from Italy since the fifteenth century were seized by the university's chancellors, especially by Bishop John Fisher of Rochester (*c.* 1469–1535). Study in the Latin west was becoming transformed by a renewed desire to understand Greek as well as Hebrew, trends that were spurred on through the fresh technological triumph of print. Important patrons, including King Henry VII's mother, Lady Margaret Beaufort (1443–1509), endowed new colleges. The undergraduate degree course in Arts was revised in 1488 and then it was revised again in 1495. The scholastic foundations of the trivium and quadrivium were infused with the study of languages. Philosophy was partially demoted, and literature was stressed instead. This was the intellectual climate that greeted the young Cranmer at Cambridge.[18]

His experience of learning as an undergraduate was a stimulating fusion of medieval tradition blended with the new trends. Lectures continued to be the means by which undergraduates were introduced to the higher levels of intellectual engagement. Undergraduates in Arts attended lectures during term times for about four years. Most lectures were delivered in the Schools (some portions its buildings are still visible today behind the Senate House) across the High Street from the University Church (now known as Great St Mary's). A lecture was what its name implied: a reading in Latin on a specific subject from a set text. The lecture was amplified by explanations and commentary. Learning was presented in the dialectical form that owed much to the Socratic Method and to Platonism. The meaning of texts was investigated by the lecturer's dialogue through discussion and reasoning. Often lectures began in the early morning. A lecturer or reader was usually a 'regent master', a fellow from one of the colleges who had only recently completed his master's degree in Arts. The regent masters were still young men, and they were amongst the hardest-working members of the university. Many had not yet completed their final degrees. They were post-graduate students who were still attending lectures, and they continued to be tested in their disputations and debates. This meant that while they were teaching the undergraduates, the regent masters themselves were still learning.

In the Schools, the lecturer sat in a position of eminence on a raised platform, enthroned above his students. Lectures fit into two broad categories: cursory or ordinary. Cursory lectures were less demanding. The material was taken up only lightly, mainly to increase understanding. The text was read in Latin and the meanings of the words were explained. In ordinary lectures, the material was examined more closely. Paraphrases of the more difficult passages were introduced. The philological points of the text would move into higher, more abstract realms of the subject.

For the first two years of their curriculum, undergraduates in Arts heard ordinary lectures in humane letters, with an emphasis on Terence (d. 159 BC). Then they spent a year attending lectures in logic, and a fourth in philosophy. As an undergraduate, Cranmer heard Dr Robert Ridley (d. *c.* 1536), the uncle of Nicholas, when he lectured in philosophy.

Although Cranmer arrived at university in 1503 slightly younger than most students, he proceeded to his bachelor's degree in Arts rather later than usual. Twelve terms (or four years) were the usual length of time that an undergraduate needed to complete the Arts course, but Cranmer needed longer. He did not go up for his first degree until 1511. Seven years was, as his biographer Diarmaid MacCulloch has suggested, 'a surprisingly long time', which fed the assumption that he was always a mediocre scholar.[19] For some biographers, Cranmer's entire career at Cambridge 'was surprisingly undistinguished'. Patrick Collinson (1929–2011), Regius professor of history at Cambridge, dismissed him as having the sort of mind 'which would have been awarded an upper second, not a first, in a modern tripos examination', even though (as he wrote in another context) high levels of originality were not looked for then in undergraduates or even in the highest ranks of society.[20] Cranmer's slow or broken progress towards his first degree meant that when he finally took his degree in 1511 in a group of forty-two, he stood amongst some much younger men, including Latimer and his friends Benson and Goodrich.[21]

Cranmer's first marriage

The most probable reason that Cranmer went up for his first degree so late was not due to inability but rather, because he married. Now that I have discovered his ordination records, we can know that Cranmer's first marriage must have taken place earlier than Morice thought: not after he proceeded to his master's degree in Arts in 1515, because that was the year Cranmer became a priest. Probably he did not relinquish a fellowship at Jesus College in order to marry. Cranmer probably married before he completed his first degree in 1511.

From Cranmer himself, we learn almost nothing about his first marriage. According to John Foxe, his wife was 'a gentleman's daughter', though that seems doubtful. Neither Morice nor Matthew Parker (1504–1575) recorded her name. More likely,

Cranmer wed the daughter of a Cambridge townsman, in the same way, a generation later the young William Cecil (1521–1598) wed Mary, the sister of John Cheke (1514–1557), whose mother ran a wine business on Market Hill. In 1556, Cranmer's enemies accused him of marrying 'one Joan, surnamed Black or Brown'. Because their information was incorrect in other regards, we cannot even be certain that her Christian name really was Joan.[22]

Much remains puzzling about Cranmer's first marriage. Agnes Cranmer sent both her younger sons to Cambridge. Edmund proceeded to his bachelor's degree in Arts only two years after his brother.[23] We do not know if she wanted them to enter careers in the Church. Cranmer's marriage suggests that he had not intended to enter the priesthood. Yet he did not altogether abandon his studies, for according to Parker, he went to lectures at the Schools as before. In the early sixteenth century, a married scholar who persisted in staying at university was an anomaly. Cranmer became 'the common reader at Buckingham College' which was the Benedictine house at Cambridge (now Magdalene College). Presumably he would have been paid by the monk-students for tutoring them or delivering lectures, and Parker described Cranmer's married life as being close to destitution.[24] He placed his wife in lodgings in the Dolphin Inn in Bridge Street, which was run (according to Foxe) by one of his wife's relatives (which seems likely) or (according to Parker) by one of his mother's relatives. This too is difficult to explain, and probably we will never be certain about the details. Cranmer may have married out of a sense of family duty, even though he was inconvenienced by a lack of ready funds. His annuity from his father's estate, as we have already observed, was only one pound a year, which would have been insufficient to support them. Even a poor person at the beginning of the sixteenth century needed an annual income of at least three or four pounds in order to live a bare sort of existence, and Cranmer would have needed much more than that to establish an independent household with his wife, complete with servants, that would befit his rank as a gentleman.

They were married one year or not even one year (according to Morice) when their first child was expected. Parker said that the marriage lasted at least one full year, probably (as MacCulloch has suggested) to remove any suspicion that they had had to marry hastily. Seen from this perspective, Cranmer's first marriage looks like a youthful indiscretion. We will never know what really happened. Perhaps his first marriage was not fully anticipated any more than was his second, but if Cranmer caused Joan to fall pregnant, he did the honourable thing and he married her, even if he had to sacrifice his prospects. The simplest explanation for their marriage was that he loved her.

But Joan did not survive the hazards of childbirth. Both she and the baby died in labour. To his friends, Cranmer never hid the fact that he had been married before he became a priest. Morice knew and Parker knew: in fact, it was no secret at either Cambridge or Oxford. What pursued him in his later career was his reputation for having had sexual experience in an era when priests were supposed to be blameless and without a 'past'. Virginity was the preferred ideal, especially for the priesthood, and matrimony was considered to be a debased state. Opposition to a married clergy remained strong at many levels of society until the latter half of the sixteenth century. Cranmer was not a priest at the time he married Joan, but his desire to pursue his studies despite his marriage was unusual. Much later, after his secret second marriage was revealed, his sexual relations became the subject of comment and envy amongst his colleagues. His first marriage highlights the extraordinary unconventionality that marked his entire career. Cranmer was never ashamed that he had married, and his willingness to marry then, and later, was instrumental in introducing a married clergy into the English Church.

Jesus College

Morice's confusion about the timing of Cranmer's first marriage has created considerable difficulties in establishing his earliest affiliation with Jesus College. According to a long-held tradition, Cranmer was first an undergraduate at Jesus, and then a fellow. However, no records were made then to show when he matriculated at Cambridge or at Jesus. The earliest reference to his fellowship dates to 1522.[25] Morice wrote that Cranmer was already Master of Arts and a fellow of Jesus when he married, and therefore he was 'constrained' to leave his fellowship. But either Morice was mistaken or he deliberately misinformed his readers, perhaps because he too wished to protect the uncomfortable details concerning Cranmer's first marriage.

Following his wife's death, Cranmer turned definitively to a career in the Church. He embarked on a fresh round of gruelling endeavour for his master's degree in Arts. The curriculum here had also been recently expanded, beyond what had been the traditional program in philosophy, centred on Aristotle (d. 322 BC). Now it embraced lectures in mathematics: one year of arithmetic and music, a second in geometry and perspective, and a third in astronomy. The lecturers in mathematics were Henry Bullock (d. 1526) and Humphrey Walkenden. At the same time that they were lecturing Cranmer in mathematics, they were also learning Greek from Erasmus.

In 1515 shortly before he took his master's degree in Arts, Cranmer went up to the priesthood. He was twenty-five. Every spring, university men returned to their home dioceses where they were ordained. The register of Thomas Cardinal Wolsey (1471–1530) for the archdiocese of York shows that Thomas Cranmer was admitted to the subdiaconate on Sunday, 24 March 1514/15 in the city of York. His 'title' or his guarantee of support (a prerequisite for ordination) came from the Benedictine monastery of St John in Colchester. Then he was ordained to the deaconate on Easter Sunday, 7 April 1515, in York Minster. The ordination list gave his first name now as 'John' but that was a simple mistake. Again, his title came from the monastery of St John in Colchester. On 2 June 1515, Thomas Cranmer was ordained to the priesthood at the conventual church of the Dominican friars in York, when once more he was guaranteed by the monastery of St John in Colchester. Later that summer Cambridge's Grace Book *B* recorded that Cranmer went up for his master's degree in Arts.[26]

Colchester in Essex is only fifty miles from Cambridge. Now Cranmer had his reward for the time he spent while married in instructing the Benedictines. His seriousness must have impressed the monks, and they were willing to invest in his future as a priest. In early 1515, Cranmer was probably not yet a fellow at Jesus, for otherwise the college would have been his sponsor, just as Latimer's title, when he was ordained in Lincoln that same spring, came from Clare College, where he was already a fellow.[27] Three years later, Edmund Cranmer followed his brother's route, and he was admitted to the priesthood in the same church, Blackfriars in York, on 20 March 1517/18. It is not surprising that Edmund's title came from the White Canons of Welbeck Abbey.[28]

When Cranmer went up for his master's degree in Arts in 1515, after fulfilling his obligations and paying the necessary fees for the mathematics lectures, in a rush of disputations, Masses, dinners, gift-givings and other ceremonies, he was allowed 'to incept', which, as the word implied, marked a new beginning of his life as a lecturer.[29] It was probably at this point also that he was admitted to a fellowship at Jesus College. When the college was surveyed in 1522 for the purposes of a tax subsidy, his name appeared on the list of fellows.[30]

Jesus College was the earliest of the new foundations that in Cranmer's lifetime transformed Cambridge from its medieval beginnings, dominated by its religious houses and student hostels, into a true collegiate institution. The college was founded specifically for the study of Theology, and it represented the greatest advancement for the university until St John's College was perfected by Fisher in the early 1530s. But in its early years, Jesus College was poor. The fellowship was small, set originally at eight, and in its early years it could probably not afford the full number of fellows that its first statutes allowed. Lady Margaret assisted the college in 1503 with a large gift of twenty-six pounds to be used towards the rebuilding of the parish church that served as Jesus's chapel. She came to visit the university frequently. If Cranmer was an undergraduate at Jesus, he may have been able to make the acquaintance of James Morice (d. 1557), Ralph's father, who was Lady Margaret's clerk of works. Cranmer's friendship with the younger John Markham (d. 1559), who served in her household, may have started seriously then.[31] The generosity of Margaret's long-time friend Lady Katherine Bray (d. 1506) created special studentships for undergraduates at Jesus. The college's *juvenes*, as undergraduate scholars were known, were permitted to study in the faculty of Arts, and they served as organists, sacrists, bible clerks, and gatekeepers. They waited on tables in hall. We might speculate, as others have, that as an undergraduate the fatherless Cranmer could have been introduced into one of these special positions. Later, the college youths were given preference for elections to fellowships. Cranmer's studentship may have gained him eligibility for his election to a fellowship after the death of his wife and thus prepared his return to Jesus College.

Like all other colleges at Cambridge, Jesus was a religious community. In its chapel, Cranmer sang and prayed. As a priest, he celebrated Mass at its altars. In his early life, he believed as the Church taught: that when the words of consecration were spoken over the bread and the wine, through the miracle of transubstantiation, they changed into the same body and blood of Jesus Christ that had been crucified.[32]

As a regent master, Cranmer lectured as he studied towards his first degree in Theology, which he gained in 1521.[33] He lectured on Lombard's great standard, the *Sentences*, and he probably delivered cursory lectures on Scripture at least ten days each term. Already he had begun to gather the books he needed into a collection that ultimately became one of the premier libraries in the Europe of his time. He acquired Latin Bibles and the vast compendium of scriptural commentary known as the *Glossa Ordinaria*. He had, as David Selwyn, the historian of his library, informs us, commentaries on the *Sentences* by at least seventeen scholastic authors, including Albertus Magnus (d. 1280), Duns Scotus, Robert Holcot (d. 1349), and William of Ockham (d. 1347). In time Cranmer also collected a large number of books on the liturgy, which he used to develop the *Book of Common Prayer*. John Bale (1495–1563) was tutored at Jesus, and he remembered later that its fellows represented the true spirit of holiness. He observed that Cranmer stood first amongst them as the most learned of men.[34]

Cranmer as a biblical humanist

It is crucial for us to ascertain how orthodox or traditional Cranmer was in his thinking at this stage of his career and if he was persuaded before he left Cambridge in 1529 to believe as Martin Luther and Philip Melanchthon (1496–1560) of Wittenberg did. The evidence is difficult to interpret, and recent historians have not agreed. His biographer Jasper Ridley suggested that Cranmer was 'already an incipient heretic' in the 1520s and that he held no strong views in favour of the papal supremacy.[35] MacCulloch argued that the comments Cranmer wrote in the margins of his books proved that he was a 'papalist' in the 1520s, and that we cannot see him as evangelical much earlier than 1531.[36] Collinson believed Cranmer's thinking did not move within a Lutheran framework until he was sent on embassy to Nuremberg in 1532.[37]

But I would like to suggest that we might look again at an important clue that the author of the 'Life' provided. Before Luther appeared, when Cranmer was in his twenties, even while he was married so briefly, he devoted himself to the works of 'Faber, Erasmus, [and] good Latin authors'.[38] Faber was Jacques Lefèvre (*c.* 1455–1536), better known as Faber Stapulensis from his birthplace in the French port town of Etaples, across the English Channel from Lydd in Kent. He taught philosophy and mathematics at the University of Paris at the Collège du Cardinal Lemoine at the same time that Desiderius Erasmus of Rotterdam (1466–1536) was a student there in Theology at the Collège de Montaigu. We would be surprised if Cranmer did not know their work very well, especially as Fisher persuaded Erasmus to come to Cambridge in 1511 to re-ignite the study of Greek. Erasmus taught a select group of scholars, many of whom (like Bullock and Walkenden) were at Queens'. Erasmus also spent some months in delivering lectures in the Schools on the Epistles of St Jerome (d. 420), as well as Jerome's *Apology against Rufinus*. Cranmer did not learn his Greek from Erasmus (probably he studied with Richard Croke (1489–1558), who succeeded Erasmus as Cambridge's Greek professor). Nor can we know if Cranmer ever had the opportunity to hear Erasmus lecture, though for two years the great man was a conspicuous presence at the university, and fond of riding on Market Hill just for the exercise.[39] But I would suggest that from his reading in the works of Lefèvre and Erasmus, Cranmer imbibed his earliest form of biblical humanism, sometimes called evangelicalism.

Lefèvre and Erasmus are amongst the most famous of the humanists of northern Europe. They insisted that classical texts, and especially the Bible, must be understood in their historical contexts, and through their literal senses, with the guidance of the Holy Spirit. They shifted the framework of scriptural study away scholastic commentaries towards close textual analysis. Lefèvre and Erasmus were willing to sacrifice, albeit reluctantly, the traditional fourfold apparatus of scholastic methodology. Scripture's literal sense was paramount for them. Erasmus and Lefèvre's approach was an innovation for its time, and it has helped to form the foundation of the study of modern languages.

For Lefèvre, the literal sense of Scripture coincided with its spiritual sense, and its true meaning was the one in which the Holy Spirit spoke through the Psalms. His most influential works were his *Quincuplex Psalterium*, or *The Fivefold Psalter* (1509 and 1512) in which he expounded the devotional significance of each Psalm. He established a permanent standard: that Holy Scripture must be understood primarily in its most direct meaning as literal truth.

Lefèvre also issued a commentary on Paul's Epistle to the Romans concerning the manner in which sinners are saved or justified. Drawing on Psalm 13, Paul noted that when the Lord looked down from heaven to see if there were any people who understood him and sought him, he saw that not even a single person did what was good. Their mouths were full of cursing and bitterness, and their feet were swift to shed blood. Paul used Psalm 13 to illustrate that no one was able to justify himself before God, because no one was just. Rather, justification was not achieved through any human endeavour or good efforts. No good works availed for salvation. Rather, justification was offered freely by God on behalf of a flawed people through his own sacrifice of himself in Jesus Christ on the cross. God's grace was freely given, but it was not available through any effort on the part of sinful human beings. Redemption was possible, but it was offered only through Christ, who shed his blood for all humankind. Those who believed in him and had faith in the saving power of his blood were justified by their faith. Lefèvre struggled with the implications of Paul's words, and he used the example of the penitent thief who was crucified alongside Jesus as an illustration that it was possible to be saved only by faith without any good works. The sinner was not justified by his own actions, but solely through the sacrifice of God on behalf of humanity. Justification occurred through God's grace alone. Salvation could not be earned. No one saved him- or herself by their own actions, though good works were still expected of a Christian as a sign of faith. What the Christian must do was to express faith and love.[40]

Before Luther appeared, Lefèvre had already highlighted the implications of Paul's teachings. His *Commentaries on St Paul's Epistles* were a landmark and they were recognized immediately as essential. Fisher gave a copy to St John's College in 1513. Huldrych Zwingli of Basel owned a copy of the *Quincuplex Psalterium* which he annotated heavily. Luther relied on Lefèvre's work when he prepared his own exegesis of the Psalms and Paul's Epistles. Cranmer owned *The Fivefold Psalter* and many of Lefèvre's other books.[41] Foxe wrote that by reading Lefèvre and Erasmus, Cranmer 'did daily rub away his old rustiness on them, as upon a whetstone'.[42]

The kind of evangelicalism that Lefèvre and Erasmus advocated was meant to bring about spiritual renewal from within, as a type of individual spiritual exercise. Their evangelicalism was not an organized movement, but rather it was a private intellectual discipline that allowed scholars to learn from and then to teach sacred texts using fresh methods with language, history, and divine inspiration as their guides. Scholasticism was not completely overwhelmed by humanism. There was nothing to prevent a scholar from being evangelical and a 'papalist' at the same time, especially as neither Lefèvre nor Erasmus challenged the authority of the papacy or the role of the sacraments in salvation in an overt or substantive manner. They believed (as Cranmer also did then) in the real presence of Christ in the sacrament of the altar, and that the Mass was both miracle and sacrifice. Nothing about this type of evangelicalism was perceived to be at odds with the teachings of the Church or with the papacy, until Luther emerged in late 1517 to challenge the stability of western Christianity in his *Ninety-five Theses* and thereafter by criticizing the authority of the pope. We will see that Erasmus and Lefèvre permanently impressed Cranmer's thinking and teaching.

We will also have more to say about Luther's doctrines in later chapters, but our purpose now is to explore the immediate effects that his appearance had on Cranmer's career. On 15 June 1520, Pope Leo X (1475–1521) issued his bull *Exsurge Domine*, which threatened Luther with excommunication unless he submitted before the end of the year. Luther was told that he must repudiate his teachings, burn his own books, and recant within sixty days of the receipt of the bull or else face the penalties of heresy.

But Luther did not submit. With the approval of friends like Melanchthon, Luther answered Leo's sentence by kindling his own fire at Wittenberg. He burnt scholastic texts, copies of canon law, and the papal bull itself. By burning Leo's bull, Luther denounced the pope as the real heretic. Leo's sentence of excommunication against Luther was imposed at the beginning of January 1521. Three months later at the Diet of Worms, Luther appeared before the young Emperor Charles V, and he was questioned harshly. But once again he refused to submit. In the Edict of Worms, Charles echoed the pope and declared Luther a heretic.

In England, the news that Luther had been excommunicated was greeted by the king and Cardinal Wolsey. By now, Wolsey was both lord chancellor as well as papal legate. Luther's books were banned across western Europe. On 12 May 1521, Wolsey came in great state to Paul's Cross, the pulpit in the churchyard of St Paul's Cathedral in London. For two hours, Fisher preached in denunciation of Luther as his books were thrown into the flames. To show to the vast crowd, Wolsey held up a draft of a tract that the king had been writing: a preliminary copy of his *Assertio Septem Sacramentorum*, a defence of the Seven Sacraments, that would be finished later that summer and that would win for Henry the accolade from the pope *'Fidei Defensor'*.

Luther's books were also burned at Cambridge, and perhaps as a response to the threat that he posed, the university elected Cranmer as one of its Preachers in 1520. On occasions that we may regret were not recorded, he was obliged to preach at Paul's Cross.[43]

Although Cranmer had delivered cursory lectures on Scripture for a number of years, in the present crisis, he did not think that he was sufficiently equipped to face the challenges that Luther posed. It is not possible to be fully certain of the timing of events, but if we can trust the author of the 'Life', Cranmer's study now took an intense turn. He was struck by the gravity of 'the great controversy' that Luther had engendered 'in matters of religion'. Luther's criticism of the doctrines of the Church were not 'trifles', but rather they concerned 'the chiefest articles of our salvation'. The truth needed to be discerned, understood, and taught so that souls could be saved. It may be only now, after Luther appeared, that Cranmer's biblical studies intensified, but as an Erasmian, not as a Lutheran. He became convinced that he could not judge 'indifferently in so weighty matters' without greater knowledge of Holy Scripture, and now he may have taken up an innovative lectureship at Jesus College whose founders asked that ordinary lectures be delivered on the New Testament, in preference to the Old Testament, and that the meaning of Scripture should be explained either in English or Latin, which was unusual, for Scripture was usually expounded at the university in Latin, rather than in the mother tongue. As the author of the 'Life' noted, Cranmer 'applied his whole study three years to holy scripture', and he continued, 'till he were made doctor of divinity' in 1526. Cranmer was now thirty-seven years of age, and one of the men who took a doctorate with him at the same time was Edward Crome (d. 1562), who was an important figure in his career, as we will observe later.[44]

It is curious to note that Cranmer approached the new questions in doctrine impartially. According to the 'Life', he decided to 'try out the truth' by wrestling with their implications, and to make up his own mind for himself, 'before he were infected with any man's opinions or errours'. Thus Cranmer did not take up any controversial questions until he was saturated in Scripture, a method that Erasmus taught was essential for preachers and scholars. Only then did Cranmer give 'his mind to good writers both new and old'. Although the pope, the king, the cardinal, and the university's chancellor all spoke with one voice against Luther, Cranmer did not simply accept their prohibitions until he tested them for himself. He proceeded with a remarkable independence of mind, and it was this quality that eventually led him to revise his opinions about the mercy of God, the Eucharist, and eventually, the fundamentals of the English Church.[45]

In the 1520s, Cranmer was quite evidently a man still on the rise. After he received his doctorate in 1526, he began to take up new responsibilities that spoke to the trust he enjoyed at the university. He was one of the auditors who reviewed annually the contents of the university's Common Chest, what would be the equivalent today of Cambridge's main bank account.[46] He was a demanding examiner who would allow no man to proceed to a degree in Theology unless he had fully immersed himself in scriptural study. For three years until 1529, all of the candidates for Theology degrees came before him, many of whom, like Bale,

Benson and Holbeach, would later play important roles in the Reformation. Cranmer 'was neither in fame unknown, nor in knowledge obscure'. Amongst his friends was Nicholas Hawkins (*c.* 1495–1534), the nephew of the bishop of Ely, who later worked closely with him as a diplomat. Another was William Gonell (d. 1560), a local schoolmaster, who had learned Greek with Erasmus and who had returned to Cambridge after tutoring the children of Sir Thomas More (1478–1535).[47]

But Cranmer was also unusually private and cautious. In the 1520s, Lefèvre and Erasmus were distressed by the possibility that Luther's condemnation might inadvertently overshadow their legacies. Foxe described Cranmer as a 'scholar of Pythagoras' (d. *c.* 485 BC) who was famous not only for his work in Euclidean geometry but also for his clandestine religious teachings. Cranmer 'weighed all men's opinions with secret judgment'.[48] Whatever his opinions were, Cranmer did not disclose them. If he respected the prohibitions against reading Luther's books, there were others at Cambridge who did not. Soon Luther's friends began to urge English scholars to join them. If we can believe the account supplied to Foxe by Miles Coverdale (1488–1569), Latimer and Bilney were part of a circle of scholars, known privately as 'the brethren', who met regularly to discuss matters of religion and news from the continent at Cambridge's White Horse Tavern near King's College. Foxe made the White Horse Tavern famous as the university's 'Little Germany'.[49] But Cranmer does not seem to have been one of the brethren.

More than once, Cranmer was almost attracted into Wolsey's orbit. His sponsor was William Capon (*c.* 1480–1550), the cardinal's almoner, who was elected master of Jesus in 1516. When Wolsey founded Cardinal College at Oxford, he drew men from Cambridge. They included John Frith (1503–1533), who was elected to a fellowship at Cardinal College in 1525. Richard Taverner (d. 1575) left Corpus Christi to join a kinsman at Cardinal College. Richard Cox (*c.* 1500–1581) and Parker were also invited to Oxford, and so was Cranmer, upon Capon's recommendation.[50]

But Cranmer decided not to exchange Cambridge for Oxford. According to Morice, he 'utterly refused' to take up the offer because he preferred to stay at Jesus. In 1525 he was only a year away from completing his doctorate, and this fact may have had a bearing on his decision. Cranmer became convinced that there was greater scope for Theology at Jesus than there would be at Wolsey's new college. But it could have been too that Cranmer was warned that his kind of ideas would not be welcomed in Oxford. Most curiously, Parker noted that Cranmer actually set out for Cardinal College. But then he was warned by a friend to turn back. There is the merest hint from some later evidence that the warning came from a member of the Markham family, who shared Cranmer's evangelicalism.[51] Neither Cranmer nor Parker left Cambridge with Frith.

Perhaps that was just as well. Immediately after Rome was sacked in May 1527, Bilney and a friend set out from Cambridge to make a provocative preaching tour to London. As they travelled through Suffolk they denounced pilgrimages and prayers to the saints. So inflammatory were Bilney's sermons that he was pulled out of the pulpit more than once. Shocked by their effrontery, English bishops redoubled their efforts to suppress heresy. Few colleges at the universities were spared scrutiny, and early in the following year, Wolsey was embarrassed when more than a score of young scholars at Cardinal College, Frith amongst them, were discovered to have prohibited books in their possession. Held prisoner for many weeks, several died. Frith escaped to the continent. At Cambridge, Capon was empowered to search out heretics as Wolsey's agent. In 1528, Latimer, already implicated, was sent to London to be questioned by the cardinal himself, but Wolsey was so impressed by his self-assurance and his knowledge in the writings of Augustine that he was quickly released. There is no reason to believe that Capon searched his own college. Cranmer remained undisturbed. No Cambridge man died for heresy in 1528.[52]

Capon was also responsible for introducing Cranmer to Thomas Cromwell in October 1528. Now that we know that Cranmer was not sent on any diplomatic mission until 1530,[53] Capon's introduction was the first real indication we have that Cranmer's career was beginning to move beyond the university onto a larger and more important stage. Cromwell was Wolsey's senior legal advisor. Wolsey refounded a grammar school at his birthplace in Ipswich in Suffolk with Capon as its dean. In 1528, as Cromwell waited for Cardinal Lorenzo Campeggio (1474–1539) to arrive in England to hear Henry's suit against his marriage to Katherine of Aragon at the legatine court at Blackfriars, he came to Ipswich to open the school in September for the cardinal. With his own hands, Cromwell set up benches in the school's hall and he put up the wall hangings. With him was Stephen Gardiner (*c.* 1495–1555), the future bishop of Winchester, who was already well known to Cranmer from their days at university. Gardiner had just returned from Rome and acrimonious audiences with the pope about Henry's suit for an annulment from his marriage. A little later, Capon sent Cranmer to London on matters of business. In October, Capon wrote Cromwell to thank him for a letter that Cranmer brought back to Ipswich. This modest episode marked the start of Cranmer and Cromwell's long association that ended only with Cromwell's execution in 1540. Cranmer's rise could begin in 1529 because his talents were already well known amongst those who had the power to make decisions.[54]

So it seems that Cranmer's opinions by the late 1520s were already complicated. Although he was probably not yet a Lutheran, it is likely he was evangelical in the senses that Erasmus and Lefèvre were, and therefore his opinions were sufficiently dangerous in the present climate to call for prudence. Some of his friends, like Latimer and Crome, embraced controversial opinions sooner and with greater openness than did Cranmer. In 1529, at Cranmer's next known meeting with Gardiner at Waltham, we can see how far he moved away from his former papalism when he was to make a suggestion that would change the course of Henry VIII's efforts to obtain a new marriage. It was the making of Cranmer's career.

Notes

1 Thomas Cranmer's collect for the saint's day of St Thomas the Apostle: *The booke of the common praier and administration of the sacramentes, and other rites and ceremonies of the churche: after the vse of the Churche of Englande* (London: Richard Grafton, March 1549, RSTC 16268), 100v–101r.

2 The date of Cranmer's birth was recorded in the 'Life', 218.

3 Morice, 23–40.

4 The names of some of the Cranmers' neighbours in Aslockton are listed in TNA:PRO, SP 1/46, 117r (*LP*, 4, no. 3819).

5 Cranmer and the Markham family: TNA:PRO 1/46, 117r (*LP*, 4, no. 3819); *LP*, 18 (2), 334–5; MacCulloch, *Cranmer: A Life*, 24.

6 G. Baskerville, 'A Sister of Archbishop Cranmer', *EHR*, vol. 51 (1936), 287–9.

7 Agnes Hatfield: 'Lyfe', BL, Harley MS 417, 90; *Narratives of the Days of the Reformation*, 218. Unquietness: Cranmer to Thomas Cromwell, 28 April 1534, printed in *Miscellaneous*, no. 107.

8 The Register of Archbishop Thomas Savage, BIHR, Register 25, 151v.

9 Cranmer's 1533 letters to his brother-in-law Harold Rosell, printed in *Miscellaneous*, nos. 41, (12 October 1533) 62; *VCH*, Nottinghamshire, 2, 189.

10 Cranmer's Archiepiscopal Register is preserved in Lambeth Palace Library. Whitwell's deposition concerning Goodrich's character is found on 86v.

11 The will of Cranmer's father, Thomas Cranmer gentleman, of Aslockton, made 27 May 1501 and proved 1 October 1501, printed in *Testamenta Eboracensia*, 4, *Surtees Society*, 53 (1869), 194–5.

12 The tomb of Cranmer's father has been pictured as the frontispiece of P. N. Brooks, *Cranmer in Context: Documents from the English Reformation* (London, 1989), and MacCulloch, *Cranmer*, ill. no. 1.

13 *Thoroton's History of Nottinghamshire*, ed. John Throsby, 1 (London, 1797), 264.

14 *The Itinerary of John Leland in or about the Years 1535–1543*, ed. L. Toulmin Smith, 1 (1964), 97.

15 'Life', 218.

16 'Life', 218–19. Cranmer's scholarship: B. Hall, 'Cranmer's Relations with Erasmianism and Lutheranism', in *Thomas Cranmer: Churchman and Scholar*, eds. P. Ayris and D. Selwyn (Woodbridge, Suffolk, 1993), 3–37. For the books Cranmer owned: D. Selwyn, *The Library of Thomas Cranmer*, Oxford Bibliographical Society, third series (1996), nos. 38 (*Quincuplex Psalterium*), 193 (*Liber trium*), 179 (Nicholas of Cusa).

17 Cranmer, *Lord's Supper*, 305.

18 For the state of learning and the University of Cambridge in general: D. Riehl Leader, *A History of the University of Cambridge*, 1, *The University to 1546* (Cambridge, 1989), 104–5, 170–91; B. Smalley, *The Study of the Bible in the Middle Ages* (1964); B. Cummings, *The Literary Culture of the Reformation: Grammar and Grace* (Oxford, 2007), 69–78.

19 MacCulloch, *Cranmer*, 19.

20 J. Ridley, *Thomas Cranmer* (Oxford, 1962), 23; P. Collinson, 'Thomas Cranmer and the Truth' in *From Cranmer to Sancroft*. (London, 2006), 13, and Collinson's '"A Magazine of Religious Patterns": An Erasmian Topic Transposed in English Protestantism', in *Godly*

People: Essays on English Protestantism and Puritanism (London, 1983), 499–525.

21 Cranmer took his B.A. in 1511: *Grace Book B I*, 254–5.

22 Morice, 240; Cranmer, *Miscellaneous*, 557.

23 Edmund Cranmer went up for his B.A. in 1512–1513, only two years after Thomas took his first degree. *Grace Book B I*, 15–16. Edmund incepted for the M.A. in 1520: *Grace Book B II*, 79.

24 Matthew Parker, *De Antiqvitate Britannicae Ecclesiae et Priuilegiis Ecclesiae Cantuariensis, cum Archiepiscopis eiusdem 70* (London: John Day, 1572, RSTC 19292), 387; MacCulloch, *Cranmer*, 21–2.

25 The 1522 subsidy at Cambridge listed the members of the colleges: TNA:PRO, SP 1/233 (*LP*, Add. 1, pt. 1, no. 357).

26 Cranmer's ordination: BIHR, Register 27 (Wolsey's Register), 167v, 168v, 169v.

27 LAO, Register 25, fols. 112r–115r.

28 Edmund's ordination to the deaconate occurred on 28 February 1517/18 and to the priesthood on 20 March 1517/18: BIHR, Register 27 (Wolsey's Register), 179v, 180r.

29 He incepted for his M.A. (as 'Granmer') in 1515: *Grace Book B II*, 32, 34, 36.

30 TNA:PRO, SP 1/233 (*LP*, Add. 1, pt. 1, no. 357).

31 Jesus College: A. Gray and F. Britten, *A History of Jesus College* (1979), 34–5, 45–7, 51–6. Also helpful has been the website for Jesus College 'Thomas Cranmer: A Questioning Note': www.jesus.cam.ac.uk/about-jesus-college/history/pen-portraits/thomas-cranmer/ (accessed 2014).

32 Cranmer, *Miscellaneous*, 217; P. Brooks, *Thomas Cranmer's Doctrine of the Eucharist: An Essay in Historical Development* (London, 1965), 2.

33 Cranmer's B.Th. (1521): *Grace Book Γ*, 101, 103, 115, 193–4, 236–7; and *Grace Book B II*, 95.

34 The 1522 subsidy at Cambridge listed the members of the colleges: TNA:PRO, SP 1/233 (*LP*, Add. 1, pt. 1, no. 357).

35 Ridley, *Cranmer*, 21.

36 MacCulloch, *Cranmer*, 27–33, 59.

37 Collinson, 'Cranmer and the Truth', 1–24.

38 'Life', 219.

39 For the requirements Erasmus was supposed to perform towards his Cambridge D.Th.: *Grace Book Γ*, 46; CUL, MS UA, *Grace Book B*, 238, printed in *Grace Book B I*, 222. Erasmus and Greek: Leader, *Cambridge*, 253–4; *Grace Book B II*, 10; Richard Croke, *Orationes duae* (Paris, 1520), a2r–a2v, a4v–a5v, c5r, d2v–d3v; R. Rex, *The Theology of John Fisher* (Cambridge, 1991), 51, 55–6.

40 Psalm 13:3; Romans 13:11–28; P. E. Hughes, *Lefèvre: Pioneer of Ecclesiastical Renewal in France* (Grand Rapids, 1984), 35–7, 75–8, 97.

Also, E. F. Rice, ed., *The Prefatory Epistles of Lefèvre d'Etaples and Related Texts* (New York, 1972); E. Ives, 'Anne Boleyn on Trial Again', *JEH*, 62 (2011), 766–8.

41 Selwyn, *Cranmer's Library*, lxxv, nos. 38, 188–92, 401, 491.

42 Foxe 1563, 1470.

43 Cranmer's election to the office of University Preacher (as Craynmeyr): *Grace Book B II*, 77; Paul's Cross, *Grace Book Γ*, 193–4, 225. Cambridge preaching licenses: Leader, *Cambridge*, 278–81; S. Wabuda, *Preaching during the English Reformation* (Cambridge, 2002), 116–19.

44 Cranmer's lectures: Selwyn, *Cranmer's Library*, lxxiii, no. 29 (*Complutensian Polyglot*); 'Life', 219; Hall, 'Cranmer's Relations with Erasmianism and Lutheranism', 3–37; Theology Lecture at Jesus: *Documents relating to the University and Colleges of Cambridge*, 3 (London, 1852), 120; 'vel materno vel Latino sermone interpretandam'; Leader, *Cambridge*, 273. Cf. MacCulloch, *Cranmer*, 23.

45 Erasmus on study habits: Wabuda, *Preaching during the English Reformation*, 68–70. For Cranmer: G. W. Bromiley, *Thomas Cranmer* (Oxford, 1956), 12–13; Brooks, *Cranmer's Doctrine of the Eucharist*, xvi, 5; G. Cuming, *The Godly Order: Texts and Studies relating to the Book of Common Prayer*, Alcuin Club, 65 (1983), 77; Hall, 'Cranmer's Relations with Erasmianism and Lutheranism', 3–37.

46 Cranmer as university auditor: *Grace Book B II*, 120 (1523), *Grace* 139 (1527), 147 (1528), 153 (1529).

47 His friendship with William Gonell: See S. F. Ryle's entry on in the *ODNB;* MacCulloch, *Cranmer*, 31–2.

48 Foxe 1563, 1470.

49 S. Brigden, 'Thomas Cromwell and the "brethren"', in *Law and Government under the Tudors*, eds. C. Cross, D. Loades, and J. J. Scarisbrick (Cambridge. 1988), 31–49.

50 John Frith: *Grace Book Γ*, 221.

51 *LP*, 18 (2), pp. 334–5.

52 S. Wabuda, 'Cardinal Wolsey and Cambridge', *British Catholic History*, 32 (2015), 280–92.

53 MacCulloch has corrected his previous account of a diplomatic mission Cranmer was supposed to have made to Spain in 1527: 'Thomas Cranmer and Johannes Dantiscus: Retraction and Additions', *JEH*, 58 (2007), 273–86.

54 Cranmer and Cromwell met for the first time: BL, Cotton MS Titus B/1, 281r–282r (*LP*, 4 (2), nos. 4778 and 4755); TNA/PRO SP 1/50, 203 (*LP*, 4 (2), no. 4872); *Grace Book Γ*, 237.

3 The king's 'great matter', 1527–1533

'Almighty God, which by thy blessed son didst call Matthew from the receipt of custom to be an Apostle and Evangelist: Grant us grace to forsake all covetous desires and inordinate love of riches, and so to follow thy said Son: who liveth and reigneth now and forever, amen.'[1]

Waltham, August 1529

The crisis of what is sometimes referred to as Henry VIII's 'Divorce' from his first wife Katherine of Aragon (1485–1536) was already more than two years old when Thomas Cranmer became one of the king's theological advisors. Henry's attempts to gain an annulment that would have permitted him to remarry had become stalemated first in 1527 following the Sack of Rome, and then again in mid-1529 after the meeting of a special legatine court at Blackfriars. Cranmer's suggestions opened new courses of action that the king pursued so that he could marry Anne Boleyn (c. 1500–1536). By allying himself with Anne and by working closely with Thomas Cromwell, Cranmer became instrumental in encouraging the king to sever England's ancient allegiance to the papacy.

By chance, in early August 1529, Cranmer met Edward Fox (1496–1538), provost of King's College Cambridge, and Stephen Gardiner, now the king's principal secretary, at the house of the Crecy family in Waltham in Essex, where they had all taken refuge during a difficult summer. Heavy downpours threatened the harvest through much of England, and bread was in short supply. Then the plague broke out. When a fellow of Jesus College died suddenly, Cranmer helped to settle his estate.[2] He assisted at Cambridge's annual financial review as usual, but within days one of auditors also sickened and died.[3] Two sons of the Crecy family were students at the university, and alarmed for their safety, Cranmer brought them home to Waltham. Their mother was another of Cranmer's distant relatives. Waltham's Abbey of Holy Cross was a royal foundation, and when Henry heard about the plague while he was on his way to his summer hunting exercises, he stopped briefly at the abbey. Gardiner and Fox were assigned lodgings in the comforts of the Crecy household, and according to Ralph Morice, they joined Cranmer at the table.[4]

On their 'first night at supper', Morice recorded that the 'great and weighty cause of the king's divorcement' became the topic of conversation. Fox and Gardiner were eager for new ideas because every avenue that Thomas Cardinal Wolsey had pursued to release the king from his marriage had failed. Because Katherine had been married briefly to Henry's elder brother Arthur (1486–1502), the king had latterly come to believe that his marriage was defective from its beginning under prohibitions recorded in the Old Testament book of Leviticus: 'He that marrieth his brother's wife, doth an unlawful thing, he hath uncovered his brother's nakedness: they shall be without children'.[5] Although Henry and Katherine had had many sons, all of them died as infants. Their only surviving child was Mary (1516–1558), whom Henry reluctantly considered his heir. In early 1527, when the king first asked Wolsey to take up the question of the validity of his marriage, Katherine was forty-one years old and she had not conceived for nearly a decade. Without a son to succeed him, Henry feared that England would be overwhelmed by its more powerful neighbours.

But the king has been thwarted in his pursuit to be released from his marriage, first by the Sack of Rome in 1527, which meant that Pope Clement VII (Giulio di Giuliano de' Medici, r. 1523–1534) did not dare to render a determination that would offend Katherine's nephew, the Emperor Charles V. Prolonged negotiations by Fox and Gardiner with the pope in Orvieto had at last led Clement to allow a special legatine court to meet at Blackfriars in mid-1529. However, the Blackfriars court had just been adjourned on a flimsy technicality without a resolution, and Henry was exposed to open humiliation.

It was with this in mind that at dinner Morice said Cranmer launched into harsh criticisms about the way that the case had been handled. He told Fox and Gardiner that the frustrating 'delays of these your courts', had achieved 'small effect'. They had been 'beaten' in their dealings with the pope. Moreover, he did not believe that the papal courts could solve the problem of the king's marriage, and he rejected the authority they assumed. Rather, Cranmer suggested that theologians at the universities should debate the doctrinal questions that disturbed the king. Their opinions could be 'soon known'. The king's uneasy conscience would be quieted and then Henry could do what 'shall seem good before God'. Assuring the conscience of the king was the goal 'which we all chiefly ought to consider and regard in this question and doubt'.[6]

We cannot know how much of Morice's story was accurate. He was not present at the dinner, and there are difficulties with his account. The views that he said Cranmer expressed to Fox and Gardiner read very much like some of the arguments that appeared in 1532 in *A Glasse of the Truthe*, a little tract that promoted Henry's cause to his subjects, which possibly Cranmer helped to write.[7] Morice may have also developed his story from documents he saw after he entered the archbishop's employment. Morice may have borrowed a good deal from information he gained long afterwards when he wrote of the evening that launched Cranmer's career.

In reality, in August 1529 Cranmer could not know what the king actually wanted. We also do not know if Cranmer had heard the news that had filtered into England that summer from the Imperial Diet at Speyer. In April, the Elector of Saxony, Duke John (1468–1532) and the Landgrave Philip of Hesse (1504–1567), with several other princes and city magistrates, had banded together to defend Martin Luther against renewed opposition by the papacy and the Habsburgs. They called for greater freedom to worship as they thought right. Their petition has become known as the famous 'Protestation' that gave its name to Protestantism. Certainly Cranmer envisioned that Henry could also enjoy greater independence from the influence of the pope and emperor as part of the same trends that were taking place on the continent. Morice accurately captured Cranmer's extraordinary willingness to accommodate Henry at the expense of the papacy. This was the quality that drove Cranmer forward in his career and ultimately to the archbishopric of Canterbury.

Many years later, John Foxe noted that Fox and Gardiner liked Cranmer's ideas, and Fox brought them to the king's attention.[8] Henry was impressed, and he acted on them straightaway. Before the end of August Wolsey urgently summoned the French ambassador. Henry told him that he wanted him to go to France immediately to gather the opinions of learned men about his marriage and to send their advice back to England.[9] Henry also called Cranmer to court, but he had already left Waltham for Cambridge and then Aslockton. A post had to be sent to bring Cranmer to Greenwich in the early autumn.

Cranmer at court and Convocation

Cranmer's meeting with Fox and Gardiner had only happened by chance, which permitted John Foxe to write in hindsight that Cranmer's 'gentle nature' made him reluctant to enter the king's service.[10] However, Cambridge had prepared Cranmer to play the courtier. He had already seen the king on Henry's visits to the university, most recently in 1522, when the king spent a day or two at Cambridge accompanied by his secretary, Sir Thomas More (1478–1535) and the future archbishop of York, Edward Lee (1482–1455).[11] Henry's desire to find relief from his marriage and its diplomatic entanglements with the Holy Roman Empire provided new opportunities for evangelicals to enter the king's service. The physician William Butts (*c.* 1485–1545) had come to court from Cambridge in 1528, and he was one of a number of men Cranmer already knew who could have advised him.

Cranmer told Fox and Gardiner that he had had no opportunity to study the grounds of the king's case, and at his first audience, Henry may have confided what he wanted him to know, in the same way that he had startled Sir Thomas More two years earlier, when he abruptly revealed his doubts about his marriage as they were walking privately together in the gallery at Hampton Court. The king laid an open Bible before More and showed him the passages in Leviticus that convinced Henry that his marriage was against the laws of the Church, against Scripture, and also against the law of nature.[12]

One of the most consistent aspects of the king's case was his contention that Katherine's first marriage had been consummated, even though many years earlier Henry had acknowledged that Katherine was a virgin when he married her in 1509. Arthur and Katherine had spent no more than seven nights together. When questioned after Arthur died in 1502, she maintained at great immediate cost to herself that he had not consummated their marriage. For the rest of her life, she vigorously denied that Arthur had known her. In all likelihood, Katherine was telling the truth.[13] However, Henry's predicament was not unprecedented in the annals of Europe's dynasties. Similar doctrinal problems had been addressed by theologians for centuries. Despite Katherine's consistent denials, Henry insisted that his brother's marriage had been consummated, for otherwise he had no legal escape in his application to the pope. His whole case turned on this point. He told his advisors he believed that his soul would be destroyed if he continued in his marriage, and he may have said something to Cranmer along these lines. Henry expected Cranmer to endorse his version of the case and he instructed him to write his opinion. He sent Cranmer to live at Durham Place with the newly made earl of Wiltshire, the father of Anne Boleyn.

We cannot know to what extent Cranmer had been aware of Anne before now. In her youth, from about 1513 to 1521, she received a continental education at the French court, at a time when King Francis I (1494–1547) was interested in shielding evangelical scholars and preachers against the censures of the Sorbonne at the University of Paris. With his sister Marguerite (1492–1549), later queen of Navarre, he protected Jacques Lefèvre. When Anne returned to England in the early 1520s she was a fervent evangelical. Henry became smitten by her from about mid-1526 although she had already been promised in marriage at least once. Persistent rumors linked her with Henry Percy (*c.* 1502–1537), the heir to the fifth earl of Northumberland, a match that Wolsey forbade. The name of Sir Thomas Wyatt (*c.* 1503–1542) was also linked with Anne's. However, we cannot be certain to whom she was privately contracted in marriage. For more than five years she refused to become the king's mistress. Henry had already engaged in an adulterous affair with her sister Mary (*c.* 1499–1543), soon after Mary's marriage to William Carey (*c.* 1496–1528), a member of his privy chamber.[14] Remarkably ambitious and encouraged in her hopes by her father Thomas (1477–1539) and her brother George (*c.* 1504–1536), as well as her uncle Thomas Howard (1473–1554), third duke of Norfolk, Anne wanted to marry the king.

If Cranmer did not already have a clear idea of what was expected of him, then the period he spent with the Boleyns at Durham Place were definitive. Anne's enemies dismissed her as a Lutheran, but it would be more accurate to describe her as sharing the evangelical views that she had encountered at the French court. Her patronage became the cornerstone of Cranmer's rise. Quickly he wrote a long treatise that argued that Scripture prohibited any marriage between a man and his brother's widow, and that no pope had the authority to offer a dispensation in a matter that was prohibited by divine law. Cranmer accepted the idea that Arthur's marriage had been consummated.[15] In October 1529, Wolsey was indicted on a charge of *praemunire*, a crime that had long been defined by statute as an offence that trespassed on royal authority. He was deprived of all his royal offices and possessions (including Cardinal College and his Ipswich school). He was replaced as lord chancellor by Sir Thomas More, and Henry sent Cranmer with Fox to brief More concerning the details of his Great Matter.[16]

Meanwhile, Cranmer's treatise was circulated in manuscript, and within a few weeks it was used as a preliminary test of opinions at Cambridge even though Cranmer's university days were at an end. Henry rewarded him with the archdeaconry of Taunton in Devonshire. Because we know that he was not in service to the king before now, this was the first ecclesiastical appointment Cranmer ever received.[17] Giving Cranmer Taunton was a strategic decision, for, as archdeacon, he could support the king's plans when he sat as one of the approximately sixty members of the Lower House of Convocation, the legislative body of the province of Canterbury. Convocation held its meetings at the same time as Parliament, and it served almost as a third chamber in England's legislative system.

The first session of what has become known as the Reformation Parliament opened on 3 November 1529, and Convocation began meeting two days later with Cranmer in attendance.[18] Wolsey's fall encouraged calls for the reform of perceived abuses in the Church, but Archbishop William Warham of Canterbury, presiding over Convocation, was both fearful and reluctant to implement drastic changes. He was surprised by criticisms rising in the House of Commons that denounced pluralism and non-residency: that in holding more than one benefice, a priest might neglect some of his responsibilities for the cure of souls. Heretical books had been discovered at the universities, and Convocation ordered their examination. Little was achieved in that session, however, and Warham prorogued Convocation on 24 December. But Cranmer had had his first taste of the legislative functions of the English Church.

Impressed by his energy and abilities, in early 1530 Henry sent Cranmer to advance his cause in Rome.

Cranmer in Italy, 1530

Even now, despite nearly three years of delays and setbacks, Henry had not given up hope that Pope Clement could be persuaded to release him from his marriage to Katherine, and the king's intentions continued to be enormously complicated as a reflection of the difficult diplomatic scene. A new realignment of the great European powers had the potential of leaving Henry exposed, should the Emperor Charles and King Francis invade England together. Henry could not risk the pope's censure. To exert renewed pressure for a resolution, he sent Wiltshire as his representative at Charles's coronation in Bologna. Cranmer embarked with Anne's father towards the end of January 1530, but instead of stopping for the coronation, he proceeded directly to Rome where he took up the post of Penitentiary for England, so that English supplications for papal dispensations would come under his eye. Cranmer became fluent in Italian, and he chose capable servants who continued to keep him informed about events in Rome long after he became archbishop. If Clement had decided to find for Henry, then Cranmer's presence in Rome would have been essential.

But if Henry expected Wiltshire to make any real gains on his behalf, he was thwarted. After consultation with Charles at the coronation, Clement answered Katherine's appeal on 7 March by calling her case to the Curia, and he summoned Henry to Rome so a decision could be made there. Concerned that the king might now abandon Katherine for Anne, the pope forbade him from making any new marriage under pain of excommunication, the most fearsome penalty that he could impose. Excommunication represented not only a personal humiliation for the king, but carried with it the threat of dethronement by encouraging domestic uprisings and invasions. Two weeks later, Clement amplified his prohibition when he forbade all theologians to speak or write against the validity of Katherine's marriage.[19] The pope's threat blasted the most important aspect of Cranmer's assignment.[20]

But in the meantime, before the pope's prohibition reached the English universities, Henry's agents succeeded in pressuring Cambridge to deliver an opinion in his favour by using arguments from Cranmer's treatise. In early March Cambridge decided that the law of God prohibited a man from marrying his brother's widow. However, Cambridge shrank from explicitly denying the powers of the pope, which displeased Henry greatly. Strong measures had to be taken afterwards to make it look as if Cambridge had come out unequivocally for the king.[21] Using Cambridge's decision as a precedent, Oxford also decided reluctantly for Henry. At the same time, the king offered substantial financial inducements to Francis to encourage French universities to support his cause. Most of them did, but members of the Sorbonne were resistant until pressure and bribery gave Henry a small majority decision in his favour.[22]

At Henry's request, but with hostile reluctance, the pope allowed the question of the king's marriage to be taken up by Italian universities in the summer. John Stokesley had already been made bishop of London on the strength of his commitment to Henry's cause, and he had been sent with Reginald Pole to persuade the French universities. Now Stokesley arrived in Italy as Henry's ambassador to the imperial and papal courts, and Cranmer began to work closely with him for the first time in their careers. Cambridge's Greek scholar Richard Croke was also busy in assisting the king's cause in Italy. Bologna, Padua and a half-dozen other universities in Italy found for the king.[23]

As a reward for his service, while Cranmer was in Rome, Henry's agent, the Italian bishop of Worcester, Girolamo Ghinucci (1480–1541) collated him to the living of Bredon, one of the wealthiest in his gift. Ghinucci, like the king's confessor, Bishop

John Longland of Lincoln (1473–1547), believed that Henry's marriage to Katherine was invalid, and Ghinucci had often interceded with the pope on behalf of the king. Ghinucci's gift of Bredon probably came at Henry's suggestion as a reward for Cranmer's service, and to provide him with a good income to support his new career as a courtier. In addition, Ghinucci probably also moved Clement to grant Cranmer a dispensation that would permit him to hold four benefices at once, or three in addition to Bredon. Ghinucci may have meant this as a gesture of goodwill towards Cranmer, even though Cranmer was well aware that he could not use Clement's dispensation and he had not asked for it, since he already knew that the new legislation that had been passed while he was attending Convocation forbade pluralism on this scale.[24]

The appeal to the universities had now run its course, and Cranmer returned to England by the end of 1530.

Promoting the divorce, 1531

In England again, Cranmer returned to court. It is unlikely that he could afford to spend much time as far away as Bredon in Worcestershire, even though, for the first time in his life, he had cure of the souls of his parishioners. Rather, he was expected to employ curates who would conduct the day-to-day work of the living, though we know from a letter that he wrote to the earl of Wiltshire that he maintained considerable interest in his benefice.[25]

At the beginning of 1531, despite the apparent success of the appeal to the universities, Henry was almost no closer to a resolution to the stalemate. Now a vigorous campaign to promote the king's cause in the press was advanced by Cromwell. Cranmer also became involved in this work.

From 1527, Wolsey had commissioned written opinions on marriage law to carry the king's case through the papal courts. When Sir Thomas More became lord chancellor in 1529, he had asked to see what had already been written about it, and he probably read Cranmer's treatise.[26] While Cranmer was in Italy, Edward Fox continued to amass scriptural sources and other texts.

Now, from 1531, the documents were brought together to produce an array of printed tracts that argued that English kings had always enjoyed not only rule over the government but also complete authority over the Church in England. Fox's documents have become known as the *Collectanea satis copiosa*, and they became the centrepiece of Cromwell's efforts to promote the king's supremacy over the English Church, a difficult and dangerous new initiative that consumed the next four years before it was completely approved by both Parliament and Convocation. Fox articulated a new understanding of royal power, a legal fiction with only the thinnest reality in fact: that England was an empire that had suffered under the usurpation of the popes. The king's rule over the Church had always existed, but only now was it being expressed.[27] The purpose was first to support the king's cause, and ultimately, to endorse Henry's supremacy over the Church in England.

In April 1531, Fox's compilation of the results from the French and Italian universities was released in Latin as the *Censurae* by the king's printer Thomas Berthelet (d. 1555) for international consumption. Something similar was necessary for the domestic market. Working closely with Fox and Stokesley, Cranmer translated an English version, which was titled *The Determinations of the most famous and most excellent uniuersities of Italy and France* and printed by Berthelet in November.[28] Now also *A Glasse of the Truthe* was written to convince Henry's subjects. It took the form of a dialogue between a lawyer and a theologian that warned of the dangers England faced if the king had no son to succeed him. Cranmer probably also had a hand in preparing it, and in 1532 his friend Nicholas Hawkins was asked to turn *A Glasse of the Truthe* into Latin to take with him on embassy to the papal and imperial courts.[29]

Further, in June 1531 Cranmer wrote Wiltshire to inform him about a treatise written by Pole. At this stage of his career, Pole was still in service to the king and his tract was meant as another position paper on the king's case. It warned Henry about the dangers to the succession, but not about the potential problems should a daughter succeed him. Rather, Pole sounded an alarm about the wisdom of Henry's efforts to end his marriage, which he thought would jeopardize the stability of the realm. Cranmer thought Pole's book was eloquent and convincing. Yet, Cranmer advised Wiltshire that if it were released, it would persuade Henry's subjects against him. Pole's opinions challenged the efforts that Cromwell, Fox, and Cranmer were already making to promote royal authority. Pole wanted the king to submit his cause to the pope's judgement, and in this Cranmer thought 'he lacketh much judgment'.[30] In another year, Pole left England to pursue his studies in Italy, where he remained, beyond Henry's reach, for the rest of the king's life.

Henry's appeal to the universities had gained widespread attention and raised important interest amongst Protestants abroad. In mid-1531, the king received a visit from the humanist scholar Simon Grynaeus (1493–1541) of Basel, who arrived with letters of introduction from Erasmus to More and his other English friends. Ostensibly Grynaeus came to England to find rare manuscripts, but the real purpose of his visit was to encourage Henry to protect Protestants from the emperor. In February, at a meeting of Lutheran princes and cities in the market town of Schmalkalden, a defensive alliance was created under the leadership of Duke John and Landgrave Philip. Intrigued, and still eager to gain support wherever he could, Henry warmly received Grynaeus, and a presentation of the doctrinal grounds of his case was made by three or four of his leading theological advisors, one of whom was probably Cranmer.[31] Henry commissioned Grynaeus to send him the opinions of his colleagues, and at the same time he solicited Luther for his thinking about his case.

While he was at Cambridge, Cranmer had probably met prominent evangelicals from abroad, including Erasmus, but Grynaeus played an unusually important role as the first eminent evangelical reformer with whom he developed a lasting friendship. The visit of Grynaeus opened opportunities for Cromwell and Cranmer to build common theological positions between English and continental reformers. Once he returned to Basel, Grynaeus wrote to Martin Bucer, Philip Melanchthon, Huldrych Zwingli, and others, including perhaps John Calvin in Paris and he asked them to prepare their opinions on the grounds of Henry's case. From 1531 onwards, because of the introductions Grynaeus provided, Cranmer had extraordinary access to all of the leading figures of reform on the continent.

Almost immediately, an important split in opinion became apparent that divided the Lutherans from the rest. Zwingli was one of Grynaeus's earliest patrons.[32] They both believed that

Katherine's marriage was invalid and that Henry was already free to marry Anne. However, Luther, Melanchthon and Bucer disagreed. They decided that the prohibitions defined by Leviticus were superseded by other passages in the book of Deuteronomy that commanded a man to marry his late brother's wife. Therefore they argued that Henry had no grounds for discarding Katherine.[33] William Tyndale (*c.* 1494–1536), writing from exile, had already denounced Henry's cause in his book the *Practice of Prelates*.[34] Therefore the Lutherans concluded that the king's marriage to Katherine was binding. At the very beginning of England's approach to the Protestants, the Lutherans were unwilling to support the king while the Swiss proved quite accommodating, a pattern that Cranmer would discover again as archbishop. The English Reformation in Cranmer's lifetime would ultimately owe more to Swiss Reform than to the Lutherans.

In August 1531, English evangelicals were disturbed when Thomas Bilney was burnt for heresy by the bishop of Norwich, Richard Nix (*c.* 1447–1535). Bilney was one of the most influential of all of the Cambridge brethren, responsible for persuading Hugh Latimer and others to question traditional beliefs. Bilney had already abjured for the first time in 1527. Then he suggested that kings should assume the role of an Old Testament ruler like Hezekiah (d. 687 BC) and destroy any religious images that detracted worshippers from the sacrifice that Christ had made on the cross. He also admitted then that Luther's opinions had been justly condemned. But more recently, Bilney repudiated his abjuration. He began to preach against abuses again, and he distributed Tyndale's banned books.

His second arrest meant that very likely he would be condemned. However, Bilney made an audacious appeal to the king to hear his case as the supreme head of the English Church. The same strategy saved Edward Crome a year later when Warham accused him before Convocation of preaching heresies. But Bilney was hurried to the stake before Henry could intervene. In making an investigation afterwards, Sir Thomas More did not denounce his execution.[35] Bilney was killed as a defensive measure on the part of those who wished to defend the Church from royal control. His execution redoubled Cromwell's efforts to build the king's supremacy, and once Cranmer was archbishop, he hounded Nix for killing Bilney.

Nuremberg, 1532

Cranmer's next important appointment came in 1532 when Henry sent him as English ambassador to the court of the Emperor Charles. His assignment then was to win support from persons of influence for the king's cause. This was a task of daunting dimensions because Henry's predicament continued to be overshadowed by larger and more dangerous problems. Central Europe was still reeling not only from the Sack of Rome in 1527 but from the devastating defeat that the kingdom of Hungary suffered in 1526 at the hands of the Ottoman emperor, Suleyman the Magnificent (1494–1566) at the Battle of Mohács. The city of Buda was sacked, and King Louis II (1506–1526), the husband of Charles's sister Mary (1505–1558), was slain. The entire Hungarian nobility and sixteen thousand men died with him. Charles immediately made his brother Ferdinand (1503–1564) king of Hungary to stabilize the region. In 1531 Ferdinand became his brother's acknowledged heir to the Holy Roman Empire when he was elected king of the Romans. But in 1532 Suleyman threatened to attack again. Cranmer was sent to the imperial court in the midst of the crisis.

Charles knew that he was ill prepared to face a fresh onslaught. He had insufficient money and fighting men to repel the invaders. Thus he summoned the Imperial Diet to Regensburg (Ratisbon) where he was obliged to negotiate with Lutheran members of his own empire that he would have preferred to subdue. Charles also turned to England, France, and Poland for assistance. In March, Cromwell received word that Francis promised some fifty thousand men for the defence of Naples. But Henry had no real intention of giving Charles the money and military aid he requested.[36]

Cranmer left England in late January 1532 for Brussels to join the previous ambassador, Sir Thomas Elyot (*c.* 1490–1546), the author of the masterwork of political theory, *The Boke Named the Governour*. Together they followed the imperial court as Charles made his way from the Low Countries. The emperor was never willing to abandon his support of his aunt Katherine, and he treated Henry's ambassadors with icy courtesy. Elyot's embassy had lasted only a few months and bore little fruit.

As Elyot and Cranmer followed the imperial court from Brussels to central Europe, they passed through a complicated patchwork of semi-autonomous principalities and free cities that belonged to the Holy Roman Empire. Each had their own local rulers, their own customs, their own styles of dress, their own forms of German, and increasingly, their own religious allegiances and liturgies. One region remained loyal to the papacy, while the next town was thoroughly imbued with Lutheran ideas. They were knit together in a loose confederation, united only by their allegiance to their elected emperor and the agreements that were forged during the sessions of the Imperial Diet.

In Worms, Elyot noted in a letter to Norfolk that the town was almost completely 'possessed' by Lutherans, as well as by a large Jewish population, while the rest were so 'indifferent' that the local bishop did not know how to address the challenges of his situation. In Speyer, the people kept their Catholicism.[37]

The free city of Nuremberg was different still. On the River Pegnitz in Franconia, Nuremberg was the third largest city of the Holy Roman Empire, and important for its extensive trade and printing industry. Its leaders had been won over quickly to Luther's theology, and they refused to accept his condemnation as a heretic by Pope Leo X and by the emperor's Edict of Worms. Nuremberg was so vulnerable to suppression by Charles, however, that it feared political isolation and therefore it could not afford to join the League of Schmalkalden. The Imperial Diet moved to Nuremberg during the summer of 1532. The friendships that Cranmer made there were definitive for his developing theology and for his private life. Nuremberg shaped the ultimate direction of his career.[38]

Elyot caught Cranmer's immediate fascination with Nuremberg's new liturgy. Cohesion in religious worship was lost in the Holy Roman Empire as many imperial cities abandoned the Latin Mass. In 1523, Luther and Zwingli each attempted his own revisions of the Latin liturgy, and then Luther took a bold step in 1526 when he prepared a *Deutsche Messe* that was influenced by the service Bucer had written for Strasbourg. In Nuremberg, the Mass had recently been revised by Johann Brenz (1499–1570) with Andreas

Osiander (1498–1552), the influential chief pastor of the church of St Lorenz.

In March 1532, Cranmer and Elyot observed this new service a year before it was printed. As Elyot wrote Norfolk, the priest sang the Mass in Latin, but he omitted the traditional petitions to the saints. When he read the Epistle in Latin, the subdeacon went into the pulpit and read the text to the people in their own language. Then the priest read the Gospel verses softly in Latin, and as he did so, the deacon went into the pulpit and read them 'in the Almain tongue'. Immediately intrigued, Cranmer made inquiries, and he told Elyot that the Epistles and Gospels were not kept in the same order as they were in England. Every day one chapter of the New Testament was taught. Then the priest and the choir sang the Creed 'as we do'. The priest sang the words of the consecration 'with a high voice'. After the elevation the deacon turned to the people and told them in German ('a long process', Elyot observed) how they should prepare themselves to take communion of the flesh and blood of Christ. Then anyone who desired could come up to receive without first going to confession. But Elyot and Cranmer left the church without taking communion, and Elyot joked in his letter to Norfolk that the worshippers perhaps wondered whether their visitors were greater heretics than they were themselves.[39] When the time came for Cranmer to devise a new liturgy for the English Church, he drew upon what he learned from Nuremberg.

Over the summer Cranmer became a welcome visitor at Osiander's house, and they spent hours amongst the books in his study. Osiander was engaged in developing a *Harmony* of the four gospels, a 'great labor' that had never been undertaken before. When Osiander dedicated the book to Cranmer in 1537 he wrote of Cranmer's great love for the Gospel and his devotion to true religion.[40] They went to meetings of the Imperial Diet. Cranmer also wanted to discuss the king's cause with the new elector of Saxony, Duke John Frederick I (1504–1554), which prepared the groundwork for the later attempts that he made as archbishop to bring about agreements between the Lutheran princes and his own king.[41]

According to the author of the 'Life', Cranmer was remarkably persuasive in convincing members of the imperial court that

Henry's cause was just. Cranmer made an excellent impression. He was gracious to all he met. One of those he persuaded was the theologian Henricus Cornelius Agrippa von Nettesheim (1486–1535), who 'confessed' to Cranmer that the Aragon marriage was 'nought', though he dared not say so openly for fear of both the emperor and the pope.[42] John Cochleus (1479–1552) of Meissen also enjoyed Cranmer's company, though later he repudiated their friendship. Cranmer was also a favourite amongst the ambassadors, and he struck up a friendship in Vienna with the Polish ambassador Johannes Dantiscus (1485–1548), who listened to him patiently when Cranmer told him 'all my mind concerning the bishop of Rome'. Many times, Dantiscus seemed to agree. He entrusted Cranmer with a student to send back to England for education.[43] Almost alone amongst the Lutheran leaders, Osiander was convinced that Henry's marriage to Katherine was invalid. He urged Luther and Melanchthon to reconsider their opinions of Henry's case. Later Osiander wrote a pamphlet on the subject, which he told Cranmer at the beginning of 1538 had to be suppressed to avoid giving offence to the emperor.[44]

When they arrived in Nuremberg in March 1532, Elyot reported to Norfolk that 'all the priests have wives' and they were 'the fairest women of the town'.[45] From the mid-1520s, Lutheran clergymen discarded the standard of celibacy that was required in the Catholic Church as part of the special discipline that was expected of all men in holy orders. In redefining the sacraments, the Lutherans argued that marriage was a right for the laity and clergy alike. Their marriages became public acts of defiance against the papacy. Luther married Katharina von Bora (1499–1552) in 1525, and she played a pivotal role in running his extensive estates and in presiding at his table as he entertained important guests.[46] Zwingli and Bucer also took wives. Osiander married three times, and he established a dynasty of theologians who were influential well into the seventeenth century.

Cranmer turned forty-three in 1532. Although the details elude us, he probably met Osiander's wife Katharina Preu when he visited their house. She had a young unmarried niece, Margarete (d. *c.* 1575), who may have been twenty. We do not know if Cranmer had learned German, or if Margarete knew any Latin.

In the course of Cranmer's visits, Osiander arranged for them to wed. Probably he solemnized their union.

Cranmer's decision to marry in Nuremberg was so great a watershed in his life that it signals how far he had moved beyond his early evangelical views. Now he embraced Lutheran teachings: that salvation was by faith alone, and that believers were justified by their faith, and not by their works. He accepted that the Mass was not a sacrifice. Like Luther and Osiander, he rejected the dogma of transubstantiation because it could not be proved by Scripture, but for the next fifteen years he continued to believe, with the Lutherans, that Christ's body and blood were really present in the sacrament of the altar.[47]

Under canon law in the Catholic Church, Cranmer's marriage was illegal, and offensive to the imperial court to which he was accredited. We cannot know if his marriage became widely known, but in Vienna Dantiscus knew or suspected that Cranmer had a wife. His marriage was also disrespectful to his own king. Cranmer's second marriage, even more than his first, complicated his career. He had reason to believe that he would serve as Henry's ambassador for a long time to come. Perhaps he would not have married again had he anticipated that Henry and Anne Boleyn might want him to become archbishop of Canterbury.[48]

Most of his biographers have emphasized Cranmer's willingness to enhance Henry's powers, but few have recognized that Nuremberg provided him with the strategies to maintain his own opinions despite the hostility of his prince. Osiander and Nuremberg's other leaders protected its Lutheran identity despite the emperor's repeated threats to the city's independence.[49] Others wrestled with the problem of how to place their loyalty to God ahead of their duty to their prince. Luther was protected from the wrath of the papacy and the emperor by the electors of Saxony. In contrast, Cranmer did not enjoy Henry's unconditional protection. From Canterbury, Cranmer carefully observed the career of Hermann V von Wied (1477–1552), archbishop of the free city of Cologne. In the 1530s and 1540s Hermann emerged as that greatest of rarities: a Protestant archbishop in the Catholic Church. He invited the advice of Melanchthon and Bucer. Despite the emperor's opposition, Hermann instituted evangelical reforms in Cologne until he was deprived in 1546.[50] Remarkably, at many junctures,

Cranmer chose, like Osiander and Hermann, to accommodate his prince without relinquishing his own private opinions and purpose.

Cranmer wrote Henry regularly with diplomatic news. In the autumn, he followed Charles and Ferdinand from Regensburg to Vienna and to southern Austria, where he witnessed a frightening military disaster, as he reported in October 1532. The Italian troops that Charles had taken such great measures to marshal mutinied because they had not been paid. They turned their anger against the unprotected towns of southern Austria. Cranmer told Henry that many of the townspeople fled to the mountains in fear. Villages were burnt, women raped, and many were killed. The harvest was destroyed. 'Thus is this country miserably oppressed by all parties, but much more by them that came to defend this country, than it was by the Turks'. Cranmer passed through a battlefield strewn with bodies, where as many as two thousand lay dead, by his estimate. Although he was in real danger, he was fully prepared to follow the emperor into Italy and then to Spain.[51]

While Cranmer was writing to the king, he could not know that Henry was sending Hawkins as his replacement. Cranmer had not yet heard that Archbishop Warham had died in August. In the following month, Henry raised Anne to the marquisate of Pembroke and settled on her a substantial income. In November, she accompanied Henry to Calais for a meeting with King Francis. On that visit, now certain at last that the king would marry her, Anne became pregnant. When her condition became apparent early in the new year, immediately the king wanted to ensure that her child would be recognized as his legitimate heir. So secretly was their marriage solemnized in the third week of January that Cranmer did not learn for a fortnight that they had wed.[52]

When Cranmer remembered in 1555, six months before his execution, how he had been suddenly recalled to England, he told his examiners that no candidate had ever been more reluctant to take up an archbishopric than he. He did not wish to leave his studies, and he said he delayed his return by half a year or 'seven weeks at the least' in the hope that he would be forgotten.[53] But this was not what actually happened. Cranmer wanted to become archbishop, and when summoned, he travelled to London as quickly as the icy winter conditions allowed. Only a few weeks elapsed between the time he was recalled and his arrival around

10 January. According to Charles's highly capable ambassador Eustace Chapuys (*c.* 1492–1556), many people were astonished when they learned that Cranmer was the king's choice to succeed Warham as archbishop of Canterbury.

As his very first act as archbishop elect, Cranmer continued the pension Warham had granted Erasmus. On 7 February 1533, Erasmus wrote Sir Thomas More (who had resigned the lord chancellorship in the previous year) that his pension from the living of Aldington in Kent had been extended. Although it is doubtful that Erasmus knew who Cranmer was beyond the fact that he had succeeded Warham, Cranmer's generosity earned the great man's gratitude and a stream of compliments in his letters. Cranmer's decision was an open sign of his intent to continue to associate the English Church with evangelicalism.

Cranmer's consecration, 1533

In the first weeks following his return, Cranmer met with Henry's lawyers to consider the political implications of his consecration. This was the first time in a generation that there would be a new archbishop of Canterbury; Warham had occupied the throne of St Augustine since 1503. For centuries, bishops and archbishops had customarily sworn oaths of fealty to the pope as well as to the king. In March 1532 Henry had raised objections against the oaths the bishops made to the pope. During a furious argument in the House of Lords, Henry had accused Warham of *praemunire*. A few weeks earlier Warham had publicly repudiated anything that had been done since the start of the Reformation Parliament in 1529 that violated the rights of the papacy or the privileges of his metropolitical see. He decided that he would rather run the risk of punishment for misprision of treason under the *praemunire* charge than be guilty of perjury for breaking his oath to the pope. Only his death on 22 August spared him further consequences.[54]

Cranmer did indeed want to be archbishop, but not at the cost of *praemunire* if he swore obedience to the pope. Nor did he wish to accept the pallium, the narrow woollen stole that popes bestowed upon their metropolitans as the greatest symbol of their office, which Luther had denigrated as an empty extravagance.

But in 1533 the king could not afford to insult the pope openly. There was still an extremely small chance that Clement might, even now, make a determination in Henry's favour. Now that he had married Anne, the threat of excommunication hung heavily over him. England was awash with rumours that Charles was preparing to invade. Strong domestic support continued for Katherine and Mary. Henry had to pursue conflicting policies to safeguard the realm. The fourth session of the Reformation Parliament opened on 4 February 1533. Convocation began its meetings the next day without Cranmer. Until the full agenda of legislation that Cromwell was planning could be passed, Henry would not be sufficiently secure to repudiate the papacy completely. The king wanted Cranmer to receive all of the necessary approvals from the pope that would make him generally accepted as the legitimate archbishop of Canterbury, and he was even willing to pay the substantial expenses for the papal bulls that would be required. The king also wanted Cranmer to have the pallium.

Left to his own devices, Cranmer would have accepted the archbishopric from the hands of the king without invoking the papacy. Cranmer dismissed the papacy as an intrusive foreign power. Paradoxically, Henry's efforts to end his marriage to Katherine reinforced the idea that the king, as well as everyone else, was bound by the law of God as it was now interpreted by Scripture. Although he was not always successful, Cranmer endeavoured to hold Henry to this standard, as much as he was constrained to obey the king as the chosen agent of God. Cranmer did not have a lawyer's perspective (as we will note again), but at length they came to an agreement: at his consecration, Cranmer would protest against the authority of the pope but without jeopardizing his installation in the eyes of Rome. The king called several civil lawyers to devise the means to bestow the archbishopric upon him without 'enforcing me nothing against my conscience'. As was the usual practice, a proctor was sent to the pope to swear oaths on Cranmer's behalf.[55] When he gave him the archbishopric, Henry presented Cranmer with a ring that had once belonged to Wolsey.[56] This was the first ring of several that played symbolic roles in Cranmer's career as signs of promise, reward, and protection.

Henry's application for the bulls for Cranmer's consecration was hurried along, much to the distress of Chapuys, and he warned Charles that once Cranmer was consecrated he would dissolve Katherine's marriage. In a state of anxiety, Chapuys recommended that the bulls be delayed, but they were not. An unusually large number of papal bulls were sent to England in early March to allow Cranmer to be consecrated, and one of them specifically absolved him, as archdeacon of Taunton, for an unspecified problem, which may have been related to the early steps Convocation had taken, in conjuncture with Parliament, against papal rights.[57]

Cranmer's consecration as the sixty-eighth archbishop of Canterbury occurred on 30 March 1533. In a semiprivate ceremony in the chapter house of St Stephen's College in the old Palace of Westminster, Cranmer made a formal protestation in the presence the canon lawyer Richard Gwent (d. 1543), dean of the Court of the Arches, and other witnesses, that it was not his intent to be bound by any oaths that were contrary to the law of God or against the king and his laws. No oath that he was about to take would prevent him from reforming those things in the Church of England that seemed to him in need of reform. Whatever had been sworn by a proctor in Rome on his behalf he declared null and invalid. He also promised to pursue heretics, schismatics, and rebels.[58]

Then Cranmer entered St Stephen's Chapel, a royal space *par excellence* whose walls were illuminated with portraits of the family of King Edward III (1312–1377) kneeling in devotion to Christ and his mother. St Stephen's Chapel was lost when the Houses of Parliament burned in 1834, but there can be no doubt that Cranmer's consecration was held in a sacred space dedicated to the power of England's kings.[59] He was consecrated by the bishops of Lincoln, Exeter, and St Asaph. Longland of Lincoln was the king's confessor, to whom Henry had confided his first doubts about his marriage to Katherine. In 1532, the pressure of consecrating Henry Standish (d. 1535) of St Asaph had triggered the catastrophic breakdown between Archbishop Warham and the king. Longland read the oath, and Cranmer declared he would take it only according to the protest he had just made. Then he swore. Before he accepted the pallium, Cranmer again referred to his protest. A third time, he asked all those present to bear witness that he took his oaths in accordance with his protestation, which was duly written into his Register following the papal bulls, although it did not become widely known at the time.[60]

Historians have struggled to reconcile the inconsistencies concerning Cranmer's consecration and many have concluded that his actions were unethical. He benefited substantially by accepting the primacy of all England from Pope Clement VII even though he had no intention to abide by papal law. Twenty-two years later, Reginald Pole, now a cardinal and poised to succeed him as archbishop of Canterbury, angrily accused Cranmer of 'a double perjury' because he had 'forsworn afore you did swear'.[61] When he was examined at Oxford before his execution, some of his opponents thought Cranmer had no conscience at all.

Some of the problems that Cranmer's consecration presented were addressed in 1534, when the Act Restraining the Payment of Annates was passed by Parliament, which disallowed papal bulls for a bishop's consecration. Cathedral chapters were now to elect the man that the king chose to be the next bishop, and candidates had to swear their loyalty to the king and to no other authority. As we will see in future chapters, other inconsistencies were raised at his consecration that Cranmer had to address in due course.[62]

Dunstable

In April 1533, after Parliament and Convocation were prorogued, Cranmer once again acknowledged that he owed his office to the king when he made a formal request to address the 'uncertainty of the succession' and to provide a 'final determination' in the king's Great Cause.[63] The most important piece of legislation, the Act in Restraint of Appeals to Rome, had been passed by the Reformation Parliament in the previous month. It asserted that England had always been ruled by its king as the one supreme head who held authority over all people, laity and clergy alike. It denied the power of the papacy and criticized its interference in the king's marriage. The new law also disallowed Katherine's appeal to the papal courts.[64]

Two days after his consecration, Cranmer began to preside over Convocation in the chapter house of old St Paul's Cathedral, and the theological grounds of the king's case were discussed. Under heavy pressure from the king, both houses agreed that it was unlawful for a man to marry his brother's widow if the first marriage had been consummated, and that such a marriage was forbidden by divine law.[65]

The way was now clear for Cranmer to pass a final sentence. He summoned Henry and Katherine to his court at Dunstable Priory. On 10 May, assisted by Longland and Gardiner, Cranmer opened the proceedings. Katherine refused to recognize the legitimacy of his court and she had no intention of appearing. Cranmer declared her contumacious and he made the business as brief as he could because Anne's coronation was 'so near at hand'. On 23 May 1533 he passed sentence that the king had never been lawfully married to Katherine.[66]

Coronation of Anne Boleyn

Anne was crowned at Westminster Abbey on Whitsunday, 1 June 1533, the feast of Pentecost. The finest account we have of her coronation comes from Cranmer's letter to Hawkins when he described the great show the livery companies of London made on the Thames with decorated barges, music and tableaux, and how Anne rode through the streets of London in a horse litter with her hair streaming down her back. That she expected a child was plain for all to see. Supported by Stokesley and Gardiner, Anne approached the high altar of the Abbey, where 'I did set the crown on her head'.[67]

Thomas Cranmer had been created by the king's Great Matter and by Anne Boleyn. He had been instrumental in resolving a dynastic predicament that had threatened the king and the realm since the beginning of Henry's reign. To the queen he crowned he owned his promotion to the archbishopric of Canterbury even more than to the king whom he had sworn to serve. At the coronation banquet, as the king watched from a gallery, Cranmer alone sat on the dais with the queen, with the nobility and bishops of England and Wales at their feet. Together they represented a new future that would ultimately become a fundamental and permanent break from the papacy and its centuries of tradition.

Notes

1 Cranmer's collect for the feast of St Michael in *The booke of the common prayer and administracion of the sacramentes and other rites and ceremonies of the Churche: after the vse of the Churche of England* (London: Edward Whitchurch, March 1549, *RSTC* 16267), 115v.

2 Mr Ashton's death at Jesus College: CUL, University Archives, VC Probate Wills I, fol. 49r.

3 Cranmer as university auditor in 1529: *Grace Book B Part II: Containing the Accounts of the Proctors of the University of Cambridge, 1511–1544*, ed. M. Bateson (Cambridge, 1905), 153 (1529). George Stavert of Pembroke was the auditor whose death prompted Cranmer to leave Cambridge for Waltham. CUL, University Archives, VC Probate Wills I, fol. 49v.

4 The comforts of the Crecy household are indicated in the will of Margaret Crecye of Waltham Holy Cross made when she was a widow on 9 November 1553 and proved 18 October 1554. TNA:PRO PROB 11/37, fols. 68v–69v. Morice, 241–2. John Foxe incorporated Morice's story of Cranmer's meeting at Waltham in his 1570 edition of the *Actes and Monuments* (London: John Daye, *RSTC* 11223), at pp. 2033–5.

5 Leviticus 18:16, 20:21.

6 Morice, 241–2.

7 See especially the comment 'And yet there is but one truth in this matter', which Morice ascribed to Cranmer at dinner: *A Glasse of the Truthe* (London: Thomas Berthlet, 1532, *RSTC* 11918), sig. B3r; Morice, 242.

8 Foxe 1570, 2033. Gardiner made no references to Cranmer in his letters to the king in 1529.

9 *LP*, 4, no. 5862.

10 Foxe 1570, 2034–5.

11 *Grace Book B I*, 219–20, 223; and B *II*, 108; S. Wabuda, 'Receiving the King: Henry VIII at Cambridge', in *Henry VIII and the Court: Art, Politics and Performance*, eds. T. Betteridge and S. Lipscomb (Farnham, 2013), 163–78.

12 More to Cromwell, 5 March 1534, printed in *Correspondence*, no. 199 (493–4).

13 H. A. Kelly, *The Matrimonial Trials of Henry VIII*, (Stanford, 1976), 60, 213–15, 219–21.

14 Kelly, *Matrimonial Trials*, 16–17; M. Dowling, 'Anne Boleyn and Reform', *JEH*, 35 (1984), 30–46; R. J. Knecht, 'Francis I, "Defender of the Faith"?' in *Wealth and Power in Tudor England: essays presented to S. T. Bindoff*, eds. E. W. Ives *et al.*, (London, 1978), 106–27.

15 John Bale listed the two-volume 'De non ducenda fratria' amongst Cranmer's works in *Scriptorvm Illustriu[m] maioris Brytanniae, quam nunc Angliam & Scotiam uocant: Catalogus.* (Basel: Joannis Oporium, 1557, 1559), 691.

16 More to Cromwell, 5 March 1534, printed in *Correspondence of More,* no. 199.

17 Morice, 243. MacCulloch has corrected his early supposition that Cranmer had been sent on embassy to Spain in the late 1520s: 'Thomas Cranmer and Johannes Dantiscus: Retraction and Additions', *JEH,* 58 (2007), 273–86.

18 S. E. Lehmberg, *The Reformation Parliament 1529–1536* (Cambridge, 1970), 69, 76–89, 100–1.

19 *LP,* 4, no. 6256, 6279, also *Calendar of State Papers, Spanish,* 4, nos. 315, 396; Scarisbrick, *Henry VIII,* 255–8.

20 *LP,* 4, no. 6531.

21 Lamb, 20–4.

22 Knecht, 'Francis I', 115. Scarisbrick noted that the University of Angers found for the queen. *Henry VIII,* 255–8. *LP,* 4, no. 6370.

23 *LP,* 4, nos. 6428, 6446.

24 I am indebted to the late Maria Dowling for this information. See also Morice, 243; MacCulloch, *Cranmer,* 49–50. Pluralism statute: 21 Henry VIII c. 13; Lehmberg, *Reformation Parliament,* 93. Cranmer's letter to Wiltshire, *Miscellaneous,* no. 1.

25 Cranmer, *Miscellaneous,* letter, no. 1 (from 1531); MacCulloch, *Cranmer,* 53.

26 More to Cromwell, 5 March 1534, printed in *Correspondence,* no. 199 (495–6).

27 Graham Nicholson, 'The Act of Appeals and the English Reformation', in *Law and Government under the Tudors,* eds. C. Cross, D. Loades, and J. J. Scarisbrick (Cambridge, 1988), 19–30.

28 *Grauissimae, atque exactissimae illustrissimarum totius Italiae, et Galliae academiarum censurae . . . .* (London: Thomas Berthelet, [1531] RSTC 14286); *The determinations of the moste famous and mooste excellent vniuersities of Italy and Fraunce . . . .* (London: Thomas Berthelet, 7 November 1531 *RSTC* 14287).

29 *A Glasse of the Truthe* (London: Thomas Berthlet, 1532, *RSTC* 11918); MacCulloch, *Cranmer,* 55–9. See also D. G. Newcombe's account of the life of Hawkins in the *ODNB.*

30 Cranmer to Wiltshire, Hampton Court, 13 June 1531, *Miscellaneous,* letter no. 1.

31 *LP,* 5, nos. 145, 287; MacCulloch, *Cranmer,* 60–7; R. McEntegart, *Henry VIII, the League of Schmalkalden, and the English Reformation* (London, 2002), 39.

32   Simon Grynaeus, *Epistolae*, ed. G. T. Streuber (Basel, 1874), 48, 57, 60.

33   Deuteronomy 25:5–10: 'When brethren dwell together and one of them dieth without children, the wife of the deceased shall not marry another: but his brother shall take her, and raise up seed for his brother'.

34   Melanchthon: *OL*, 2, 556–7; [William Tyndale], *The practyse of prelates* ([Antwerp, 1530, *RSTC* 24465), H4v–K1v. M. Dowling, 'Humanist support for Katherine of Aragon', *Historical Research*, 57 (1984), 46–55; McEntegart, *League of Schmalkalden*, 39–41.

35   *The confutacyon of Tyndales answere*, ed. L. A. Schuster *et al.*, in *The Complete Works of St. Thomas More*, 8, pt. 1 (New Haven, 1973), 22–5.

36   MacCulloch, *Cranmer*, 74–5; McEntegart, *League of Schmalkalden*, 11–14.

37   Sir Thomas Elyot to Thomas Howard, duke of Norfolk, 14 March 1532, BL, Cotton MS Vitellius B XXI, 58r–59r (*LP*, 5, no. 869).

38   G. Seebass, 'The Importance of the Imperial City of Nuremberg in the Reformation', in *Humanism and Reform: The Church in Europe, England, and Scotland, 1400–1643: Essays in Honour of James K. Cameron*, ed. J. Kirk, *SCH*, subsidia 8 (Oxford, 1991), 113–27.

39   Elyot to Norfolk, 14 March 1532, BL, Cotton MS Vitellius B XXI, 58v–59r (*LP*, 5, no. 869); G. J. Cuming, *A History of Anglican Liturgy* (London, 1969), 39–41, 326; B. A. Gerrish, 'The Reformation and the Eucharist', in *Thinking with the Church: Essays in Historical Theology* (Cambridge, 2010), 229–58.

40   See the dedicatory epistle in Andreas Osiander's *Harmoniae Evangelicae Liber IIII Graece et Latine* (Basel: Johannes Froben, 1537). His remarks were quoted by John Bale, *Illustrivm Maioris Britanniae Scriptorvm . . . Summariu[m]*. (Ipswich: John Overton. [Wesel: Dirick van de Straten], 1548, *RSTC* 1295), 238v–239r.

41   Cranmer to Henry VIII, 20 October 1532, printed in Miscellaneous, letter no. 3.

42   'Life', 221.

43   MacCulloch has corrected his early supposition that Cranmer and Dantiscus met in Iberia as early as 1528. 'Thomas Cranmer and Johannes Dantiscus: Retraction and Additions', *JEH*, 58 (2007), 273–86. See also his *Cranmer*, 72–3. H. de Vocht, ed., *John Dantiscus and his Netherlandish friends as revealed by their correspondence 1522–1546* in *Humanistica Lovaniensia*, 16 (Louvain, 1964), 280–3, 325–6. See also Cranmer's 1540 letter to Wriothesley, *Miscellaneous*, no. 271.

44   Osiander to Cranmer, 24 January 1538: BL, Harley MS 6989, 80 (*LP*, 13 (1), no. 140 and also no. 648); MacCulloch, *Cranmer*, 70–1, 74–5;

G. Cuming, *The Godly Order: Texts and Studies relating to the Book of Common Prayer*, Alcuin Club, 65 (1983), 72.

45 Elyot to Norfolk, 14 March 1532, BL, Cotton MS Vitellius B XXI, 59r (*LP, 5*, no. 869).

46 I owe this suggestion to Susan C. Karant-Nunn.

47 Cranmer to Joachim Vadian, 1537, *OL*, 1, no. 7; *AM*, 5, 54; P. Brooks, *Thomas Cranmer's Doctrine of the Eucharist: An Essay in Historical Development* (London, 1965), 3–37.

48 Cranmer to Henry VIII, 20 October 1532, printed in Miscellaneous, letter no. 3; Ridley, *Cranmer*, 46–7.

49 Seebass, 'Nuremberg in the Reformation', 113–27.

50 Hermann and Cranmer: Cuming, *The Godly Order*, 68–90; MacCulloch, *Cranmer* 385, 393.

51 Cranmer to Henry VIII, 20 October 1532, printed in *Miscellaneous*, letter no. 3.

52 Cranmer's letter to Hawkins, 17 June 1533, *Miscellaneous*, no. 14.

53 Cranmer, *Miscellaneous*, 223; Foxe 1583 (1880); *AM*, 8, 55.

54 J. M. Gray, *Oaths and the English Reformation* (Cambridge, 2013), 100–5; see also J. J. Scarisbrick's entry on Warham in the *ODNB*.

55 Cranmer, *Miscellaneous*, 223–4.

56 Alexander Ales to Elizabeth I: TNA/PRO, SP 70/17, 11v (*Calendar of State Papers Foreign, Elizabeth*, 1, no. 1303); MacCulloch, *Cranmer*, 84.

57 LPL, Cranmer's Register, 1r–5v.

58 LPL, Cranmer's Register, 4v, translated in Gray, *Oaths*, 102.

59 Roy Strong, *Lost Treasures of Britain* (London, 1991), 203–8.

60 LPL, Cranmer's Register, 4r–5v; Cranmer, *Miscellaneous*, 224; Gray, *Oaths*, 103.

61 Pole to Cranmer, *Miscellaneous*, 538.

62 Gray, *Oaths*, 105.

63 Cranmer to Henry VIII, Lambeth Palace, 11 April 1533, *Miscellaneous*, no. 5.

64 24 Henry. VIII c. 12 (1533).

65 Lehmberg, *Reformation Parliament*, 176–8; Kelly, *Matrimonial Trials*, 198–203;

66 Cranmer's letters to Henry VIII, Cromwell and Hawkins, *Miscellaneous*, nos. 10–14.

67 Cranmer's letter to Hawkins, 17 June 1533, *Miscellaneous*, no. 14.

4   The new archbishop, 1533–1535

'Almighty God, whom truly to know is everlasting life: Grant us perfectly to know thy son Jesus Christ, to be the way, the truth, and the life, as thou hast taught Saint Philip, and other the Apostles: Through Jesus Christ our Lord.'[1]

The office of the archbishop of Canterbury

When Thomas Cranmer was made archbishop of Canterbury in 1533, he became the beneficiary of an array of powers and privileges that had accrued to his office ever since the sixth century, when the mission Pope Gregory the Great (d. 604) sent to the British Isles made Canterbury a metropolitan see. Cranmer's title was *Totius Anglie primas*: Primate of all England. He exercised extensive jurisdictional powers over Canterbury and thirteen dioceses in England and another four in Wales that made up the southern province. When a diocese fell vacant at the death or deprivation of the bishop, Cranmer administered it until a new bishop could be elected. He had the power to inhibit the business of bishops in their own dioceses during his visitations.[2] The French diocese of Thérouanne had been granted to Canterbury in the fourteenth century, so Cranmer's authority also extended over the English Pale of Calais. The province of Canterbury, as we have already observed, had its own bicameral legislature, known as Convocation, over which he presided. Its meetings were held at the same time as Parliament. So extensive was Cranmer's authority at the start of his archiepiscopate that some scholars have been tempted to think that he was as powerful as the prince-archbishops that ruled over cathedral cities on the continent, like Hermann V von Wied of Cologne.[3]

Cranmer was also the 'ordinary' bishop over his own diocese of Canterbury, which was located in eastern Kent, where no other bishop exercised any rule. Canterbury also enjoyed several jurisdictional 'peculiars' or deaneries of immediate jurisdiction beyond Kent that were exempt from the local bishops' control. They included the deaneries of the Arches in London; Croydon in Surrey; and Hadleigh in Suffolk. Cranmer administered several courts: the Prerogative Court of Canterbury, where the wills of the wealthiest men and women of the realm were proved; the Court of Canterbury in the deanery of the Arches, where clerical cases for the province were taken up; and the Court of Audience, where appeals or complaints were heard.

As archbishop, Cranmer outranked senior members of the aristocracy. He held the lordship of extensive properties. Canterbury, Lambeth, and Knole were the most distinguished of his twenty-one palaces, but Croydon and Otford were almost as splendid. He had other estates along the River Thames at Wimbledon and Mortlake.[4] Cranmer had his own barge and servants to row him across the river. He maintained extensive stables, and he hunted deer in his parks. The tenants of his properties were numerous. At Canterbury, the archbishopric had a mint. In 1535, the archbishop's annual income was estimated by the *Valor Ecclesiasticus* as £3093. He could not always collect the full amount, but his income placed him, at least in theory, in the company of peers of the realm.[5]

Most of the powers and possessions Cranmer enjoyed owed their origins to the archbishop's role as the representative of the pope in England. But from the beginning of his archiepiscopate, he was unusually dependent upon Henry VIII's goodwill, a fact he acknowledged at his consecration, as we have already observed. With the rest of the English Church, the archbishopric was becoming subordinated to the king, a process that had already begun under his predecessor William Warham.

Cranmer was in Italy in 1530 when Henry mounted his first great challenge against Warham's authority. Two months after Cambridge was canvassed for its opinion in the Divorce, Henry interposed himself in his role as Defender of the Faith when

Convocation examined heretical books. William Tyndale's first translation of the New Testament of 1526 was denounced as dangerously corrupt and it was banned. But surprisingly, at the conclusion of their deliberations, Henry embarrassed Warham and lord chancellor Sir Thomas More by announcing that he would commission a more accurate translation of Holy Scripture that he intended to give to his people with his own hands, once they demonstrated that they were sufficiently prepared to receive it. His promise was one of the first indications that Henry intended to take a direct role in the spiritual lives of his subjects in exchange for their loyalty, and he probably was encouraged to take this step by Anne Boleyn.[6]

When Cranmer was on embassy in May 1532, he was not present also for the episode that has become known as the Submission of the Clergy, one of the pivotal moments in the history of the English Church, when Warham made a desperate attempt in Convocation to protect ecclesiastical privilege against the king. The crisis began during a review of the canons, the laws governing the Church, the most important assessment of canon law that had been attempted for nearly two hundred years. Warham wanted to improve clerical discipline and education, and his review might have led to substantial corrections. However, as we have noted in the previous chapter, he was interrupted when Henry charged him with *praemunire*. Initially, Bishop Stephen Gardiner of Winchester sided with Warham. As a canon lawyer, Gardiner defended Convocation's right to make laws independently for the Church in England without royal intervention or approval by Parliament. But Warham and Gardiner did not succeed. The Church lost its ancient powers of making its own laws without interference. Henry presented Convocation with an ultimatum and, under intense pressure, Warham and the members of the Upper House capitulated. The Submission of the Clergy was one of the contributing causes that led to Sir Thomas More's resignation from the office of lord chancellor on 15 May 1532, and Gardiner's outspoken defiance of the king probably cost him the archbishopric of Canterbury when Warham died in August.[7] The Submission of the Clergy helped to deliver the Church into the hands of the king. As archbishop, Cranmer knew he was limited by Convocation's subordination to royal authority and parliamentary oversight.

Although Cranmer's title *Totius Anglie primas* made him Primate of all England, in actual terms the kingdom was divided into two provinces, Canterbury and York. In the fourteenth century, long and acrimonious disagreements about precedence were settled when the archbishops of Canterbury were allowed to call themselves 'Primate of all England', while the archbishops of York were termed more simply 'Primate of England'. The archbishop of York at the start of Cranmer's tenure was Edward Lee, who succeeded Cardinal Wolsey in 1531. Each province had its own Convocation that met separately, though York's tended to ratify Canterbury's decisions. The independent action of the two Convocations meant that during the middle ages the English clergy had not been able to unify into one body that might have become an additional and even dominant chamber as part of Parliament. As a consequence, especially after the defeat of 1532, the Convocation of Canterbury was permanently weakened.[8] In political terms, because its authority was limited to the southern province, Cranmer had almost no power in the north. As we will see, Henry gave Thomas Cromwell greater authority over the entire Church in England than he allowed to Cranmer, and the king permitted his archbishop of Canterbury almost no direct political influence in lay affairs.

Over time, Cranmer developed a modest 'affinity' of clients and dependents. Unlike many bishops, he had never been head of a college, which would have given him valuable experience and an extensive network of friends to place in positions of influence. He drew members of his own family and men from various Cambridge colleges into his service. Eventually he was able to advance friends into high places. William Benson became abbot of Westminster and later its dean. Others rose to bishoprics, including Edward Fox of Hereford, who brought him to Henry's attention. John Capon (d. 1557), the brother of the master of Jesus College, became bishop of Salisbury. Other Cambridge men advanced by Cranmer included John Bale, George Daye, Nicholas Heath, John Ponet, Hugh Latimer, and Nicholas Shaxton. The most prominent amongst them was Thomas Goodrich, who was both bishop of Ely from 1534 and lord chancellor from late 1551. Gradually Cranmer was able to extend the range of his influence, especially under Henry's son Edward. However, Cranmer lacked the resources and perhaps the personal ability to develop what historians call a faction: a tight-knit group of people who were dedicated to the success of certain specific policies or causes. In the absence of organized political parties, factions became increasingly important, especially in the last decade of Henry's reign. Too often Cranmer was disappointed by his friends' deaths, dismissals, or defections. His loyal secretary Ralph Morice discounted some of Cranmer's bishops as 'rabblement' who abandoned him during various crises, including the passage of the Act of Six Articles in 1539.[9] So ineffectual has Cranmer seemed in political matters that some historians have characterized him as of 'little use in a political struggle' or said that he was 'of little value as a political operator',[10] even though he was able to demonstrate considerable (but self-effacing) acumen throughout his career.

Inside the Church, Cranmer faced formidable challenges in administering his office. Immediately after Warham's death, Richard Gwent was appointed to the key position of dean of the Arches, and he remained in that post until his death in 1543. Cranmer inherited an administrative system in Canterbury that he could not fully control, in part because Warham's relatives and clients continued to enjoy offices that gave them lifetime sinecures. Kent formed the only archdeaconry in the diocese of Canterbury, and its archdeacon was responsible for its administration. He sat in the Lower House of Convocation, and he carried out the policies that the archbishop promoted. So sensitive was the relationship between the archbishop and his archdeacon that for many years Warham employed his nephew (sometimes described as his illegitimate son), who occupied the office at Cranmer's entrance. Few of Warham's men could be dislodged unless death deprived them, and they owed the new archbishop nothing. The same was true of the church livings that were in the archbishop's gift. Traditionalists occupied the wealthiest livings, like the active preacher Rowland Philips, who presided as vicar of Croydon on Cranmer's own doorstep. Enemies spread rumours that Cranmer was as ignorant as a gosling that wandered on the village green. Gibes from the time of his early marriage came back to haunt him. They said Cranmer was fit only to keep an inn, and they sneered that his wife had been the tapster at the Dolphin.[11] Cranmer knew that 'priests report the worse of me'. They spread 'mere lies and tales'.[12]

The cathedral chapter at Canterbury also posed difficult problems that Cranmer could not overcome. It was ruled by Benedictine monks of the Priory of Christ Church, one of the oldest, wealthiest and most powerful religious houses in England, and the monks feared (with good reason) that the new archbishop was arriving as their nemesis. Cranmer struggled against withering opposition in Canterbury. As we will see in later chapters, even after the cathedral chapter was refounded and secularized, the former monks came close to destroying him in 1543. Then, after the accession of Queen Mary in 1553, they were instrumental in creating the final crisis that led to Cranmer's arrest and his ultimate destruction.

Cranmer's purposes as archbishop

In the protest Cranmer made before taking the oath at his consecration, he referred to his desire to reform those things in the Church that seemed to him in need of reformation.[13] He had plans for the English Church that he was not always at liberty to express, and that he was not always successful in realizing, but may be summarized here.

The duties of a bishop were encapsulated by St Paul's epistles, and especially in his letters to Timothy and Titus. Cranmer believed that the instruction of the laity was one of his greatest responsibilities, which he interpreted in light of Paul's teaching in Romans 10:8–17 that 'faith cometh by hearing, and hearing by the word of God'. Cranmer was a frequent and impressive preacher, a fact that has not always been noted because, rather surprisingly, his sermons have not survived. He oversaw all preachers in his province. He offered licenses to those he trusted, and he inhibited many. Most clergymen in the 1530s were 'massing priests', rather than trained preachers. For those who were unused to writing their own sermons and preaching in their own words, Cranmer wanted to supply homilies that they could read to their parishioners.

Under the royal supremacy, Cranmer worked to create what we now understand was a national Church. His great goal was to evangelize the English people. Like Queen Anne Boleyn, he wanted the legalization of an English Bible, and he and the queen offered Tyndale as much protection as they could. Secretly, using

agents in his employ, Cranmer supported Tyndale and other trans-
lators who were working in exile in Antwerp and in other places
on the continent. In late 1534, when Tyndale released his revised
translation of the New Testament, Anne was sent a lavish copy,
specially printed for her on vellum and inscribed '*Anna Regina
Angliae*'. Tyndale's New Testament was a daring present to give
and for the queen to keep, especially as he was a hunted exile and
his translation was an illegal book.[14] In the last months of her life,
the queen kept a copy of Miles Coverdale's English Bible on a
desk, and she read from it openly before her household.[15]

Cranmer also wanted the liturgy to be in English, and we have
already observed his fascination with the services he observed in
Nuremberg. Because he believed that the Mass was not a sacrifice,
Cranmer wanted to remove all those practices that he thought
distracted from the honour that was due solely to the one sacrifice Christ had made on Calvary. He dismissed traditional prayers
like the rosary as unprofitable 'lip labour'.[16] Like the queen, he
favoured the transformation of the religious houses into centres
of preaching, teaching, and relief of the poor. He opposed pilgrimages and other traditional devotional practices. Like Thomas
Bilney, he favoured the removal of religious imagery, including
crucifixes and the images of saints, and in his iconoclasm he
sharply differed from his Lutheran colleagues, who saw nothing
objectionable with holy pictures or statues.

Cranmer also wished to work for doctrinal and political consensus amongst Protestant leaders, and he wanted to create an
international Protestant power bloc that would rival the papacy
and Catholic powers abroad. He wanted the English Church to
have a definition of faith that was in concert with those of other
Protestant Churches. He wanted to complete the long-desired
revision of canon law that Warham had started, an ambitious and
time-consuming project which occupied his attentions at several
lengthy intervals. Domestically he wanted obedience from the
king's subjects and conformity from members of the clergy.

However, Cranmer was not allowed to introduce all of the
changes he wished to implement in the English Church, even
though his Cambridge friends encouraged him to seize the great
opportunity that God had sent. Immediately after his consecration, George Joye (d. 1553) suggested that Latimer write Cranmer

and 'animate him to his office'. The archbishopric of Canterbury was 'a perilous place', but a 'glorious' one 'to plant the Gospel'.[17] Although Henry expected Cranmer to continue to denigrate the papacy with the same success that he brought to invalidating his first marriage, the king was indecisive, and moreover Henry was resistant to doctrinal innovations he did not understand. As we will observe in greater detail in the next chapters, Cranmer's original intentions for the English Church may never have been possible to achieve without the continued presence of Anne Boleyn. He entered into the archbishopric with expectations that would not be fulfilled following her destruction in 1536. Instead, Cranmer was eclipsed by Cromwell, whose superior skills in creating policy and legislation led the king to make him vicegerent in spirituals at the beginning of 1535, first to conduct a royal visitation of the religious houses, and then to exercise broad powers over the English Church in both provinces as his vicar general from July 1536.[18] After Anne's fall, Cranmer adjusted his expectations, and he and Cromwell worked together to bring the English Church into closer alignment with the Lutheran princes of the League of Schmalkalden. Cranmer was disappointed again when Cromwell was destroyed in 1540. Thereafter, Cranmer was able to revive partially some plans he had deferred since Anne's destruction, but continued pressure from the king meant that he did not have a freer hand until after Henry's death in 1547.

Troubling ambiguities about the source of Cranmer's powers as archbishop would pursue him until the end of his life. By separating the archbishopric from the papacy, and by impugning the power of the pope in England, the essential weakness of his office under the royal supremacy was revealed within a few years of his consecration. The autonomy of the Church in England was sacrificed, and the office of the archbishop of Canterbury was diminished. Cranmer was often outflanked by formidable opposition from other bishops, especially from John Stokesley of London and Stephen Gardiner of Winchester. Henry allowed Cromwell greater powers as vice gerent than Cranmer was ever permitted to exercise. As a consequence, too often Cranmer was reduced to the status of a government functionary, the vulnerable servant of a king whose supremacy he had willingly created by sacrificing himself.

John Frith

Immediately after Anne's coronation, the king instructed Cranmer to examine John Frith. After his escape from Oxford in 1528 (which we observed in Chapter 2), Frith joined Tyndale in Antwerp, where he may have helped him with the translation of the Bible. In 1529 Frith was in Marburg in Hesse, where he attended Martin Luther and Huldrych Zwingli's debate about the nature of the presence of Christ in the sacrament. Frith was the first English author to express a Reformed opinion about the Eucharist, which was at odds with traditional dogma as well as Lutheran opinion. In 1531 he released a provocative attack against Sir Thomas More and John Fisher in *A disputacion of purgatory*, which displayed his name prominently on the title page. When he returned to England that year, More seized him and sent him to the Tower, where Frith continued to write to Tyndale and the other 'brethren'. His papers were stolen and delivered to More, who denounced him as a follower of Oecolampadius (1482–1531), who had been deeply influenced by Zwingli's thinking that the presence of Christ in the Lord's Supper is spiritual and a commemoration of his sacrifice on the cross. Frith argued that 'This is my body', the words Christ spoke at the Last Supper, should not be understood as a literal statement. More wrote that for Frith, the Eucharist was 'only bare bread and wine', and merely 'a remembrance of Christ's passion'.[19]

Not long before Cranmer's consecration, in a Lenten sermon delivered at court, one of the king's chaplains denounced the dangers that English sacramentaries posed, and he drew attention to Frith, who was still in the Tower. Henry ordered that Frith be examined by Cranmer in a panel that included Stokesley and Gardiner, as well as his brother-in-law Charles Brandon (d. 1545) the duke of Suffolk; the new Lord Chancellor, Thomas Audley (1488–1544); and the earl of Wiltshire, the queen's father. According to a story that Foxe recounted many years later, as Cranmer's agents brought Frith from the Tower to be questioned at Croydon, they felt a great reluctance to convey him 'as a sheep to the slaughter'. Frith was a Kentish man, and at Brixton they encouraged him to run away to his friends. It is unlikely that Cranmer secretly urged them to give Frith a chance to escape, and in any case he refused their offer.[20]

In the same letter in which Cranmer detailed Anne's coronation to Nicholas Hawkins, he described Frith's examinations. His eloquence and charm made a good impression even though his opinions isolated him from the support he might have otherwise enjoyed. His examiners would have preferred to 'dispatch' him, except that his opinion was 'so notably erroneous' that they felt that they had to let Stokesley pass judgement against him. But rather than let Frith be condemned at once, Cranmer sent for him three or four times and tried to persuade him on his own. He concluded (like More) that Frith had drawn his opinions from Oecolampadius, for Frith said that it was not necessary to believe as an article of Christian faith that the host had within it the very corporeal presence of Christ. Nothing Cranmer or the other examiners said would make him leave his opinion. Because they believed that the actual body and blood of Christ was present in the Eucharist, in 1533 Cranmer was actually closer to More's opinion than he was to Frith's.[21]

By refusing to submit, Frith placed his own conscience ahead of his obedience to the king and he violated existing statutes against heresy. Because Henry had sent Anne's father and Suffolk to examine him, Frith had been given unusually generous opportunities to fall into line. Cranmer had also gone to extraordinary lengths to interview him privately. He was only too well aware that English evangelicals were surrounded by enemies, and Frith's case could not be allowed to endanger the possibility of bringing about doctrinal change in the future. In 1533, Stokesley began to enhance his own power and influence, and he inhibited Latimer from preaching in London, which was an indication of his real opinion of the evangelicals. Cranmer's own position was precarious, for the other examiners could easily report him to the king if they thought he was making a stubborn case to save Frith. His death was a dreadful warning that evangelicals could not exceed the strictures that Henry placed on them as the Church's head. Cranmer and his friends had done their utmost for Frith. Had he been willing, he might have been spared, but he refused to equivocate or temporize. Therefore his examiners realized they had no choice but to relinquish him to Stokesley as his ordinary to pass sentence and to hand him over to the secular powers for punishment. Condemned with him for the same opinion was Andrew Hewet, a London tailor. In the same letter Cranmer wrote to Hawkins about Anne's coronation, he noted that Frith 'looketh every day to go unto the fire'. Frith and Hewet were burnt together at Smithfield on 4 July 1533.

In later years Frith was admired as one of the great sacrificed heroes of the early Reformation. Cranmer meant Hawkins to share his news at the Emperor Charles's court, and therefore his letter conveyed official thinking disguised as a friendly missive. But Hawkins was also truly a friend, and he would have become bishop of Ely had not he died in Aragon in 1534 while still on embassy. Reading through the lines, he would have known what Cranmer may have meant privately about Frith. Probably they had both known him at Cambridge. Cranmer's letter hints that he had sympathy for Frith, a feeling that he knew Hawkins would share, and moreover he felt deep regret that Frith had been lost, or rather that he had thrown himself away, despite the opportunities he had been offered to submit and to save himself. Cranmer's position was clear: he would put English law and the will of the king ahead of exposing himself to save Frith, despite the remorse he may have felt for the condemned man. Frith's execution was meant to demonstrate to Pope Clement VII and the Emperor Charles that Henry would uphold the fundamental tenets of Christian belief against heretics in England.

The Nun of Kent

At the beginning of his archiepiscopate, Cranmer's most immediate practical problem was lack of funds. After Warham's death, valuables belonging to the archbishopric were carried off or damaged by neglect. Although the king promised Cranmer the loan of one thousand marks (about £666) in his first summer as archbishop, he was worried by a shortage of money so acute that he was forced to sell wood from his properties.[22] When he made the gift of a buck to William Capon for the fellows of Jesus College, he could not send with it the small sum necessary for its baking.[23] Cranmer accepted the sons of important people into his service, and then he realized 'I have overcharged my house with servants' whom he could not afford to feed. So many deer had been killed in the archbishop's parks while the see was vacant that he had no venison.[24] Desperate for assistance, Cranmer summoned

Harold Rosell, his sister Dorothy's husband, to become clerk of his kitchen, an important financial position that involved the supply of his household.[25] In the months between his consecration and his enthronement, he called into his service other relatives from Nottinghamshire and friends from Cambridge, including Nicholas Heath as his chaplain.[26] Morice may have eventually joined his service upon the recommendation of Anne's brother, Lord Rochford. Shortly before his enthronement, Cranmer learned that the king had reduced the loan he had promised him to no more than £500, and he was forced to turn to the queen's father and others for assistance.[27] Cranmer's financial position did not improve for another five or more years.[28]

At the beginning of September 1533, Cranmer was in attendance at court for Anne's lying in at Greenwich. On 6 September the queen was brought to bed of a girl instead of the expected prince. Had Anne given birth to a son, Henry would have greeted his heir as the indubitable sign of God's favour, and Anne would have been secure. Cranmer was godfather for the infant Elizabeth.

Just five weeks before her birth, Rochford brought stunning news from the continent that Pope Clement had at last issued a ruling in the king's case. The pope found in Katherine's favour, and he ordered Henry to take her back or be excommunicated.[29]

At this dangerous moment, Henry embarked on daring new diplomatic overtures. For the first time, he sent requests to the elector of Saxony, Duke John Frederick, and Landgrave Philip of Hesse that English ambassadorial posts be created at their courts. To ward off papal retribution, Henry asked King Francis I of France to mediate with the pope on his behalf. He instructed Cranmer to warn the English ambassadors in France that Clement intended 'to make some manner of prejudicial process against me and my church'.[30] Henry also decided to call for a meeting of a General Council, whose aim would be the reduction of the power of the papacy and the reform of long-standing abuses in the Christian Church. In the distant future, Henry's suggestion bore fruit in the Council of Trent, which began to sit (without English participation) in 1545. Taking further defensive steps, in December 1533, the king's council determined that the pope henceforth should be referred to merely as the diocesan bishop of Rome. Official English documents no longer made any mention of 'the pope'.[31]

In an atmosphere of rising urgency, threats had to be eliminated, and Cranmer had a central role in removing one of the king's most formidable opponents: Elizabeth Barton, the visionary known as the Nun of Kent. Barton had achieved wide fame in the 1520s for her revelations. At the outset, her predictions concerned personal matters of the soul, and she offered advice to the men and women who came to her for guidance. She was brought to Warham's attention by one of his chaplains, Henry Gold (d. 1534), the incumbent of Aldington in Kent (important as the parish that provided Erasmus's pension), who as a Cambridge theology student in the late 1520s had asked Cranmer to examine him.[32] Warham placed Barton in a Benedictine convent in Canterbury and Dr Edmund Bocking (d. 1534), one of the monks of Christ Church, collected her utterances for publication. Many people regarded her as a living saint, and thousands of pilgrims on their way to St Thomas Becket's shrine in Canterbury Cathedral stopped at her convent to visit her.

But in time Barton began to criticize the king's desire for a divorce, and the extensive clientele who revered her for what Sir Thomas More called her 'good inspirations and great revelations' allowed her to reach the very highest audience chambers. Warham introduced her to Wolsey, and she warned them against their involvement in the king's Great Matter. She sent letters to Pope Clement to warn him of disaster should he assist the king's designs. More than once she was brought to court to meet Henry. Cranmer concluded later that her influence was so great that she managed to delay the business of the 'Divorce'.[33]

Barton's greatest prophesy concerned the divine punishment that would be meted out should Henry marry Anne: within a month, he would no longer be king in the eyes of God, and then England would be laid waste by the plague. Some of her revelations were already in print, and Bocking was about to release the rest when More warned Barton that she should refrain from speaking about matters that pertained to princes. But he was too late.[34]

In mid-July 1533, once the news arrived of Clement's threat to excommunicate Henry, Cranmer summoned Barton for questioning. At first she would confess nothing, although he encouraged her, in an unhurried fashion, to confide in him just as she had confided in Warham. Later, More found the mildness of Cranmer's technique remarkably disconcerting.[35] Bocking was seized, and Barton's contact with the pope's ambassadors in England was revealed. She had been helped by a scribe employed by Archdeacon Warham. At length, Cranmer, Latimer, and Cromwell exposed her as a fraud. Cranmer wrote Hawkins, who was still with the imperial court, that the nun confessed 'that she never had a vision in all her life'. She had invented everything to impress her friends.[36]

In November 1533, Lord Chancellor Audley brought Barton before an assembly of the king's councilors, bishops, and noblemen, and when he finished denouncing her, there were cries that she should be sent to the stake. For centuries, the special penalty that women paid for treason or for murdering their husbands (which was understood as a form of 'petty' treason) was execution by burning, but Barton's case represented something new. Cranmer decided that those who stubbornly supported the papal supremacy could be condemned as heretics because they were enemies of the Gospel.[37] For both heretics and women convicted of treason, the penalty was the same: death by burning. Further, Sir Thomas More and Bishop John Fisher were implicated as Barton's friends.

On 23 November 1533, the day after Cranmer wrote that the king wanted to call a General Council, Barton, with nine of her followers, including Bocking and Gold, were exposed at Paul's Cross. In a grim act of humiliation, they were made to stand on a scaffold next to the pulpit. The preacher was John Capon, Cranmer's nominee for the bishopric of Bangor, and his sermon castigated Barton for encouraging Henry's subjects to think that God no longer accepted him as a righteous king who deserved to be obeyed. Sir Thomas More was amongst the thousands in the audience that day. Horrified by what he heard, he immediately tried to shield himself from impending disaster. He sent his servant to the Charterhouse monks to inform them that Barton 'was undoubtedly proved a false deceiving hypocrite'.[38]

The suppression of the Nun of Kent and her supporters played an important part in Cranmer's enthronement at the end of the year. When he entered Canterbury for the first time, he came as the king's man. On 3 December 1533, Cranmer was enthroned by the monks in the cathedral's Trinity Chapel. Only a few steps away towered the jewel-encrusted shrine of his greatest predecessor, the martyred St Thomas Becket, murdered in 1170 at the behest of King Henry II (1133–1189) for his allegiance to the papacy. In its shadow, Warham had been interred just a year ago. The irony of the situation was not lost on Christ Church's prior Thomas Goldwell. His house was threatened by Bocking's arrest. At the enthronement banquet, Goldwell served swans, an impressive but inexpensive dish that was wholly inadequate for the occasion. Up to the last, Cranmer was sending out pleas for venison.[39]

On 7 December, the Sunday following Cranmer's enthronement, Barton and her followers were exposed to humiliation once again in Canterbury. The preacher on this occasion was Heath, who repeated Salcot's sermon with additions that had been prepared by Cranmer himself. He emphasized her crimes of idolatry and heresy. Barton had told her followers that from heaven, Mary Magdalen had sent her a letter, illuminated in gold with the Names of Jesus and Mary. Cranmer wrote the king that Heath 'grievously rebuked' Barton and her supporters for their crimes. Cranmer also reported that the people of Canterbury seemed glad that the nun's 'false and forged matters' had been exposed.[40]

Immediately Cranmer began a visitation of the diocese of Canterbury. He 'diligently examined' the monks of Christ Church to discover how deeply they were implicated with Bocking and the Nun, and he was able to inform the king that few had had anything to do with Barton's 'false revelations'. Fearful of Henry's disfavour, Goldwell asked Cranmer to intercede for Christ Church, and offered the king two or three hundred pounds for his clemency, although (as Cranmer noted) the house was already heavily in debt.[41]

Cranmer's visitation was also noteworthy for its iconoclasm. From the Abbey of Boxley near Maidstone, he took down a huge crucifix known as the Rood of Grace that once had moveable features, and he sent it to Westminster to show to the king.[42] This was the first occasion of many in which Cranmer or his officers removed religious imagery to prevent them from being objects of devotion.

The defeat of Barton and her allies in Canterbury meant that at one blow Cranmer intimidated the senior members of Canterbury's diocesan clergy into a kind of spiteful acquiescence that lasted long enough for him to strengthen his own position over them, at least for the time being.[43] In early 1534, Cranmer was able to pension off Warham's nephew (who was fortunate to escape) and he collated (or named) his brother Edmund to the archdeaconry of Canterbury.[44]

Edmund's lifelong support of his brother has not always been fully appreciated. We should think of the two Cranmers as inseparable, working together in mutual interest. Edmund served as the archbishop's consultant, confidant, and protector. In step with him, he shared his brother's opinions in religion as they developed over time. Edmund pursued Kentish clergy who affirmed the authority of the pope.[45] He handled matters that were too delicate to be entrusted to anyone else, including the sifting of controversial religious tracts.[46] Edmund was essential to his brother. Cranmer also brought their sister Alice out of her Cistercian convent in Lincolnshire. She was elected prioress of the Benedictine house of Sheppey in Minster in the Isle of Thanet, even though she had to change her religious order.[47] The Cranmers were completely devoted to each other and, as we shall see, they defended and built on their family's prosperity whenever the opportunity arose.

The Act of Succession

The threat against the king's security that Pope Clement continued to pose convinced Henry and his advisors that not enough legislative and administrative measures had been put into place to guarantee his headship over the Church, and especially to ensure the loyalty of the English people. In November 1533, the king asked some of his bishops if they would consent to reject papal authority in England. The special protest that Cranmer made at his consecration meant that he had no hesitancy in consenting to the king's request now. But others refused, mindful that they had taken oaths when they entered into their bishoprics to be loyal to the pope.[48]

The next session of the Reformation Parliament opened on 15 January 1534. Cranmer attended the House of Lords almost every day, more often than any other bishop. His help was essential in securing the passage of the king's new legislation.[49] Towards the end of February a bill of attainder was sent to the House of Lords against Barton, Bocking, Gold and her other associates. At the insistence of the king, Fisher and More were also named in the bill. They sprang to defend themselves from the charge of treason. More was examined for the first time at the beginning of March by Cranmer, Cromwell, the duke of Norfolk, and Lord Chancellor Audley. More distanced himself so ably from any association with 'the wicked woman of Canterbury' that he was able to deflect the attainder, at least for the present, though he remained frantically worried. Fisher was too ill in Rochester to appear in his own defence, but he was also able to escape for the time being by paying the enormous sum of £300 as a penalty.[50] Barton was attainted by Parliament.

In 1534 Parliament created a new Faculty Office that empowered the archbishop of Canterbury to issue the kind of licenses, dispensations or grants that were handled by the papal courts. Previously, wealthy or influential people had routinely sent suits to Wolsey as legate.[51] After he fell, as we have already seen, Cranmer had overseen this kind of business at Rome in 1530 when he was briefly Penitentiary for England. The Faculty Office continued the process of claiming powers for the English Church that had originally rested with the papacy. It offered Cranmer a vital extension of his authority that was not, however, designed to infringe upon similar powers that the archbishop of York and the other bishops already enjoyed over the clergy and laity in their own dioceses. In mid-April 1534, the Faculty Office began to issue its first dispensations.[52]

Parliament reduced Katherine's style to Princess Dowager, to reflect the fact that as Arthur's widow she had never been truly married to the king. Those who recognized her as princess dowager tacitly accepted Cranmer's verdict and thus they denied the authority of the pope in England.[53]

The most important piece of legislation that was passed in the early session of 1534 has become known as the first Henrician Act of Succession. Its preamble denounced the popes for usurping powers that rightfully belonged to England's kings. It stated that Henry's marriage to Katherine was against the law of God, and it could not be dispensed by any earthly power. It validated the king's marriage to Anne, and the statute denounced the pope for interfering with England's succession. The throne was to pass to the male heirs that Henry might have with his lawful wife Anne, or failing them, to his sons with a subsequent wife. Should the king have no sons, their daughter Elizabeth would succeed, and her children after her, and then any other daughters yet to be born to Henry and Anne, and their issue after them in the order of their birth. Anyone who wrote against the Act would be guilty of the capital offence of treason. Anyone who spoke against it would be guilty of misprision of treason and liable to imprisonment at the king's pleasure. Katherine's daughter Mary was not mentioned in the statute, and thus she was implicitly excluded from the succession.[54]

The Act of Succession also stipulated that the king's subjects should, at a time appointed, take an oath in the presence of the king or his officers, and swear that they would 'without fraud or guile' to observe, maintain, and keep the provisions of the Act upon pain of misprision of treason and imprisonment. Katherine remained extremely popular, and in light of Clement's ruling in her favour, the government feared widespread unrest by her demotion.[55]

Henry came to the Lords when the session closed on 30 March 1534 to watch as the oath was administered by Cranmer and the dukes of Norfolk and Suffolk. Its text was prepared by Cromwell and Audley after the Succession Act passed. Each man signed his oath to bear his 'faith, truth, and obedience' only to the king and his heirs, and not to any foreign authority, prince or potentate'.[56] The next day Convocation met at St Paul's to vote on the proposition that the bishop of Rome had no greater jurisdiction in England, given to him by God in Scripture, than did any other foreign bishop. Cranmer and ten bishops signed, followed by ninety-one clergymen.[57]

Meanwhile, in Rome, the Consistory agreed with Clement's decisions, and it ruled on 23 March 1534 that Katherine's marriage to Henry was valid. The French had frustrated the decision for as long as possible. The verdict arrived in England just after Parliament was prorogued, and Henry reacted to the news with vindictive fury.[58] Immediately Cranmer inhibited all preachers licensed in his province to prevent them from raising doubts concerning 'the prince, his laws, or succession'.[59] In one of the most shocking events of the reign, on 20 April 1534, Barton and her associates, including Bocking and Gold, were brought out of prison and dragged on hurdles through the streets of London.

They were taken to Tyburn (near Hyde Parke Corner in the present day), where they were hanged.[60]

The news from Rome created fresh impetus for the succession oath to be administered. It became the ultimate test of loyalty that identified those who refused to side with the king. The succession oath was a potent weapon that carried with it the threat of perjury as well as eternal damnation for those who swore against good conscience. Bishop Fisher had not attended the Lords or Convocation. At the end of February he was still in Rochester. But now he was summoned, and he made his way to Lambeth Palace on 13 April 1534, when London's clergy assembled to swear the oath. More noted that he was the only layman to be called that day. The commissioners took great effort to secure his submission. Cranmer was assisted by Cromwell, Audley, and Benson. More was shown the oath under the great seal. He was given the printed roll of the Act of Succession, which he read very carefully 'secretly by myself'. Then he said that although he would swear to the succession, his conscience would not permit him to take the oath, for he feared the damnation of his soul. Audley told him that he was the first to refuse, and showed him the signatures they had taken from the Lords and the Commons. Still More refused to sign. Then Fisher was called. He too would not sign. More watched as most of the clergy of London swore 'without any sticking', even Rowland Philips, vicar of Croydon, who before now had been a staunch defender of Katherine's marriage. Only Nicholas Wilson (d. 1548) also held out. Then More was shown how many had signed while he was waiting, and when he refused again the commissioners accused him of obstinacy. Then they asked him why he refused. Perhaps this was a trick to trap him into speaking against the Act and thus make him liable to misprision of treason. But More answered that he feared that if he told them he would only exasperate Henry further.[61]

Then Cranmer tried to persuade him, using a 'subtle' argument, that since he knew he must obey the king, he should abandon his doubts, and 'take the sure way in obeying your prince, and swear it'. Again More decided in his conscience that he could not, and that this was one of those cases when he should not obey his prince. He believed that the price of his soul was too much to pay for his life. Benson told him that his opinion was erroneous, and Cromwell declared that he would rather his only son should lose his head than More should refuse to take the oath. Then Cromwell used a threat: now the king would believe that More was responsible for what Elizabeth Barton had done. When More repeated that he was willing to swear to the succession but he would not take the oath, he was sent to the Tower. Afterwards, Cranmer wrote Cromwell that he concluded that Fisher and More did not wish to repudiate 'the authority of the bishop of Rome' or Katherine's 'pretensed matrimony'. He suggested that they be persuaded to swear to the Act of Succession but not its preamble, and then let it be known that they had sworn without reservation. Then Henry could 'stop the mouths' of Katherine's defenders, especially the Emperor Charles. However, Henry rejected Cranmer's suggestion. The king insisted that More must submit to the full statute. More and Fisher remained in the Tower.[62]

The metropolitical visitation

The rest of Cranmer's first year as archbishop was spent on a visitation of every diocese in his entire province. Before he set out in May 1534 Cranmer released the most important order he issued to preachers during Henry's reign: a long set of instructions that established the form for the 'bidding prayer' that they should use as they led their audiences in prayer for the king and the 'most gracious lady queen Anne his wife'. Cranmer ordered the clergy to preach 'against the usurped power of the bishop of Rome'. To avoid dissension, he ordered no one to preach on matters that had not yet been defined for the English Church: the existence of purgatory, the honouring of saints, clerical marriage, or justification by faith. He ordered preachers to 'purely, sincerely, and justly preach the scripture and the word of Christ'.[63]

Visitations were expensive, time-consuming, and intrusive. No diocesan ever welcomed a visitation by his metropolitan, for the process challenged every bishop's authority in his own jurisdiction. Warham had not visited his province in recent memory. Moreover, Cranmer's metropolitical visitation was 'an enormous task' made even more challenging, because it involved the administration of the oath of succession to the king's subjects across southern England, a project that was itself so vast that one historian has recently described it as 'Herculean' in its ambition.[64] Cranmer's officers sent out citations across the province that inhibited the diocesan bishops' powers for the length of the visitation. Henry ordered all secular officials to assist his archbishop.[65]

Cranmer's first destination was Rochester, where he wanted to investigate any 'special matters' that deserved particular scrutiny in light of Fisher's arrest. He met no resistance there. However, in Norwich the aged Bishop Nix (who had burnt Thomas Bilney) was accused of *praemunire*, and he was imprisoned briefly.[66] In August and September 1534 Cranmer and his men were in the west of England. Because Bishop Girolamo Ghinucci had been deprived as a consequence of the royal supremacy,[67] diocesan officials in Worcester were anxious not to offer the archbishop any difficulties.

Diocese by diocese, Cranmer and his assistants called the clergy together in the chapter houses of the cathedrals or the religious houses. In his visitation sermons, he warned the clergy to leave the old deceitful ways that they had pursued under the papacy, to set aside their avarice, and to rededicate themselves to love and care for the people's salvation. The oath of succession was administered. To refuse it meant exposure and immediate arrest. Each man signed an attestation that he had sworn. Many of the still-surviving sets of signatures, comprising thousands of names, were gathered during Cranmer's visitation.[68]

The challenge

At the beginning of the visitation in London, Cranmer ran into serious difficulties when he was confronted by a 'revolt' against his authority by Bishop Stokesley.[69] The citations that were sent out in Cranmer's name used the titles that described him as Primate of all England and papal legate. In the fourteenth century, *Apostolice sedis legatus* had become a standard part of the archbishop's style at the same time as did *Totius Anglie primas*. The mandate that the king sent for secular officers to assist Cranmer in his visitation also designated the archbishop as legate of the apostolic see, and Cranmer had been using both titles as a matter of course from the beginning of his tenure, including in his decision that invalidated Katherine's marriage.[70]

Inadvertently, Cranmer's style continued to reflect the very same source of his authority that the new legislation and his own efforts were designed to discredit. Under the circumstances this was an error, for it permitted Stokesley to exploit ambiguities concerning the source of the archbishop's authority. An ugly episode occurred when Cranmer came to the chapter house of St Paul's Cathedral, and Stokesley refused his authority out right. In front of the assembled clergy of the entire diocese, Stokesley declared that he would neither accept Cranmer as legate nor obey his visitation because the powers he claimed went against the king's crown and the law. Stokesley defended his own jurisdiction, and he referred to the statute that created the Faculty Office, which guaranteed the existing rights of bishops without extending to the archbishop new authority over them. When Stokesley insisted that his protest be recorded in the records of the visitation, Cranmer commanded his man to make no mention of it.

Stokesley refused to be inhibited, and in June and July 1534 he continued to conduct routine matters of diocesan administration even after Cranmer excommunicated some of his officers. Stokesley complained to the king that Cranmer acted against Holy Scripture and he used illegal means that exceeded anything the bishops of Rome had attempted at their most tyrannical. Stokesley argued that people would think that Cromwell exercised his powers as vicegerent by the king's authority, but that Cranmer's came from the bishop of Rome. Thus Stokesley was able to portray himself as having greater loyalty to Henry and his Church than did the archbishop of Canterbury.[71] In response, Cranmer replied that he was visiting London diocese by virtue of his right as primate and metropolitan, and that he was undertaking nothing that could be construed as a derogation of the king's powers or the statutes of the realm: a statement that Stokesley recorded in his register but did not accept.[72]

On 4 November 1534, Cranmer appeared in Convocation and he repudiated the title *Apostolice sedis legatus*. He announced that from henceforth he would be known simply as metropolitan. But his renunciation was not enough. As his visitation proceeded to Winchester in April 1535, Gardiner and his archdeacon

Nicholas Harpsfield protested against Cranmer's use of 'primate of all England' which they said was an insult to Henry's headship. In May, Cranmer wrote to Cromwell to defend himself by saying that he cared for his title, name, or style no more 'than I do by the paring of an apple' and no further than they served to set forth God's word and will. He suggested that Gardiner tendered the king's interests less than he tendered his own. Cranmer suspected that the bishops preferred to have the archbishops' titles and powers taken away so that all might be equal together. Turning around the idea from *Apostolice sedis legatus*, Cranmer wished that Henry's bishops would rather call themselves 'apostles of Jesus Christ'.[73]

The New Testament

In the same session that Cranmer renounced his title, Convocation voted to censure Tyndale's second translation of the New Testament. However, Cranmer managed to press Henry to make an important concession. When the king came to prorogue the session, the Upper House petitioned him to sponsor the trustworthy translation that he had promised in 1530, and the king agreed.[74]

In early 1535, Cranmer assigned the books of the New Testament for revision. He did not initiate an original translation, for that would have been a larger effort than he could have been able to mount. Rather, Tyndale's New Testament was to be 'thoroughly corrected' by comparison with the original Greek. He asked the 'best learned bishops' to make 'a perfect correction'. Gardiner was sent the Gospels of Saints Luke and John, which cost him such 'great labour' that he feared for his health. Stokesley was given the Acts of the Apostles, but he handed his portion back to Morice uncorrected, saying that he was surprised that Cranmer would abuse the laity by giving them liberty to read the Scriptures in English, which did 'nothing else but infect them with heresies'. He told Morice 'I will never be guilty' of bringing 'the simple people into errour'. When Cranmer was shown that Stokesley had done nothing towards completing his assignment, he marvelled to his chaplains that the bishop of London was so uncooperative that he 'will not do as other men do'.[75]

The executions of Fisher and More

The oath of obedience, to which the Commons and many others had sworn in 1534, was not part of the original Act of Succession. Rather, it was devised by Cromwell and Audley after the statute passed, and thus it had no real standing in the law.[76] This was an oversight that permitted Fisher and More to evade condemnation temporarily. Late in 1534 Cromwell perfected a set of procedures that allowed for no escape. The sixth session of the Reformation Parliament passed the Act of Supremacy in November with the exact wording of the oath. The new Act demanded that the king's subjects must renounce the powers of any foreign authority or potentate, and that they must repudiate any oath to a foreign power that they had already taken.[77] It was a weapon to ensure the obedience of all the bishops who had arrived on the bench before 1534 and who had taken their oaths to the pope as a matter of course at their elevation, as Cranmer had refused to do. It was also aimed against the members of the religious orders, who had sworn fealty to the pope at the time they entered religion.

The king moved remorselessly against those who would not take the oath of supremacy. The sixth session of the Reformation Parliament also passed a harsh new treason law for use against More and Fisher if they continued to refuse to submit. High treason was defined not only by an actual attempt to injure the king or queen or their heirs, but by any simple expression of a malicious wish that they might suffer some harm. It was high treason if someone maliciously deprived them of their titles: if someone denied that Anne was queen or refused to acknowledge Henry as supreme head of the Church. It was high treason to call the king a heretic, a tyrant, or a usurper. As the bill for the treason law was discussed in the Commons, its severity was denounced. Only the word 'maliciously' might stand between an unguarded opinion expressed during a casual conversation and an accusation of high treason. Many people could become subject to the fearsome penalty of being tortured to death in public and having all their property confiscated unless they could show that they had no real malice in their hearts. Despite obvious reluctance in the Commons, the bill passed into law.[78] Fisher and More and all who refused to take the oath were now in extreme peril.

Like every person in a position of authority, Cranmer was required to detect offences against the law, and he sent Cromwell evidence of treasonous talk. The archbishop sent Cromwell a priest who had asked for vengeance on the king for the new tax of the First Fruits and Tenths that passed late in 1534. He also sent Cromwell a woman who was accused of saying that there had never been so much despoiling of the realm 'since this new queen was made'.[79]

In April 1535, the priors of three Carthusian monasteries were accused of treason under the new law for their failure to accept the king as supreme head of the Church, or for 'depriving' him of his title because they would not take the oath. They were John Houghton (d. 1535) of the London Charterhouse; Robert Lawrence (d. 1535) of Beauvale and Augustine Webster (d. 1535) of the Axholme Charterhouse in Lincolnshire. Accused with them was the scholar Richard Reynolds (d. 1535) of Syon Abbey, England's only Bridgettine house. They were tried at Westminster on 28 and 29 April before Cromwell, Audley, and Norfolk. The monks knew the law, and in their defence they referred to the only small exception it allowed: Houghton said that they denied the king's supremacy only as a matter of conscience. They had not done so out of any malice. The members of the jury did not want to convict, and Cromwell had to threaten them into returning a guilty verdict.[80]

On 30 April 1535, Cromwell and several members of the Council examined More in the Tower and told him that Henry wanted his full answer. Although he knew the monks had been condemned for treason, More said that he would not 'meddle' with the question of the king's or the pope's titles.[81] On the same day Cranmer wrote Cromwell that he was shocked to hear of the plight of the condemned men, especially as there was no other charge but treason against them. He knew that Reynolds was a capable theologian. Moreover, Cranmer took a special interest in Webster, a Lincolnshire man, who had promised that he would never openly defend the authority of the pope. Cranmer asked if the king would permit him to examine them, for 'I suppose I could do very much with them' by persuading them with 'sincere doctrine' to leave their 'ignorance'. If he succeeded they could 'publish' their change of heart to the world, and be an example to others to accept the supremacy. Better that they could be persuaded, Cranmer thought, than to suffer death in the ignorance they now professed.[82]

But Cranmer was not permitted to speak with Reynolds or Webster. On 4 May 1535 the Carthusian priors and Reynolds were dragged on hurdles from the Tower to Tyburn, where they were hanged in their habits, then cut down alive and disembowelled while they still breathed. Then they were beheaded. Their bodies were hacked apart, and their members were impaled on spears and displayed across London.[83]

Fisher had always taken a much more open line of opposition than More to Henry's repudiation of Katherine and the supremacy. When Cromwell questioned him after the Carthusians suffered, he continued to refuse to make even the slightest accommodation to the king. Fisher told Cromwell plainly that he could not consent to take the king as supreme head of the Church, which made him guilty of speaking treason.[84]

At almost the same time, the new pope Paul III (Alessandro Farnese, r. 1534–1549) made Fisher a cardinal in acknowledgement of the books he had written against Luther, and he asked King Francis to intercede with Henry for Fisher's release. Henry received the news vindictively. On 3 June, Cromwell returned to the Tower, this time bringing with him Cranmer, Wiltshire, Suffolk, and Audley. Cromwell told More the king was not satisfied with the answer he had given before the Carthusians were executed, and now Henry commanded him to say whether or not he thought the Act of Supremacy was lawful. This was almost More's last chance. When he refused to say anything further than he had in April, Cromwell reminded him of the measures he had taken as lord chancellor to suppress heretics. The news had just arrived in England that Tyndale had been seized and imprisoned in the Castle of Vilvorde near Brussels. Cromwell pressed More. If Bilney, Frith, and Tyndale, all whom he had pursued, had been compelled to make answers about the primacy of the pope, then More should be required give his opinion about the supremacy of the king. But More refused to answer.[85]

Later that same day, 3 June 1535, Cromwell sent every bishop a clear order that in all dioceses, the clergy must preach every Sunday in all public places that the 'usurped' power of the bishop of Rome was extinguished in England. The king was now to be recognized by every subject as 'supreme head in earth, immediately under God, of the Church of England', a fact that had been acknowledged with the agreement of Parliament, Convocation, and both universities. All schoolmasters were to teach the supremacy to their students. The bishop of Rome was not to be prayed for as pope, and the word *papa* was to be stricken out of all Mass books in every church and chapel in England.[86]

That Cromwell, and not Cranmer, issued this order marked a new phase in the ascendancy of the king's chief minister. For the first time, a layman was given the authority to annex the power of the pulpit in service to the state. That the archbishop seems not to have been consulted about the order in advance is likely. When Cranmer received Cromwell's letter at Lambeth Palace the next day, he had doubts about it that he sent back orally by messenger. Only a year earlier in his Bidding Prayer Order, Cranmer had commanded preachers to denounce the usurped power of the pope, if not every week, then habitually, using a strong evangelical message. This aspect of the new orders was now stripped away. The king through Cromwell reduced the topics of sermons to a narrow consideration of the supremacy, without the evangelicalism that was a pronounced feature of the instructions Cranmer had given. Angered by the heroic opposition of the Carthusians and the sympathy they evoked as they went to their deaths, Henry concluded that previous measures had been insufficient. His supremacy had not been planted in the hearts of his subjects. Cromwell's order marked a new feature in the long series of encroachments that the royal supremacy made on ecclesiastical privilege. When Cranmer received his letter he pledged to do all in his power to satisfy the king's 'express commandment'.[87] Mindful that Fisher was about to follow the Carthusians, the other bishops hastened to ring endorsements of the king's supremacy from every pulpit. In Mary's reign, Cranmer could tell his examiners with some truth that he had opposed More and Fisher's executions, but he could not deflect the king from taking revenge upon them. On 19 June 1535, a second group of Carthusians were dragged to Tyburn to suffer. Bishop Fisher was beheaded on 22 June. Sir Thomas More was killed on 6 July.

The impasse created by Fisher and More's resistance was overcome when Henry strengthened Thomas Cromwell's authority over Archbishop Thomas Cranmer and the other bishops. Stokesley's and Gardiner's challenges to Cranmer's visitation were essential in demonstrating that the archbishop's powers were too weak to be effective. The present crisis required a stronger and more comprehensive approach across both provinces by a vicar-general whose authority could not be challenged because it came exclusively from the king. In the next chapter, we will examine Cranmer's problematic relationship with Cromwell. The royal supremacy separated the archbishop of Canterbury from his symbolic role as the representative of the pope in England, and as a result Cranmer lost much of the authority and prestige that his office had long enjoyed.

Notes

1 The collect for Saint Philip and James day, 3 May, written by Thomas Cranmer, for the second prayer book: *The boke of common praier, and administracion of the sacramentes, and other rites and ceremonies in the Churche of Englande* (London: Richard Grafton, August 1552, *RSTC* 16285), 107v.

2 The essential study on the powers of the archbishops is *Canterbury Administration*, by I. J. Churchill (London, 1933). See also D. M. Smith, *Guide to Bishops' Registers of England and Wales* (London, 1981), 1–19.

3 Prince-bishop: P. Ayris, 'Thomas Cranmer and the Metropolitical Visitation of Canterbury Province 1533–1535', in *From Cranmer to Davidson: A Church of England Miscellany*, ed. S. Taylor, Church of England Record Society, 7 (1999), 1–46, especially 25.

4 P. Hembry, 'Episcopal palaces, 1535 to 1660', in *Wealth and Power in Tudor England: Essays Presented to S. T. Bindoff*, eds. E. W. Ives *et al.*, (London, 1978), 146–66.

5 *Valor Ecclesiasticus*, 1 (London, 1810); G. Alexander, 'Victim or Spendthrift? The Bishop of London and his income in the sixteenth century', in *Wealth and Power in Tudor England*, 128–45; MacCulloch, *Cranmer*, 166–7. Tenants: Cranmer, *Miscellaneous*, letters nos. 31, 74.

6 J. F. Mozley, *William Tyndale* (London, 1937), 264; D. Daniell, *William Tyndale: A Biography* (New Haven, 1994), 110–34, 361; S. Wabuda, 'A day after doomsday': Cranmer and the Bible translations of the 1530s', in *The Oxford Handbook of the Bible in England, c. 1530–1700*, eds. K. Killeen, H. Smith and R. J. Willie (Oxford, 2015), 23–37.

7   M. Kelly, 'The Submission of the Clergy', *TRHS*, 5th series, 15 (1965), 97–119.

8   S. E. Lehmberg, *The Reformation Parliament 1529–1536* (Cambridge, 1970), 64–7, 72–3, 177–8.

9   Morice, 248.

10   G. R. Elton, 'Thomas Cromwell's Decline and Fall', *HJ*, 10 (1951), 151; R. McEntegart, *Henry VIII, the League of Schmalkalden, and the English Reformation* (London, 2002), 103.

11   Morice, 269–72.

12   Cranmer, *Miscellaneous*, letters, nos. 14, 118.

13   J. M. Gray, *Oaths and the English Reformation* (Cambridge, 2013), 102; LPL, Cranmer's Register, 4v.

14   Mozley, *Tyndale*, 264–7, 289–91. M. Dowling, 'Anne Boleyn as Patron', *Henry VIII: A European Court in England*, ed. D. Starkey (London, 1991), 107–11; and the same author's 'Anne Boleyn and Reform', *JEH*, 35 (1984), 30–45.

15   M. Dowling, ed. 'William Latymer's Chronickille of Anne Bulleyne', Camden Miscellany, 30, CS, 4th series, 39 (1990), 62–3.

16   'Cronickille of Anne Bulleyne', 58; Cranmer, *Miscellaneous*, 339.

17   Joye to Latimer, 29 April 1533: SP 1/ 75, f. 210 (*LP*, 6, no. 402).

18   F. D. Logan, 'Thomas Cromwell and the Vicegerency in Spirituals', *EHR*, 103 (1988), 658–67.

19   More, *Correspondence*, no. 190. The preacher was Dr Richard Curwen: *LP*, 6, no. 168; Foxe, *AM*, 8, 695–6; *LP*, 6, no. 168. See D. Daniell's entry for Frith in the *ODNB*; A. Ryrie, 'The Strange Death of Lutheran England', *JEH*, 53 (2002), 74–5.

20   Foxe, *AM* 8, 695–6.

21   Cranmer to Hawkins, Croydon, 17 June 1533, printed in *Miscellaneous*, no. 14, 246.

22   Cranmer, *Miscellaneous*, letters nos. 53, 56, 59.

23   Cranmer to William Capon, from Croydon, 16 June 1533: *Miscellaneous*, letter no. 16.

24   Cranmer, *Miscellaneous*, letters nos. 17, 24, 38 (his request to Lord Arundel for stags).

25   Cranmer, *Miscellaneous*, letters nos. 41, 61–2, 170.

26   Cranmer, *Miscellaneous*, letters nos. 35–6, 70, 97.

27   Cranmer to Rochford, *Miscellaneous*, letter no. 52.

28   Foxe, *AM*, 8, 20.

29   Scarisbrick, *Henry VIII*, 317–18.

30   Cranmer to Bonner, *Miscellaneous*, letter no. 76; McEntegart, *League of Schmalkalden*, 14–25.

31   R. Rex, 'The Crisis of Obedience: God's Word and Henry's Reformation, *HJ*, 39 (1996), 880, 889.

32 Gold: Foxe 1570, 2033; *AM*, 8, 4. *Grace Book B II*, 137, 143, 150; TNA:PRO, SP 1/73, 30r (*LP*, 5, no. 1700); MacCulloch, *Cranmer*, 43.

33 TNA: PRO SP 1/82, 89–96 (*LP*, 7, nos. 71–2); L. E. Whatmore, ed., 'The Sermon against the Holy Maid of Kent and her Adherents', *EHR*, 58 (1943), 463–75; D. Watt on Elizabeth Baron in the *ODNB*; Cranmer, *Miscellaneous*, letters no. 83; More, *Correspondence*, no. 197. Aldington was the parish that supplied Erasmus with his pension. Gold was a Cambridge man, and many years earlier he had requested that Cranmer dispute with him when he went up towards his degree. MacCulloch, *Cranmer*, 103–7.

34 More, *Correspondence*, nos. 192, 197; Scarisbrick, *Henry VIII*, 320–2.

35 More, *Correspondence*, no. 200 at 505.

36 Cranmer, *Miscellaneous*, letter no. 83; Richard Moryson, *Apomaxis calumniarum* (London: Thomas Berthlet, 1538, *RSTC* 18109), 73r–84r.

37 Whatmore, 'Holy Maid of Kent', 473, n. 1; P. Marshall, 'Papist as Heretic: The Burning of Friar Forest', *HJ*, 41 (1998), 351–74 (at 357–8).

38 More, *Correspondence*, nos. 192, 197; Scarisbrick, *Henry VIII*, 320–2.

39 'Chronicle of the years 1532–1537, written by a monk of St Augustine's, Canterbury', printed in *Narratives of the Days of the Reformation*, ed. J. G. Nichols, CS, 77 (1859), 279–81; Goldwell's account of the feast in his letter to Thomas Cromwell, *LP*, 7, 1520 (misdated); Cranmer, *Miscellaneous*, letter no. 79.

40 Cranmer, *Miscellaneous*, letter no. 81; R. Rex, 'Paul's Cross and the Crisis of the 1530s', in *Paul's Cross and the Culture of Persuasion in England, 1520–1640*, eds. T. Kirby and P. G. Stanwood, Studies in the History of Christian Traditions, 171 (Brill, 2014), 107–27.

41 Cranmer, *Miscellaneous*, letter no. no. 81.

42 Wriothesley, *Chronicle*, 1, 74.

43 MacCulloch, *Cranmer*, 107–9.

44 LPL, Cranmer's Register, 343v–35r; Cranmer, *Miscellaneous*, letter no. 75; dispensation for Edmund: *FOR*, 1; Churchill, *Administration*, 45.

45 TNA:PRO, SP 1/91, 89r–92v (*LP*, 8, nos. 386–7); G. R. Elton, *Policy and Police: The Enforcement of the Reformation in the Age of Thomas Cromwell* (Cambridge, 1985).

46 In a well-known case, Edmund and Latimer examined Tristam Revel's translation of François Lambert's controversial *Farrago Rerum Theologicarum* when he asked to be allowed to dedicate it to Queen Anne Boleyn in early 1536. She recognized that it was too dangerous for her to endorse. François Lambert, *The summe of christianitie*, trans. Tristam Revel (London: John Redman, 1536, *RSTC* 15179); *LP*, 10, no. 371; Dowling, 'Anne Boleyn and Reform', 44; Ives, *Anne Boleyn*, 283.

47 *FOR*, 2, 72; Cranmer, *Miscellaneous*, letters nos. 30, 103–4.
48 Gray, *Oaths and the Reformation*, 56.
49 Lehmberg, *Reformation Parliament*, 38, 257.
50 More, *Correspondence*, no. 198; Lehmberg, *Reformation Parliament*, 195–6.
51 P. D. Clarke, ed., 'Rivalling Rome: Cardinal Wolsey and Dispensations', in *Papal Authority and the Limits of the Law in Tudor England*, Camden Miscellany, 36, CS, fifth series, 48 (2015), 3–100.
52 25 Henry VIII, c. 21, printed in *Statutes of the Realm*, 3, 464–71; *FOR*, xi.
53 25 Henry VIII, c. 28.
54 25 Henry VIII, c. 22 printed in *Statutes of the Realm*, 3, 471–4; Wilkins, *Concilia*, 782–3; Lehmberg, *Reformation Parliament*, 194–9, 213–14.
55 25 Henry VIII, c. 28.
56 25 Henry VIII, c. 22 printed in *Statutes of the Realm*, 3, 471–4; Gray, *Oaths and the Reformation*, 57–8 and Appendix D1; Lehmberg, *Reformation Parliament*, 194–9, 213–14; MacCulloch, *Cranmer*, 121–2.
57 Ayris, 'Metropolitical Visitation', 14, 23.
58 Scarisbrick, *Henry VIII*, 332–3, and footnote 2 on 332.
59 Cranmer, *Miscellaneous*, letter 100.
60 *Chronicle written by a monk*, printed in *Narratives of the Days of the Reformation*, 281.
61 Gray, *Oaths and the Reformation*, 58. Fisher: see his itinerary in *Humanism, Reform and the Reformation: The Career of Bishop John Fisher*, eds. B. Bradshaw and E. Duffy (Cambridge, 1989), 247. More, *Correspondence*, no. 200.
62 More to Margaret Roper, April 1534, *Correspondence*, no. 200; Cranmer to Cromwell, 17 April 1534, *Letters*, no. 105; MacCulloch, *Cranmer*, 137.
63 Cranmer, *Miscellaneous*, 460–2.
64 Ayris, 'Metropolitical Visitation', 4; Gray, *Oaths and the English Reformation*, 59.
65 Ayris, 'Metropolitical Visitation', 16–20; Cranmer, *Miscellaneous*, letter no. 118; MacCulloch, *Cranmer*, 72–3.
66 Cranmer, *Miscellaneous*, letter no. 66.
67 25 Henry VIII, c.27; Lehmberg, *Reformation Parliament*, 185.
68 Cranmer, *Miscellaneous*, letters nos. 118, 122; J. E. Foster, ed., *Churchwardens' Accounts of St Mary the Great, Cambridge, from 1504 to 1635* (Cambridge, 1905), 77; Ayris, 'Metropolitical Visitation', 16–20; MacCulloch, *Cranmer*, 72–3. Cranmer's sermons: Jacobus Gislenus Thalassius to Cromwell, written from Heidelberg, 6 June 1535 (*LP*, 8, no. 831).

69 Ayris, 'Metropolitical Visitation', 5, 8–10.
70 Wilkins, *Concilia*, 31–2; Churchill, *Canterbury Administration* 155–7; Ayris, 'Metropolitical Visitation', 16–20; Cranmer, *Miscellaneous*, 243, n. 3 and letter no. 118; MacCulloch, *Cranmer*, 72–3.
71 Ayris, 'Metropolitical Visitation', appendix 1B.
72 Ayris, 'Metropolitical Visitation', 6 and appendix 1A.
73 Wilkins, Concilia, 769; Cranmer, *Miscellaneous*, letter no. 145.
74 Lehmberg, *Reformation Parliament*, 214; Mozley, *Tyndale*, 266.
75 BL, Harley MS 422, 87r–87v; printed in 'The Answers of Mr. Thomas Lawney', in *Narratives of the Days of the Reformation*, 277–8.
76 Lehmberg, *Reformation Parliament*, 203.
77 26 Henry VIII, c. 2.
78 Treason: 26 HenryVIII, c. 13; Lehmberg, *Reformation Parliament*, 203–6.
79 Cranmer to Cromwell, written from Lambeth 7 June [1535], *Letters*, no. 149, and from Otford [15 August 1535], no. 154.
80 A. Dillon, *Michelangelo and the English Martyrs* (Aldershot, 2012), 25–6; Lehmberg, *Reformation Parliament*, 206.
81 More to Margaret Roper, 2 or 3 May 1535: *Correspondence*, no. 214.
82 Cranmer to Cromwell, Otford 30 April [1535], *Miscellaneous*, no. 143.
83 Dillon, *English Martyrs*, 26–7.
84 Dowling, *Fisher of Men*, 156–7.
85 More to Margaret Roper, May and June 1535: *Correspondence*, nos. 214, 216; Daniell, *Tyndale,* 365 from Mozley, *Tyndale*, 304–7 (*LP*, 8, no. 449).
86 No copy of Cromwell's original order is known to survive, but it was summarized in Elton, *Policy and Police*, 231–5; S. Wabuda, 'Bishop John Longland's Mandate to His Clergy, 1535', *The Library*, 6th series, 13 (1991), 255–61.
87 Cranmer's response: BL, Cotton MS Cleopatra, E. VI., fol. 236r, printed in *Letters*, no. 148 (*LP*, 8, no. 820).

5 Thomas Cromwell ascendant, 1535–1537

'Everlasting God which hast ordained and constituted the services of all angels and men in a wonderful order: mercifully grant that they which alway do the service in heaven, may by thy appointment succor and defend us in earth, through Jesus Christ our Lord.'[1]

Obedience and the Henrician Church

At the time of the executions of Bishop John Fisher and Sir Thomas More in mid-1535, the theology of the English Church was about to undergo substantial reconsiderations. However, Henry VIII was fundamentally resistant to making changes in doctrine unless he could be convinced that they were to his advantage. The king feared that disagreements among his subjects over matters of religion would lead his realm into such total confusion that the English commonwealth would be destroyed. What God expected of him was governance that encouraged agreement in only one persuasion of faith.[2] For the rest of his reign, Henry sought peace in the religious unity of his kingdom. After the Act of Supremacy was passed by Parliament in November 1534, the paramount value for Church and state became obedience to the king as supreme head. Obedience was equated with the word of God in Scripture, an idea that had initially been developed by William Tyndale and other evangelicals as a weapon to repudiate the pope. The obedience of the king's subjects was essential for the peace of the realm and for the salvation of their souls.[3]

The royal supremacy opened opportunities to reform the English Church. From the beginning of her rise, Anne Boleyn hoped to make England more evangelical, and from late 1529, as we have already noted, she tried to persuade the king to allow the legalization of the Bible in English. Thomas Cromwell as vicegerent and Archbishop Thomas Cranmer shared that goal, although they also wanted to move England closer, politically and doctrinally, to the Lutherans of the League of Schmalkalden. The historian Rory McEntegart has shown that in the 1530s only Wittenberg offered well-developed theological alternatives to Rome. Cromwell worked with all his might to bring England into the League, and at times he made overtures to the Lutherans without Henry's knowledge.[4] Had England's alliance with the League of Schmalkalden succeeded, prompt changes in doctrine and patterns of worship would have been implemented in the English Church. As we have already seen, Cranmer found his early consensus among the Lutherans. He longed to bring Philip Melanchthon to England. The visit of Simon Grynaeus of Basel in 1531 also introduced Cranmer to the leaders of Swiss Reform. Every month, letters from the continent arrived for him in Canterbury. Although only a small portion of Cranmer's correspondence survives, we know that he was in regular, often secret contact with a wide spectrum of Protestant leaders that included his wife's uncle Andreas Osiander of Nuremberg, Martin Bucer of Strasbourg, John Calvin of Geneva, and Huldrych Zwingli's successor in Zürich, Heinrich Bullinger.

Initially, Cranmer, Cromwell, and the queen thought that they would be able to persuade Henry to reform the Church. Courtiers warned each other never say no to the king, and never oppose him. They believed with Proverbs 21 that the heart of the king was in the hands of God. Just as gentle raindrops eventually wear down the hardest stone, they believed Henry could be won over in time. Anne was recognized as a 'mediatrice' with the king for many good causes.[5] Nevertheless, Henry wanted to exercise his own authority without interference, and although he weighed the evidence every side presented to him, he played one set of courtiers against the others, expecting them to get along, but without giving any side complete satisfaction. Hugh Latimer noted the difficult efforts that were required to take an idea out of the king's mind.[6] Only by persuading Henry that their ecclesiastical policies would encourage obedience did Cromwell and Cranmer make some limited progress in their goals towards the reformation of the Church. Every other effort to give the English Church greater direction remained partial and unfinished. One new initiative after another was begun, only to be cast aside with bloody violence as the king permitted one set of courtiers to destroy another.

The Church that ultimately emerged under Henry VIII was not a kind of 'Catholicism without the pope'. Conservative bishops like John Stokesley of London or Stephen Gardiner of Winchester were hard put to find a theological standard that they could rally around once they were deprived of the papacy, and like Cranmer they were forced to promote the royal supremacy through obedience.[7] From 1532 Gardiner had been out of Henry's favour after he defended Convocation's independence to make Church law. In 1535 he climbed back into the king's good graces with his book *De Vera Obedientia*.[8] The ecclesiastical historians Peter Marshall and Alec Ryrie have argued that Henry's Church was like a Lutheran Church, but without the essential Protestant tenet of justification by faith alone.[9] Henry's Church was a distinctive interval in the history of Christianity in England, unmatched by any other. Owing to the king's insurmountable opposition, in the 1530s and 1540s Cranmer could not introduce most of the changes that he suggested. Henry's reign cast a long shadow, and it gave rise to competing claims in doctrine that could not be completely reconciled, not in the next reign, nor in the reigns of his daughters, and perhaps never.

Approach to the League of Schmalkalden

The period of greatest opportunity for Cromwell and Cranmer to attempt to make substantial changes in the English Church occurred in the mid-1530s, when Henry was willing to entertain the idea of forging an alliance with the League of Schmalkalden. We have already observed that for the first time in late 1533, the king sent requests to Saxony and Hesse for the establishment of closer diplomatic ties as a means to protect himself against the threat of papal excommunication. The king's first efforts to establish ambassadorial posts did not succeed, probably because Duke John Frederick and Landgrave Philip were wary of offending the emperor. They were reluctant too because of Henry's long-standing disagreements with Martin Luther, and they refused to invalidate the king's marriage to Katherine of Aragon. Although Henry had said in 1530 that he wanted to provide his subjects with an accurate translation of the Bible, nothing had been done towards fulfilling his promise. The laity was forbidden to read the Bible in English under medieval laws that had been passed against the Lollards, the followers of John Wycliffe (d. 1384), who had made their own unauthorized translations of the Gospels into English.[10] The Lutherans made plain that Henry must promote the Gospel if he intended to join the League of Schmalkalden. Until then they could not consider the king a friend of the word of God.

But in that first approach, unknown to the king, Cromwell sent the Lutherans secret assurance that an alliance would enable those English councillors, like Cranmer, who favoured a Protestant approach to the Gospel, to have a greater chance of success in prompting Henry to bring Lutheran beliefs into England. Cromwell and Cranmer's intent was to use the Lutherans as an instrument to encourage Henry to make substantial changes in English Church doctrine, for they all stood together in their opposition to the papacy.[11]

The next overture to the Lutherans in mid-1535 offered even greater promise of success, because the dangerous diplomatic scene again threatened England. To confound the Habsburgs, King Francis I of France entered into negotiations with the Ottoman Empire. The Emperor Charles V was in Tunisia where he was conducting a successful military campaign to safeguard Italy against France's ally, the Ottoman admiral Barbarossa (d. 1546). Francis used the emperor's absence in North Africa to work towards reconciliation between the Lutherans and Rome. Francis invited Philip Melanchthon to meet him and discuss the prospect. Henry began to fear that the General Council that he had called for in 1533 might become a new tool that Pope Paul III could use against him. Alarmed that England was becoming ever more isolated, Henry instructed Cromwell to send Robert Barnes to bring Melanchthon to England.

This new approach to the Lutherans represented an important shift in English diplomatic policy. Melanchthon dedicated to Henry the latest edition of his most influential book, the *Loci communes*, and Alexander Alesius (1500–1565) was sent to England bearing copies as gifts for the king and for Cranmer. Alesius was a Scot who had gone into exile in Wittenberg. From the time of his arrival in England, the archbishop confided in him. The queen, whose connections with France had been an asset until now, was consulted for her approval for the new initiative to the Lutherans. They had refused to endorse Henry's case against his first marriage, and the king wanted them to concede that he had made a valid marriage with Anne. In Wittenberg, Barnes was able to persuade Luther to appeal to John Frederick to permit Melanchthon to go to England. In an audience with the duke, Barnes said that Henry wished to apply for admittance to the League.[12]

Many of the preparations for the forthcoming embassy were left in Cromwell and Cranmer's hands as the king and queen left Windsor for their summer's progress, which took them almost as far as Bristol, along the same route Cranmer had taken the previous year on his metropolitical visitation.[13] They were joined by Cromwell in late July, when he began his visitation of the religious houses in the initial stage of his vicegerency.[14]

The royal progress culminated at Winchester Cathedral on 19 September 1535, where Cranmer consecrated three new bishops. The diplomat Edward Fox was rewarded with the bishopric of Hereford for his many years of service in the king's Great Matter, and for bringing Cranmer to Henry's attention in 1529. Hugh Latimer became bishop of Worcester. He had been indispensable in rendering Cambridge's decision for Henry in 1530, and he served the queen as one of her chaplains. Like Fox, he was one of Cranmer's most important friends.[15] John Hilsey (d. 1539) was a Dominican friar who had come to notice first for opposing Latimer in his sermons in Bristol in 1532, and then for being converted by him. As a further insult to the papacy, Hilsey was consecrated bishop of Rochester. The martyred Fisher was replaced by a friar who enthusiastically embraced the king's supremacy over the English Church.

Fox spent the summer of 1535 at Lambeth with Cranmer preparing for the embassy he would lead to the Lutherans.[16] He was not empowered to make agreements with them, but when he reached Saxony he told officials that Henry wanted an embassy to be sent to England to discuss theological matters. Fox said that the king was interested in joining the League, and that he had no intention of restoring the pope's authority in England. A few days later, Fox made the same points when he addressed the League's Diet. In response, the Diet stipulated that the king must promote the gospel and be willing to defend the Augsburg Confession, the articles of faith that defined the League. Then Fox and his party settled down in Wittenberg for three months of strenuous theological negotiations with Luther and Melanchthon. They took up divisive questions concerning the Eucharist, private Masses for departed souls, and clerical marriage. Although Fox was not allowed to come to any resolution with the Lutherans, his embassy was essential for opening the next serious phase of the discussions between England and the League.[17]

Preaching obedience

While the court was still in Winchester, word arrived from the French ambassador that Pope Paul had responded to the executions of Fisher and More with his greatest censure: he drew up a second decree that excommunicated Cranmer and the king. The pope called for Henry's dethronement.[18] The king held an emergency meeting of the Council and decided to re-intensify the preaching campaign that Cromwell had ordered on 3 June 1535. The bishops were to command the clergy to preach the royal supremacy throughout the realm every Sunday without ceasing.

Henry's order represented a major new initiative to defend his supremacy. From this time forward, if not earlier, the sermon became a highly politicized weapon in service to the king. Cranmer welcomed the opportunity to reassert his authority in his own diocese through the pulpit, and immediately he took his chaplains to Kent. In Canterbury Cathedral, Cranmer delivered two sermons that exemplified the anti-papal rhetoric that he was now making the standard in Henry's Church. The 'bishop of Rome was not God's vicar in earth', he declared. To maintain the authority of the bishop of Rome was 'contrary to God's word'. Cranmer denounced 'the glory and pomp of Rome, the covetousness, the unchaste living and the maintenance of all vices' there. Cromwell's visitation of the religious houses had already begun in Canterbury and Cranmer insinuated that the members of the regular orders were guilty of betraying their vows of celibacy through sexual irregularities. He hinted that it was better for priests to marry than to sin. He explained that the laws of the bishop of Rome were contrary to God's laws, and did not lead to salvation. Rather, 'our sins be remitted by the death of our Saviour Christ Jesus'. To attribute remission of sins to any man's laws was to do injury to Christ himself. Nevertheless, Cranmer maintained that the king's laws were for 'good order and quietness' and they disposed men to peace and justice. For many years he had prayed daily that 'I might see the power of Rome destroyed', and 'I thanked God that I had now seen it in this realm'.[19] Obedience to the king was a matter of salvation as well as a political virtue.

Initially, Cranmer thought that his message was received quietly. But in light of the summer's events his sermons had a sensational effect. The family of Sir Thomas More's son-in-law William Roper (d. 1578) had a large house near the cathedral in the parish of St Dunstan's, and local feelings ran high against More's execution. Cranmer's sermons were answered by the prior of Canterbury's Dominican convent who preached 'clean contrary' against him. The prior said that the Church never erred. God's law was equal with the laws of the Church, or as he implied, the law of the Church of Rome. When Cranmer examined him afterwards, the prior said he knew of no vices that had been committed by any of the bishops of Rome. The prior accused him of being 'uncharitable' in his sermon. Cranmer was challenged and discountenanced in his own cathedral city. To his chagrin, he was unable to call the prior to account for more than a year because of fading support from the king and Cromwell.[20]

Henrician canons

Meanwhile, another initiative that had been necessitated by the royal supremacy was making slow progress that ground to a halt. In 1532, as a consequence of the Submission of the Clergy, the king and his advisors realized that the laws governing the Church should be re-evaluated to allow no further legal force to canons that supported the papacy or conflicted with the statutes of the realm. The existing corpus of canon law was extensive, and a review was too sensitive to be entrusted to the clergy alone. After Archbishop

William Warham died, a commission of thirty-two was proposed to take up the work, half of whom were to be clergymen and the rest from Parliament. However, the commission was never officially appointed, although a small committee, led by Richard Gwent, started the review. As we have already observed, Gwent was made dean of the Arches while Cranmer was still on embassy to the imperial court, and it is not clear that they saw eye to eye about the project. After many months of effort, 'the Henrician Canons', a draft of some three hundred and sixty new laws was ready, and Gwent asked Cromwell on 27 October 1535 for an opportunity to show it to the king.

Nothing further happened to pass them into law. Once Convocation capitulated in 1532, parliamentary statutes dominated canon law. Glaring problems, like the danger of appeals to Rome, were addressed quickly by statute. The modern editor of the Henrician canons has suggested that events were moving so quickly in the mid-1530s, especially concerning the approach to the Lutherans, that any attempt to make new laws for the Church would be out of date before they were completed. Cromwell, as vicegerent, did not wish to be hampered by an ecclesiastical law code that might not prove sufficiently supple to meet the changing needs of his office and the Church.[21] Ecclesiastical courts in every diocese ruled on marriage disputes, wills, and tithes. Parliament did not intrude upon the Church courts immediately. In fact, Roman canon law proved to be remarkably resilient in England despite the breach with the papacy.[22] As a stopgap measure, Parliament stipulated that until the review resulted in a new code of law for the Church, the existing canons would remain in force unless they defied English law or customs or infringed on royal authority. This meant that Cranmer had to work within the existing framework of canon law until 1551, when he could review the problem again in the new reign, as we will see in Chapter 9.

The religious houses and the fall of Anne Boleyn

Rather surprisingly, Cranmer lost the confidence of the king and his vicegerent towards the end of 1535. Part of the problem was his absence from court over the summer and while he was preaching in Kent. Dangerous disagreements emerged between Anne and

Cromwell concerning the fate of the immensely valuable property that was about to be confiscated when the religious houses were suppressed. Estimates vary, but perhaps as much as one-quarter of the productive land in England had been ceded over the centuries into the hands of the Church, primarily to endow Masses for souls in Purgatory, much of it invested in the monasteries. Not every religious house had the incentive to develop the economic potential of its property, even though the greatest abbots sat in the House of Lords.

Evangelicals argued, following Luther, that the religious orders had become wealthy at the expense of the rest of society. Intercessory institutions like monasteries and convents were redundant if one of their main purposes, to pray for the souls of the dead, was discredited. In cities like Strasbourg or Nuremberg, the religious houses were closed in the 1520s, because the merchant classes were persuaded by Luther's challenge to impose their own control over the Church.[23] Cranmer had been able to observe the effects of this policy in 1530 when he was in Nuremberg, and he shared many of the same ideas. In England, however, there was much less enthusiasm for closing the religious houses. Because the loyalty of the religious orders to the king was suspect, monks, friars and nuns began to be characterized as greedy drones, living in idle ignorance. Their routine of prayer was dismissed by Latimer and Edward Crome as mere 'lip labour' that did nothing to improve society.[24] They were criticized for valuing the usurped authority of the bishop of Rome more than the obedience they owed to their sovereign.

The queen, with Cranmer and Latimer, believed that once the monks and friars were turned out, many houses would have new roles to play in evangelizing England because they should be converted into places of study where the needs of the poor could be relieved. In market towns across England, the former convents and abbeys should be remade into centres of preaching and education that would prepare scholars for university. Preachers would teach the people that their duty lay in their obedience to the king and not to the bishop of Rome. By promoting the Gospel, the repurposed religious houses would provide a monumental contribution to the welfare of the entire realm. Had their plans been realized, the new institutions very likely would have had a dramatic and lasting effect.[25]

In contrast, Cromwell promoted a policy that he believed was essential in guaranteeing permanent support for the king and the royal supremacy: that the property of the religious houses should be confiscated by the Crown. The king would enjoy the immediate benefits of a huge financial windfall. Then the lands would be parcelled out to members of the local gentry (and to the merchants of market towns and London) as rewards for their support for the royal supremacy. Locally, the gentry would have a larger role to play because they would be fully invested in the regime. Those who wished to stay in religion would be sent for the time being to the larger houses of their orders. Cromwell had other plans for legislation that would relieve poverty. Poor people would be assisted in their parishes, an intention that was not fully realized until the Poor Laws were passed late in the century. Cromwell's plans had the potential of securing the loyalty of the gentry to the crown.

The disagreements between Anne and Cromwell grew so dangerous that they nearly destroyed each other. We do not know how early Cromwell decided that he had to move against Anne, but he took threatening measures against Cranmer in late 1535. Cranmer was surprised to receive a letter of warning from Latimer at the end of October that the king believed he was doing 'nothing' to promote the royal supremacy in satisfaction of the orders Henry had given at Winchester. Latimer told Cranmer that it was rumoured at court that he was only looking at the king's business through his fingers.[26] News of his preaching campaign in Kent had not filtered back to London.

Latimer's warning may have also been related to the Cranmers' dispute about property that had belonged to a house of nuns at Davington in Kent. The house had already failed, perhaps because it could not afford to pay the new tax of the Tenths. It closed a few months before legislation clarified what should happen to the property, and Cranmer relied on existing law to establish his claims. For many years, the house had held some sixty wooded acres from the archbishops of Canterbury. It had one appropriated benefice whose tithes were collected by the archdeacon. Edmund Cranmer had already taken them when his brother wrote Cromwell in mid-October to request that the lands should not go to the king. Cranmer maintained that it had to be determined before the law whether or not the property should revert to him in 'the right of the see of Canterbury'. Unfortunately, some of the facts of the case remain obscure. It may be that Edmund (or the archbishop himself) actually stayed a legal verdict that found for Henry, though Cranmer denied it. Much later, Edmund obtained some advantageous leases as the religious houses closed, including one for their sister Alice, which may have been the source of Thomas Seymour's unfounded accusation that the archbishop did not maintain due standards of hospitality because he wished to enrich his family.[27] Whatever actually happened in the autumn of 1535, Cromwell was informed that Edmund and his brother had interfered in the case to the disadvantage of the king. Cromwell instructed one of his officers to confiscate the tithes from Edmund, and he sent Cranmer a blistering letter that contained a threat: Cromwell would be sorry should Henry have to learn that the archbishop had weighed against him in this or in any other matter.[28]

What is remarkable about this episode was how far Cranmer pressed forward his interests even though the disputed property was worth relatively little. Edmund's tithes may have been no more than five shillings, but with surprising vigour, Cranmer refused to back down. At the beginning of November he asked Cromwell for the return of the tithes. He protested that neither he nor Edmund had stayed any legal verdict, even though many told him that he had a just title to the property. As for Cromwell's threat to inform the king, 'I would you saw the very bottom of my heart' because Cranmer said his sense of justice would prevent him from delivering a judgment contrary to the right against even the king's poorest subject. If he knew that it was the king's pleasure to have his title for the lands, then he would want to give it to the king more than Henry could want to have it. But what if Henry really wanted Cranmer to have the lands? Then 'if my title be good, I must needs make my claim'.[29]

This evidence should give pause to those who characterized Cranmer as unable to stand up to Henry and Cromwell. We can see that in this case Cranmer resisted an arbitrary or premature claim made on behalf of the king. With special persistence, he defended the right of the archbishopric under the law, perhaps because in recent months his see had suffered heavy losses of prestige and influence. Moreover, Cranmer energetically defended his brother. In the long term, Cranmer very likely was correct that the tithes belonged to Edmund. From the *Valor Ecclesiasticus*, we know that in due course the retired prioress received a pension from the house, and Edmund was accorded the right to take tithes from the property. We may marvel that the archbishop was willing to jeopardize the good will of the king in order to gain small tithes and sixty acres in Kent, but as we shall see, he could not dare to do so again. Disagreements over the fate of the property of the religious houses were among the most dangerous issues to emerge from the royal supremacy, and they were an important element in the destruction of the queen.

Katherine of Aragon's health broke in the closing weeks of the year, and she died in isolation at Kimbolton Castle on 7 January 1536. Henry greeted the news with joyous relief, for he believed that now it was less likely that Charles would strike against England. Anne had conceived a child towards the end of the summer's progress. Rather than mourn, and with fresh hope that this next child would be a son, the king and queen celebrated. On 21 January, while he was jousting in the tiltyard at Greenwich, Henry's horse fell. For two hours the king lay unconscious while the court erupted in a frenzy of fear.[30]

If Henry had died that day, under the terms of the Act of Succession, Anne would have been regent until Elizabeth or her next child reached the age of majority. Her baby was expected in late summer. Months of uncertainty would be spent waiting for the birth. If her pregnancy resulted in a boy, he would become king immediately. Otherwise, Elizabeth, not yet three years old, would succeed her father. Under those circumstances, it is not certain how well Anne and Elizabeth would have prevailed against Mary if, as the imperial ambassador Eustace Chapuys thought, the English people wanted to rise for Katherine's daughter. Only five days after his fall, on 29 January, the same day that Katherine's body was interred in Peterborough Abbey, Anne suffered a miscarriage. Her pregnancy was far enough along to tell that the child had been a boy.

We cannot know how much the shock of his accident may have shaped Henry's subsequent behaviour. Recent medical research has suggested that he may have suffered from McLeod's Syndrome, a rare malady that caused his health to fail gradually and painfully after the age of forty, which occasioned the irascibility and swings in mood that made him so dangerous to serve. Its origins were genetic in nature as a recessive trait on his X chromosome. Once passed to his offspring, though a first pregnancy could succeed, his wives became sensitized, which meant that their second and subsequent pregnancies had a high rate of failure.[31] We will probably never know for certain if the king suffered from McLeod's Syndrome or from some other type of illness that blasted his hopes for children. After Elizabeth's birth Anne had had at least one other miscarriage, and Henry thought briefly of discarding her, but he did not, because he would have been forced to go back to Katherine. After this miscarriage he was heard to say that he could see that God would not give him sons.[32] Alesius thought that Henry began to hate Anne because she could not give him a son. In hindsight it was understood that Anne 'had miscarried of her saviour'.[33]

Henry began to confide to his intimates that he desired to take another wife. From the beginning of the year he had become attracted to Jane Seymour (1509–1537), who served first Katherine and now Anne as lady-in-waiting. On their progress in September 1535, the king and queen stayed at Wolf Hall, the house of Jane's father near Marlborough in Wiltshire. In March 1536 Jane's brother Edward (*c.* 1500–1552) was admitted as a member of the king's privy chamber.

Meanwhile, in the first three months of the year, an intense new preaching campaign was unleashed at Paul's Cross. This had not been possible before now. Stokesley as bishop of London defended the existence of Purgatory, and he did not allow anyone to preach there who refused to lead the audience in prayers for departed souls. Several of Cromwell's preachers were turned away.[34] In December 1535, in an extraordinary demonstration of his authority as vicegerent, Cromwell removed Stokesley's prerogative to appoint the Paul's Cross preachers. He could have reassigned the authority to Cranmer, but he did not. Rather, he gave it to Bishop Hilsey of Rochester.[35] Cromwell's reassignment was almost as much a reproof of Cranmer as it was of Stokesley.

Parliament and Convocation reopened in the first week of February 1536. The series of sermons that were delivered at Paul's

Cross as the Reformation Parliament concluded were unusual for their dramatic attacks against the Carthusians, the papacy and Charles V, and for their efforts to protect Queen Anne's faltering position.[36]

Cranmer preached at Paul's Cross on 6 February. Preaching in the prophetic mode, his sermon was a daring and scathing indictment of the pope and the emperor. Although its text does not survive, we have some indication of what he said from those who heard it. He explained the diplomatic overtures that the king was making to the Lutheran princes. He denounced canonizations, dispensations, pardons, jubilees, and indulgences that he claimed the Roman Church had used to raise money by exploiting the credulity of the faithful. Cranmer declared that all of the passages in Scripture that mentioned Antichrist were references to the pope, and idea he may have borrowed from the writings of William Tyndale, who was awaiting execution in the Castle of Vilvorde near Brussels, a prisoner of Charles V's sister Mary, the regent of the Low Countries. Cranmer declared that Antichrist would appear when the Habsburg empire was ruined. And it was already ruined, he said, because few German princes still obeyed the emperor. Henry's subjects should know that the pope was the true Antichrist. Chapuys was in the audience, and he was scandalized that Cranmer, who had been entertained so generously at the imperial court, could so insult his prince.[37]

Three weeks later Cranmer returned to Paul's Cross, this time to listen to Bishop Cuthbert Tunstall (1474–1559) make a public declaration of his acceptance of the king's authority over the Church. Tunstall had been one of Sir Thomas More's closest friends. More mentioned Tunstall in the opening sentences of the *Utopia*. Together they had hunted heretics. But Tunstall had sworn the oaths. His sermon on 27 February 1536 was an open acknowledgement of his submission to the king. Cranmer and several other bishops sat beneath the pulpit where the crowd could see them. The dukes of Norfolk and Suffolk and other lords crowded behind Tunstall inside the pulpit cross. During the sermon, four Charterhouse monks were exposed to censure for their refusal to reject the papacy. They had endured months of unremitting pressure, and yet they continued to refuse to take the supremacy oath. Tunstall declared that the popes were bound to obey the terms of the eight General Councils of the early Church, but instead, they had usurped their powers over Christendom. The pope had dispensed the king to make an unnatural marriage with his brother's wife. God had given every king the power to be supreme head over the priests in their realms.[38] Tunstall made the kind of open submission that Cranmer had hoped Fisher and More might make.

The closure of the religious houses was the most important piece of business that came before the final session of the Reformation Parliament. The king and Cromwell decided to dissolve them in stages, starting with the smaller houses, which were easier to suppress. Those that had a yearly income of £200 or less were to be shut first. As an exclusionary tactic to reduce opposition, most of the abbots from the greater houses were warned against taking their seats in the Lords when Parliament assembled again. The preamble of the bill referred to the 'manifest sin, vicious, carnal, and abominable living' that was committed daily by members of the religious orders. Bishop Latimer noted that when the bill had its first reading in the Lords the 'enormities' revealed were 'so great and abominable' that there were calls in the chamber: '"down with them."' Only three abbots were present, and they did not dare to object in the hope that their own houses might be spared.[39]

The disagreements between Anne and Cromwell deepened, and she threatened to destroy him. She instructed her chaplains to deliver pointed messages in their sermons at court against the closure of the religious houses. In one of his most provocative court sermons, Latimer begged the king to convert the abbeys and priories into 'better uses' as places of learning and relief of the poor. When they heard that sermons were being delivered at court against their suppression, a delegation of priors and abbots approached the queen in a desperate bid for her protection. After she castigated them for the evils of their 'licentious life', they offered to give generous sums to her trustees to support preachers and needy students at the universities. She became even more convinced that the smaller houses should not be swept away wholesale. She believed that Cromwell and his friends were acting in their own interests under the cover of their devotion to the Gospel because they intended to take bribes and enrich themselves as the properties of the religious houses were distributed. Anne began to warn the king against Cromwell. Her chaplains began to imply in their sermons that he was one of England's 'strong thieves' who deserved to be hanged.[40]

The king came to the Commons on 11 March to present the bill to dissolve the smaller priories and convents. The Reformation Parliament came to its final end on Good Friday, 14 April 1536. As soon as the bill about the smaller religious houses passed, Cranmer spoke to Cromwell at court on behalf of his brother-in-law Harold Rosell, for whom he asked for the lease of the priory of Shelford, or for another religious house in Nottinghamshire.[41] After Easter, the archbishop went first to Knole and then to Otford. Cranmer was still in Kent at the beginning of May when Anne was accused of adultery.

Katherine's death revealed how weak Anne's position really was. Anne was an anathema to the emperor and her marriage had been condemned by two popes. She was unpopular with Henry's subjects. It was a damaging fact that the Lutherans, with whom Anne encouraged an alliance, did not want to endorse her. Doubts about the validity of Henry's second marriage dominated the negotiations in Wittenberg. Luther and Melanchthon were willing to concede that the king's arguments had merit. Osiander sent them a letter that supported the doctrinal grounds of Henry's case. But they stopped short of ruling in his favour.[42] Gardiner had been sent as ambassador to France after the new bishops were consecrated at Winchester. Writing to Cromwell in mid-February, Gardiner said the diplomatic problem was now simplified because 'God hath given sentence for the most part by the death of the Dowager', but he warned that an alliance between England and the League of Schmalkalden would cause Henry to lose his independence of action without providing him any advantages.[43]

Katherine's death also removed the impediment that prevented a new alliance between Henry and Charles, who returned to Rome from North Africa in April 1536. The emperor decided that he must protect Mary and work for her restoration in the line of succession. To conciliate Henry, the emperor prevented the release of Paul's sentence of excommunication.[44]

According to Alexander Alesius, Gardiner triggered the crisis that destroyed Anne when he wrote to warn Thomas Wriothesley, the king's secretary, that there were rumours at the French Court about the queen, and letters were discovered there that were used to accuse Anne of adultery.[45] No such letters have survived. In all probability, the charges of adultery against Anne were fabrications. Her privy chamber (like that of any court in Europe) was a hothouse of gossip, innuendo, and flirtations. The queen was probably guilty of nothing worse than minor indiscretions that her enemies manipulated to be rid of her and her most powerful supporters, including her brother George, Lord Rochford.[46] Suddenly, the queen's privy chamber was closely monitored. Alarmed, the queen entrusted the spiritual care of her daughter to her chaplain Matthew Parker.[47] Anne was accused with her brother and four other men. On 2 May 1536 Cromwell and Lord Chancellor Audley conveyed her to the Tower.[48]

Cranmer was immediately summoned to Lambeth Palace, but he was warned not to come into the king's presence, a deliberate strategy by the queen's enemies to isolate Henry from Anne's friends. Cranmer was prevented from pleading directly with the king for her life. On 3 May he wrote Henry the most difficult and controversial letter of his life. When he began it, he could not know the details of what had happened, but from what he had heard in the previous twenty-four hours he must have concluded that the queen was all but lost. A week after Easter, Cranmer had been deeply worried about the direction that matters of religion were taking, and while he was still in Kent, he had asked Cromwell for the opportunity to 'break my mind' with him, though it seems unlikely that they spoke again before the queen's arrest.[49] Cranmer could not know if Henry was willing to sacrifice evangelicalism along with Anne.

Cranmer began with a long, cautious expression of concern that the king would take all adversities from God 'both patiently and thankfully'. He noted that the king's honour was impugned 'whether the things that commonly be spoken of be true or not'. Cranmer reminded him of the example of Job, who despite being tested, remained obedient to God and was abundantly rewarded.[50] He wrote that if what people 'openly reported of the queen's grace' was true, then if they considered the matter correctly, they should think that only the queen's honour was impugned, and not Henry's. But Cranmer found what he had heard difficult to believe: 'I am in such a perplexity, that my mind is clean amazed; for I never had better opinion in woman, than I had in her; which maketh me to think, that she should not be culpable'. And yet, it was just as difficult for him to believe that Henry would have had her imprisoned if she had not been guilty.

Cranmer confessed that next to the king himself, 'I was most bound unto her of all creatures living' and he begged the king to permit him to do what 'God's law, nature, and also her kindness bindeth me unto': to pray for her so that she could 'declare herself inculpable and innocent'. However, if she was found guilty, then no loyal subject could wish otherwise than that the offence would be punished without mercy as an example.

'And as I loved her not a little for the love which I judged her to bear towards God and his gospel', then if she were really guilty, no one who loved the Gospel could support her. Rather, they must hate her, and the more they favoured the Gospel, the more they must hate her for her hypocrisy. If she was guilty, then God had sent her this punishment for pretending when she did not really live by the Gospel 'in heart and deed'. Because that cause that the archbishop and the queen had shared might be in jeopardy, Cranmer pleaded for the Gospel. Henry must recognize that like every Christian he was a sinner, and the king should be willing to admit that he had offended God before now. 'Wherefore I trust that your grace will bear no less entire favour unto the truth of the gospel, then you did before' because it had not been led by his affection for the queen, but rather, stemmed from Henry's own 'zeal unto the truth'.

Some historians have criticized Cranmer for weakness in defending the queen in such an ineffectual manner. But he took a tremendous risk in writing Henry as he did. For all he knew, England might be required to return to Rome as the price for rapprochement with Charles, and if so, Cranmer very likely would have been destroyed with Anne as the scapegoat for passing judgement against Katherine's marriage.[51]

After he closed his letter, Cranmer was summoned to the Star Chamber by Audley and other councillors, where they told him what the king wanted him to know. In a postscript, Cranmer wrote, 'I am exceedingly sorry that such faults can be proved by the queen, as I heard of their relation'. Had Cranmer truly accepted that Anne was guilty of adultery, he would have had no reason to send his letter. He would have discarded it, rather than expose himself as the queen's friend. We may conclude that Cranmer doubted that Anne was guilty, but he also did not think that she could be saved. Instead, the cause of the Gospel had to be rescued from the impending disaster.

Anne could not simply be demoted or discarded without tacitly acknowledging that Henry's marriage to Katherine had been valid all along and that Mary was rightfully his heir, which would have given the Emperor Charles an enormous advantage. After Parliament rose, Cromwell explored the possibilities that would release the king from his marriage. At the beginning of 1534, Stokesley had told the king that although Convocation had ruled the previous year that Henry's marriage with Katherine was against the law of God and could not be dispensed by the pope, Convocation had not validated the king's marriage to Anne.[52] Cromwell asked him about the feasibility of a second divorce. Stokesley replied that he would give his opinion to no one but to the king himself, and before he spoke, he would like to know what Henry wanted. Cromwell also spent four days in conference with Richard Sampson, dean of the chapel royal, for his insights about canon law. As long as Anne was alive, the legitimacy of any children Henry might have with another wife would be jeopardized.[53]

The decision to execute Anne and invalidate her marriage, therefore, was taken before Cranmer was involved, and he was given no choice but to comply with what was expected of him. The queen and Rochford were tried in the Great Hall of the Tower, and they were condemned on Monday 15 May 1536.[54] At the same time, in a chapel beneath Lambeth Palace, Cranmer convened a secret inquisition to nullify the queen's marriage. The hearing was attended by Cromwell and Audley, and Sampson once again served as the king's proctor.

On Tuesday 16 May 1536, Cranmer went to the Tower to hear Anne's confession. Before now, the queen had regularly confessed to Cranmer or Latimer.[55] The next day, when her brother and the other men went to the block, Cranmer nullified her marriage on the basis of causes that had only recently been revealed, by 'certain just, true, and lawful impediments' recently 'brought to light and open knowledge' and that were supposedly 'confessed' by Anne to Cranmer.[56]

Historians have speculated whether Anne made a damaging revelation in her confession, after she was condemned, that completed the case against her marriage. This seems unlikely. When Cranmer's decree was presented before Parliament on 10 June, the impediments that invalidated her marriage were not specified. Cranmer had been willing to bargain for lives before now, but not this time. Anne had nothing that the king wanted in exchange, and Cranmer did not offer her false hope to entrap her. She told her jailor that she was the king's true wedded wife, which would seem to preclude the possibility that one of her earlier promises of marriage – to Thomas Wyatt; or to Henry Percy, the earl of Northumberland; or to someone else – had been consummated secretly before she wed the king. Awaiting execution, Anne twice received communion from her chaplain John Skyp (d. 1552). She told those guarding her, on pain of eternal damnation, that she had never been unfaithful to Henry.[57]

It is difficult to be certain how much Cranmer could have known about the intimacies of life at court a dozen years earlier, while he was still in Cambridge, and if he had been aware before now that Henry had had an affair with Anne's older sister. Nor was Cranmer in England in 1532 when Archbishops Warham and Lee examined Northumberland about the nature of his relationship with Anne. Under the terms of the 1534 Act of Succession, with its list of Levitical prohibitions, Henry and Anne were forever ineligible to be married because of the king's affair with her sister Mary. The lack of detail in Cranmer's decree, as well as in the next Act of Succession, may have been meant to screen the king's misbehaviour. As incredible as it may seem, Henry embarked upon his marriage with Anne on the strength of a papal dispensation that Gardiner had obtained for him in 1528 that had absolved both Anne of a previous intent to wed another man, and Henry of his affinity in the first degree with her sister. Although members of the court may have known of Henry and Mary's affair when it happened, it is possible that Cranmer may have learned about it, or some other intractable problem, only now. In his study of Henry's matrimonial trials, Henry Ansgar Kelly (b. 1934) raised the possibility that there may also have been several impediments that

Clement had not dispensed that Cranmer used to nullify Anne's marriage.[58] Even if that was so, Henry and Anne's marriage was doomed both under the strictures defined by Leviticus as well as by the Act of Succession that made her children heirs to the throne. That Anne and Henry were never properly married was also later implied by their daughter, for as queen, Elizabeth made no move to have Parliament overturn her bastardization.[59]

Before dawn on the morning of 19 May 1536, Alesius went to Lambeth Palace. He wrote Elizabeth in 1559 that he found Cranmer walking alone in the garden. Alesius had been at home for several days, and he told Cranmer he knew nothing of what was going on. The archbishop raised his eyes to heaven as he said that '"She who has been Queen of England on earth will today be a Queen in heaven"', and he burst into tears.[60] At mid-morning, Anne was beheaded by a French executioner, specially brought over from Calais for his skill in wielding a sword. Before the day was over, Cranmer dispensed the king and Jane Seymour from an affinity in the third and fourth degrees and from the reading of the banns. Their marriage was solemnized at Whitehall on 30 May.[61]

In Elizabeth's reign, the years of Anne's brief ascendency were portrayed by her clients as a golden age, a moment of great promise that came to an abrupt end when the Fates 'tripped her' before half her race was run. Anne was sacrificed, as Katherine had been, for Henry's dynastic imperatives. If Alesius was correct, Cranmer's private opinion about Anne was revealed in the garden on the morning of her execution. Just as he had anointed and crowned her, in all probability he absolved her when he heard her confession. He considered her both guiltless and a martyr.[62]

The sacrifice of Anne Boleyn completed Cromwell's rise as the unchallenged leader of England's evangelicals. Anne had made many bishops, and Cranmer was her greatest. He had become archbishop of Canterbury under one set of expectations that, with Anne's death, were never fulfilled. Anne's Reformation was a lost opportunity for England.

Circumstances called for an immediate if excruciating series of readjustments. Cranmer had no other choice but to adapt to Cromwell's ascendency, for he could not be certain that he would not be destroyed also if it so pleased the king and his chief minister. Anne's fall brought home to the archbishop yet again how limited were his powers and influence, and how much the regime constrained him to do what was against his best interests and against his own conscience. In time, Cranmer accepted that he was not permitted to achieve as much for the cause of evangelicalism as could the vicegerent. Within a year, the archbishop assured Wolfgang Capito (1478–1541) of Strasbourg that Cromwell 'has done more than all others together' in 'the reformation of religion and of the clergy' in England.[63]

The Parliament and Convocation of 1536

Many people believed that Anne's destruction meant that the papacy would be reinstated and Mary restored to the succession. Less than two months after the close of the Reformation Parliament, a new Parliament opened on 8 June to complete Anne's destruction by passing a new Act of Succession. The grounds of Cranmer's decree of nullity that invalidated her marriage were not specified, but they were declared to be sufficiently proved. Elizabeth was bastardized. Yet again, Katherine's marriage to Henry was nullified on the strength of the decisions that the universities had taken in 1530, as well as Cranmer's ruling at Dunstable that her marriage to Arthur had been consummated. The Act made the king's children with Jane his lawful heirs. Failing any issue from this marriage, the Act empowered Henry to name his own heir, a startling and ultimately destabilizing innovation that had serious repercussions in the next reign.[64]

The Act Extinguishing the Authority of the Bishop of Rome, passed by this Parliament, severed England's final links to the papacy. Any expression of support for the pope's authority became an offence punishable by loss of property under *praemunire*. To refuse another round of oath-taking was treason.[65] Henry insisted that his daughter Mary acknowledge the royal supremacy and the invalidity of her mother's marriage, and when she refused, he fully intended to send her to the Tower and to her death. Her friends were arrested and marked for execution.

At enormous risk to himself, Cranmer interceded with the king on her behalf, provoking Henry's anger. For the first (but not the last) time, Cranmer was ejected from the Council. However, Mary submitted on 22 June 1536, and her friends were spared.

Cranmer also returned to the king's good graces, though according to Morice, Henry told him that he would live to regret intervening for his daughter.[66]

A double session of Convocation, in which both ecclesiastical provinces were represented, combined as a synod, opened on 9 June at St Paul's, when Cromwell was given his fullest powers as vicegerent and vicar general in spirituals in representing the king. When he entered, all members of the Upper House rose to their feet and bowed to him. Cromwell was seated with the bishops at a table, with Cranmer on one side and Archbishop Edward Lee of York on the other. On 20 June, Cromwell and every member of Convocation signed a new oath that England was an independent monarchy and an imperial see unto itself. Because Henry was supreme head, he was not bound to appear should Charles or Pope Paul call a General Council. All papal laws were invalidated in England except for those made by the first four General Councils of the Christian Church, which had been summoned by the Roman emperors of their times despite the reluctance of their popes.

The next day Cranmer's decree of nullity for Anne's marriage was introduced in Convocation. Henry's second marriage was invalidated, and with it, the past three years were negated because Anne had never been the lawful queen of England. Cranmer had set the crown upon her head, but now her coronation was undone. A few days later, her father surrendered the office of lord privy seal, and he was succeeded by Cromwell.[67] At the feast of Corpus Christi, Cranmer's friend Abbot William Benson welcomed Queen Jane to Mass in Westminster Abbey.[68]

The next most important achievement of the 1536 Convocation's was in enacting the *Ten Articles*, the first definition of the theological positions in Henry's Church, which was to be used as a guide for preachers in the parishes. Fox returned from his negotiations in Wittenberg in time to take part in the session. With Cromwell and Cranmer, he wanted the *Ten Articles* to reflect the directions that his discussions with the Lutherans took.[69] The tone for their discussions was set by the sermon Bishop Latimer delivered at the opening of the session. He accused his hearers of permitting the laity to die in superstition because they had not repaired abuses in the Church before now. He raised questions about pilgrimages,

images, and the cult of saints. His sermon's most memorable phrase, from its English translation, was 'purgatory pickpurse'.[70]

Although Stokesley, Lee and other traditionalists resisted, Cromwell and Cranmer pushed the discussions towards Lutheran positions. They were assisted by bishops Fox, Latimer, Goodrich, and Shaxton. Serious disagreements occurred about the number of sacraments. Cranmer urged the bishops to consider what Scripture meant by a sacrament. What was the true use of a sacrament? Did the sacraments justify, or were Christians justified instead by faith? Could all the ceremonies that were called sacraments compare in importance with baptism and the supper of the Lord? Were some ceremonies, like the washing of feet on Maundy Thursday, actually sacraments, as St Ambrose suggested, even though they were not considered one of the seven?[71]

Stokesley insisted that there were seven sacraments. Luther maintained that there were only two sacraments, baptism and the Lord's Supper, a point raised by Alesius, who spoke as a guest during the bishops' disputation until Cromwell and Cranmer saw that his presence offended Stokesley. Cranmer referred to the Eucharist as the Lord's Supper, as the Lutherans did. In the final version of the *Ten Articles*, they compromised on three sacraments: baptism, penance, and the sacrament of the altar.

The first four articles listed in the final document concerned baptism, penance, the sacrament of the altar, and justification. They were essential for all Christians because God commanded them as necessary for salvation. The other six articles dealt with images, the honouring of saints, praying to saints, rites, ceremonies, and Purgatory, but they were given only second place as 'laudable ceremonies' that Henry wanted to be kept for 'decent order' in the Church, even though they were not expressly required by God.

By omitting the other four sacraments, confirmation, matrimony, holy orders, and extreme unction, the *Ten Articles* implied that they were not sacraments at all and that they were rejected in Henry's Church. There were other important omissions as well. The article on the sacrament of the altar required that all people believe that the very same body and blood of Jesus Christ, born of the Virgin Mary, who suffered on the cross for redemption, was really contained and comprehended in the sacrament under the form and figure of bread and wine. However, the dogma of transubstantiation was not mentioned, nor was the traditional idea that the Mass was a sacrifice. The article on Purgatory advised that it was 'a very good and charitable deed to pray for souls departed', though the place where they were, its name, and the kinds of pains suffered there 'be to us uncertain by Scripture'.[72]

In addition to the *Ten Articles*, Convocation approved the abrogation of some popular saints' days that fell during harvest or at other inconvenient times. They included the feasts that honoured Thomas Becket on 7 July and 29 December, whose cult Henry wished to destroy as a reproach to his supremacy.

The Reformation Parliament had met over six-and-one-half years. The Parliament and Convocation of 1536 lasted six weeks. On the afternoon of the last day, Henry came to the House of Lords, where he knighted his lord privy seal and raised him to a new dignity as Baron Cromwell of Wimbledon. The new nobleman was given lands at Wimbledon and Mortlake that, until now, had belonged to the archbishops of Canterbury. Cranmer was forced to surrender them to ennoble the son of a Putney brewer.[73]

The northern risings 1536–1537

The *Ten Articles* were what the parliamentary historian S. E. Lehmberg called an exercise in 'studied ambiguity'. Mild in tone, they were meant to be inclusive and un-alarming. He discerned in them the beginnings of what would become, much later, the distinctive character of the mature English Church, especially in its ability to accommodate fine shades of opinion.[74] Cromwell opened the debates in the Upper House with the warning 'that the king studieth day and night to set a quietness in the Church'. All matters of disagreement should be concluded 'by the word of God' in 'a godly and a perfect unity'. Cranmer also said at the outset that as they considered 'weighty controversies' they must 'agree in the substance and effect'.[75]

Even so, the Ten Articles helped to provoke the greatest crisis of Henry's reign: the risings that began in the north of England in October 1536. The *Ten Articles* reached into every parish in the land, a fact that was compounded in August when Cromwell issued the first *Royal Injunctions* and the order that suppressed some of the most popular saints' days. The *Injunctions* denounced as superstitious the images and relics that had for generations inspired devotion and pilgrimages. They were not to be permitted further, because the reformers believed that they distracted people from understanding that God was the author of all goodness, health, and grace. The clergy should teach the people how to say the Paternoster, the Creed, and the Ten Commandments 'in our mother tongue'. And 'because the goods of the church are called the goods of the poor', new charges were levied in many parishes. Every priest with an income of one hundred pounds or more was to give an exhibition to a university student. Non-resident clergy who had a yearly income of twenty pounds or more were to give a tenth to distribute among the poor of the parish, under the supervision of the churchwardens. The new charges were to be levied in addition to the annual payment of the Tenths, the new tax that burdened every parish in England.[76]

The taking of the oath of supremacy in 1535 had disturbed parishioners everywhere, especially across northern England, and they were made uneasy again by the sheer number of visitations and tax subsidies that were imposed on them. In addition to Cranmer's metropolitan visitation, a visitation had been made in 1535 for the *Valor Ecclesiasticus* to assess the wealth of the Church so that the Tenths could be levied. An assize for a subsidy for the king was made, and Cromwell's vicegerential visitation of the religious houses convinced many laypeople that if the monasteries were closed, then the parish churches would follow soon afterwards. The laity would lose many generations' worth of investment and ornamentation that had been lavished on their parishes.

The *Ten Articles* and the *Injunctions* were also the first real intrusion of the royal supremacy into the daily life of ordinary churchgoers. The language of the Church was Latin. St Jerome's Latin Vulgate was the legal text of the Bible.[77] Worshippers followed the Mass in their Latin Books of Hours and their primers. Every child learned his or her Paternoster in Latin. In 1536, many people were dubious whether God would answer their petitions if their prayers were not in Latin.

The rising began at Louth in Lincolnshire on 1 October 1536, when the vicar incited the parishioners against Cromwell's agents. Rapidly the insurgency spread to Caistor and Horncastle and then to Yorkshire, where it has become known as the Pilgrimage of Grace. Ultimately six counties were involved, and more than twenty-two thousand rose in rebellion. Its leaders were important men locally: the attorney Robert Aske (d. 1537), Sir Robert Constable (d. 1537), and the baron Thomas Darcy (d. 1537).

The rebels seized Cromwell's commissary and beat him to death. They took local gentlemen hostage and made them swear a new oath of loyalty to the rising. Archbishop Lee was taken prisoner at the surrender of Pontefract Castle and he was forced to take the rebels' oath. They believed that the papacy had been repudiated over a personal quarrel between the king and the pope, and they did not want to be forced to become heretics.[78]

Against them, Henry sent armies led by his brother-in-law the duke of Suffolk, and the duke of Norfolk. The rebels vastly outnumbered their armies, but in Lincolnshire, the rebellion collapsed quickly, because the gentlemen who had reluctantly accepted the leadership that the rebels imposed upon them were no match when they were faced by the king's men. Cranmer's friend Sir John Markham held Newark for the king. In Yorkshire, heavy rains damaged the rebels' weapons, and before the end of October they asked Norfolk to sue for pardon. They explained that they were so oppressed by taxes and poverty, that if the religious houses were put down they would have neither occupation nor relief.

For a few weeks, the crisis seemed to be over, but after Christmas there was a dangerous new skirmish at Hull, led by the maverick Sir Francis Bigod who believed that reform was not happening fast enough.[79] The uprisings made further negotiations with the Lutherans impossible for the time being. Complete order was not restored until mid-1537.

The arrival of a prince

Cromwell's reaction to the northern risings was to demand further reforms. In February 1537 he summoned to Westminster a vice-gerential synod of bishops and theologians from both provinces. Archbishop Lee had emerged from the Pilgrimage of Grace with little credit, and over the next few months he continued to lose power and influence. In the negotiations that continued through the summer, Cromwell entrusted Cranmer and Fox with giving an evangelical direction to the synod. The conservatives were defeated in the Pilgrimage of Grace, but Cromwell too lost. His announcements, especially the first *Royal Injunctions* and the abrogation of saints' days, were so heavy-handed that they had contributed to the risings. By engaging prelates from the north and the south to work together, the synod of 1537 was meant to erase the independent action of the two provinces, especially to control volatility in the north. The goal of the synod was to bring about both 'union and reformation' in the entire Church of England.[80]

Through the spring and early summer of 1537, the leaders of the risings were brought to London for trial and execution. A dozen from Lincolnshire were executed in the capital, and another thirty or so in Lincoln, Louth, and Horncastle, nearly half of them monks belonging to Kirkstead or other abbeys. Constable and Ask were returned to Yorkshire for death.[81] Contagious illnesses visited London again that summer while the synod was deliberating, and Cranmer warned Cromwell that 'in Lambeth they die at my gate even at the next house to me'.[82]

In the midst of this grim business, on Trinity Sunday in May an announcement was made that Queen Jane had 'quickened' with child. A *Te Deum* was celebrated at St Paul's and Bishop Latimer preached. Across London, bonfires were lit and free wine was given out.[83]

In early August 1537, Cranmer received a new translation and printing of the Bible that was dedicated to the king, known from the pseudonym on the title page as the 'Thomas Matthew' Bible, but whose New Testament was actually Tyndale's. He sent it to Cromwell with a request that he gain the king's approval for its release. Cranmer admitted that he was not quite satisfied by the translation, although it was better than any other he had yet seen, and he warned Cromwell that it was unlikely that the bishops would ever produce a better version. When Cranmer heard that the king approved, he told Cromwell that the news did him more good than a gift of a thousand pounds.[84] At the end of the month Cromwell was brought to Windsor and made a Knight of the Garter.[85]

The work of the synod in 1537 resulted in *The Institution of a Christian Man*, known as the Bishops' Book, as a replacement of the *Ten Articles*. Its preface was written by archbishops Cranmer and Lee, in the form of a petition to the king, because the

Bishops' Book was issued before it received Henry's full approval. Its purpose was to set out 'a plain and sincere doctrine' based on Holy Scripture, that would remove errors, doubts, superstitions and abuses and that would establish 'good unity and concord', and the 'quietness' of the king's subjects in body and soul.

Its contents were more carefully arranged than the *Ten Articles*, and the *Institution of a Christian Man* was a much longer, as well as a more cautious book. The northern risings meant that reforms could not be imposed rapidly without engendering dangerous opposition. Many familiar prayers and tenets that had not been discussed in the *Ten Articles* were clearly presented in the Bishops' Book.

It began with an exposition of the Creed that included long explanatory passages. All seven sacraments appeared. The section on the sacrament of the altar was brief and like the *Ten Articles*, it avoided any mention of transubstantiation or the sacrifice of the Mass. The Bishops' Book also discussed the Ten Commandments, the Paternoster and Ave. The sections on justification and Purgatory were almost unchanged from the *Ten Articles*.[86] The Bishops' Book represented the same kind of compromise, the same useful ambiguity, the same desire for inclusiveness, the same desire for peace in the realm as the *Ten Articles* that were becoming some of the true defining features of the Henrician Church.

In the second week of October, Jane went into labour at Hampton Court Palace. To general rejoicing, she gave birth to a son on 12 October 1537. Bells were rung in every steeple in London, guns were fired from the Tower, and open barrels of wine set out for poor people to drink as much as they wanted. Three days later, in the chapel at Hampton Court, Cranmer christened the prince and confirmed him in the Christian faith. He was born on the eve of the feast of the translation of St Edward the Confessor, who remained (despite the demotion of many feast days) essential to the identity of the Tudors as the greatest of their saintly forebears. And so he was given the name Edward, and Cranmer shared with the duke of Norfolk the privilege of being the future king's godfather.[87] Jane's brother Edward was made earl of Hertford.

At long last, the birth of Henry's son gave the dynasty hope for the future that not even Jane's death from a haemorrhage on 24 October could overshadow. Just as he presided at the christening, so Cranmer conducted the solemn requiem Mass for the queen's funeral at Windsor on 12 November 1537.

Edward's birth seemed to solve the crisis of the succession. As we will see in the next chapter, Cromwell and Cranmer were emboldened to re-establish their connections with the League of Schmalkalden, only to meet unexpected disappointment.

Notes

1 Cranmer's collect for St Michael and All Angels (Michaelmas) for 20 September from the 1549 Prayer Book: *The booke of the common prayer and administracion of the sacramentes and other rites and ceremonies of the Churche: after the vse of the Churche of England* (London: Edward Whitchurch, March 1549, RSTC 16267), 117v.

2 Henry VIII to the University of Cambridge in 1530: CCCC, MS 242, 17v–18v, printed in Lamb, 26–7. Similarly, Alexander Alane [Alesius], *Of the auctorite of the word of god against the bisshop of London* ([Strasbourg: 1544], RSTC 292), A5v–A6v and the preface to the Ten Articles of 1536: *Articles Devised by the Kinges Highnes Maiestie* (London: Thomas Berthelet, 1536, *RSTC* 10033).

3 R. Rex, 'The Crisis of Obedience: God's Word and Henry's Reformation', *HJ*, 39 (1996), 863–94; R. M. Reeves, *English Evangelicals and Tudor Obedience, c. 1527–1570* (Leiden, 2003).

4 R. McEntegart, *League of Schmalkalden, and the English Reformation* (Woodbridge, 2002), 46–51.

5 William Marshall's dedication to the queen in his translation of *The forme and maner of subue[n]tion or helping for pore people /deuysed and practysed i[n] the cytie of Hypres in Flaunders* (London: Thomas Godfray, 1535, RSTC 26119), A4r.

6 *Sermons by Hugh Latimer*, ed. G. E. Corrie, PS (Cambridge, 1844), 231–2.

7 See the sermon of Stokesley's chaplain Simon Matthew made between Fisher's execution and More's *A Sermon made in the Cathedrall churche of saynt Paule of London* (London: Thomas Berthelet, 1535, RSTC 17656).

8 Stephen Gardiner, *De Vera Obedientia* (London: Thomas Berthelet, 1535, RSTC 11584).

9 A. Ryrie, 'The Strange Death of Lutheran England', *JEH*, 53 (2002), 64–92; P. Marshall, 'Papist as Heretic: The Burning of John Forest, 1538', *HJ*, 41 (1998), 351–74; Rex, 'Crisis of Obedience', 894.

10 Statutes: (1382) 5 Richard II, st. 2, c. 5; (1401) 2 Henry IV, c. 15; (1414) 2 Henry V, st. 1, c. 7. See also S. Wabuda, 'The Woman with the Rock: The Controversy on Women and Bible Reading', in *Belief and Practice in Reformation England: A Tribute to Patrick Collinson from His Students*, eds. S. Wabuda and C. Litzenberger (Aldershot, 1998), 40–59.

11 McEntegart, *League of Schmalkalden*, 20–31, 50, 154.

12 McEntegart, *League of Schmalkalden*, 26–31, 59; 'William Latymer's Chronickille of Anne Bulleyne', ed. Maria Dowling, in *Camden Miscellany XXX*, CS, 4th series, 29 (1990), 23–65; Alesius to Elizabeth I: TNA/PRO, SP 70/17, 6r–6v (*Calendar of State Papers Foreign, Elizabeth*, 1, no. 1303); *LP*, 8, nos. 1061–2.

13 McEntegart, *League of Schmalkalden*, 31–6.

14 F. D. Logan, 'Thomas Cromwell and the Vicegerency in Spirituals', *EHR*, 103 (1988), 658–67.

15 Latimer was given Worcester following the deprivation of Ghinucci: 25 Henry VIII, c.27; S. E. Lehmberg, *The Later Parliaments of Henry VIII 1536–1547* (Cambridge, 1977), 185.

16 McEntegart, *League of Schmalkalden*, 31–2, 60.

17 McEntegart, *League of Schmalkalden*, 37–8, 42, 95.

18 Scarisbrick, *Henry VIII*, 334.

19 Cranmer described his sermons in a letter to the king of 26 August [1536], *Miscellaneous*, no. 177.

20 Cranmer's letter to Cromwell, 2 November [1535]: BL, Cotton MS Cleopatra E. VI., 234r–235r, printed in *Miscellaneous*, no. 160, and his letter to the king of 26 August [1536], no. 177.

21 F. D. Logan, 'The Henrician Canons', *BIHR*, 47 (1974), 99–103; G. Bray, ed., *Tudor Church Reform: The Henrician Canons of 1535 and the Reformatio Legum Ecclesiasticarum*, Church of England Record Society, 8 (2000), xxvi–xxix, xxxviii–xliv, lxiv.

22 24 Henry VIII c. 12 (1533); 25 Henry VIII c. 19/4 (1534); Bray, *Tudor Church Reform*, lxxiii–lxxvi; R. H. Helmholz, *Roman Canon Law in Reformation England* (Cambridge, 1990), 28–54, 159.

23 M. Greschat, *Martin Bucer: A Reformer and His Times*, trans. S. E. Buckwalter (Louisville, 2004), 50–2.

24 Cranmer, *Miscellaneous*, 339.

25 Cronickille of Anne Bulleyne', 57–9; E. W. Ives, 'The Fall of Anne Boleyn Reconsidered', *EHR*, 107 (1992), 665–74.

26 Cranmer's letter to Cromwell, 2 November [1535]: BL, Cotton MS Cleopatra E. VI., 234r–235r, printed in *Miscellaneous*, no. 160, and his letter to the king of 26 August [1536], no. 177.

27 Morice, 260–4; G. Baskerville, 'A Sister of Archbishop Cranmer', *EHR*, vol. 51 (1936), 287–9; MacCulloch, *Cranmer*, 323.

28 Cranmer to Cromwell, letters of 17 October and 2 November [1535], *Miscellaneous*, nos. 157, 160.

29 Cranmer to Cromwell, letters of 17 October and 2 November [1535], *Miscellaneous*, nos. 157, 160.

30 Scarisbrick, *Henry VIII*, 348; Ives, *Anne Boleyn*, 296–7.

31 K. B. Whitley and K. Kramer, 'A New Explanation for the Reproductive Woes and Midlife Decline of Henry VIII', *HJ*, 54 (2010), 827–48.

32 Kelly, *Matrimonial Trials*, 242; Ives, *Anne Boleyn*, 191–2, 296–301; *LP*, 10, no. 282–3, 351.

33 Alesius to Elizabeth: TNA/PRO, SP 70/17, 6v; Ives, *Anne Boleyn*, 343–8; J. E. Neale, *Queen Elizabeth* (London, 1934), 17.

34 TNA/PRO, SP 1/94, 98r–99v (*LP*, 8, nos. 1054; 1019).

35 S. Wabuda, *Preaching during the English Reformation* (Cambridge, 2002), 131–2.

36 Hilsey to Cromwell, [December 1535], TNA:PRO, SP 1/99, 140r (*LP*, 9, no. 989). See also M. MacLure, *The Paul's Cross Sermons 1534–1642* (Toronto, 1958) in his 'Register of Sermons Preached at Paul's Cross, 1534–1642', 185–6.

37 Wriothesley, *Chronicle*, 1, 33–4; LP, 10, no. 283; Latimer, *Sermons*, 49–50; MacCulloch, *Cranmer*, 149–50; P. Ayris, 'Preaching the Last Crusade: Thomas Cranmer and the "Devotion" Money of 1543', *JEH*, 49 (1998), 683–701.

38 Wriothesley, *Chronicle*, 1, 34–5.

39 BL, Cotton MS Cleopatra E. IV, 131r–132v; Lehmberg, *Reformation Parliament*, 218–19, 226; Latimer, Sermons, 123.

40 Cronickille of Anne Bulleyne', 57–9; Alesius to Elizabeth, TNA:PRO, SP 70/17, 6r–6v. Remarks drawn from Latimer's sermon were included in Dorset's letter of 13 March 1536: BL, Cotton MS Cleopatra E. IV, 131r–132v (*LP*, 10, no. 462); E. Ives, 'Anne Boleyn and the Early Reformation in England: The Contemporary Evidence', *HJ*, 37 (1994), 389–400, and *Anne Boleyn*, 306–18; Wabuda, *Preaching*, 130–5.

41 Cranmer to Cromwell, Lambeth, 25 March [1536], *Letters*, no. 170.

42 See the letter that Philip Melanchthon wrote to Martin Bucer, 8 November 1531, printed in *OL*, 2, no. 258; McEntegart, *League of Schmalkalden*, 39–44.

43 Gardiner to Cromwell [February 1536], *Letters*, no. 53 (p. 75).

44 Scarisbrick, *Henry* VIII, 334, 361; Kelly, *Matrimonial Trials*, 167.

45 Alesius to Elizabeth: TNA/PRO, SP 70/17, 6r.

46 Kelly, *Matrimonial Trials*, 242–4.

47 Parker to Nicholas Bacon, 1 March 1559, printed in *Correspondence of Matthew Parker*, eds. J. Bruce and T. Perowne, PS (Cambridge, 1853), nos. 46 and 54.

48 Alesius to Elizabeth: TNA/PRO, SP 70/17, 7r–7v; Wriothesley, *Chronicle*, 1, 35–6.

49 Cranmer to Cromwell, Knole, 22 April [1536]: *Miscellaneous*, no. 172.

50 Cranmer to Henry VIII, Lambeth, 3 May [1536]: *Miscellaneous*, no. 174.

51 Scarisbrick, *Henry VIII*, 335–6; Ives, *Anne Boleyn*, 319–337.

52 Gray, *Oaths and the English Reformation*, 56–7 from SP 1/82, fol. 11r (*LP*, 7, 15); Scarisbrick, *Henry VIII*, 311–12.

53 Kelly, *Matrimonial Trials*, 243–4, 251; Ives, *Anne Boleyn*, 319–37; *LP*, 10, nos. 752–3.

54 Wriothesley, *Chronicle*, 1, 36–9.

55 Alesius to Elizabeth: TNA/PRO, SP 70/17, 3r–12r.

56 28 Henry VIII, c. 7; *Statutes of the Realm*, 3, 655; Wilkins, *Concilia*, 803–5; Kelly, *Matrimonial Trials*, 244–9, 256–7. Anne's marriage was also invalidated under 28 Henry VIII, c. 16.

57 Wriothesley, *Chronicle*, 1, 40–1; Kelly, *Matrimonial Trials*, 244.

58 Kelly, *Matrimonial Trials*, 38–54; *LP*, 4, no. 3913.

59 Kelly, *Matrimonial Trials*, 255–9; Ives, *Anne Boleyn*, 338–56.

60 Alesius to Elizabeth: TNA/PRO, SP 70/17, 7v–8r (my translation).

61 *LP*, 10, no. 915; Scarisbrick, *Henry VIII*, 349; Ives, Anne Boleyn, 338–56.

62 'Cronickille of Anne Bulleyne', 64. See also Foxe, *AM*, 5, 44. Parker also thought Anne was guiltless: Parker to Elizabeth I, 1559, *Correspondence of Matthew Parker*, no. 54.

63 Cranmer to Capito, 1537, printed in *OL*, 1, no. 8.

64 28 Henry VIII, c. 7; *Statutes of the Realm*, 3, 655; Lehmberg, *Later Parliaments*, 20–9; Kelly, *Matrimonial Trials*, 244–9, 256–7.

65 28 Henry VIII, c. 10; Lehmberg, *Reformation Parliament*, 25–9; Ives, *Anne Boleyn*, 357–64.

66 28 Henry VIII, c. 10; Morice, 259; Lehmberg, *Later Parliaments*, 25–8; Ives, *Anne Boleyn*, 357–64.

67 Alesius, *Of the auctorite of the word of God*, A5r–A5v; Wriothesley, *Chronicle*, 1, 41, 49, 52–3; Cranmer, *Miscellaneous*, 463–4; Lehmberg, *Later Parliaments*, 37; Logan, 'Vicegerency', 666.

68 Wriothesley, *Chronicle*, 1, 47–8.

69 McEntegart, *League of Schmalkalden*, 51, 58–61, 66–73.

70 Wriothelsey, *Chronicle*, 1, 47, 54; Luke 16: 1–13; *Concio quam habuit reuerediss. in Christo pater Hugo Latimerio in conuentu spirtualitum* (Southwark, 1537, *RSTC* 15285), translated in Latimer, *Sermons*, 33–57.

71 Alesius, *Of the auctorite of the word of God*, A6r–A8v.

72 *The Ten Articles* (RSTC 10033); G. Bray, ed., *Documents of the English Reformation 1526–1701* (Cambridge, 1994, 2004), 162–74.

73 Wriothesley, *Chronicle*, 1, 52; Logan, 'Vicegerency', 666; MacCulloch, *Cranmer*, 166–7.

74 Lehmberg, *Later Parliaments*, 38–9.

75 Alesius, *Of the auctorite of the word of God*, A6r–A8v.

76 The text of the First Royal Injunctions of 1536, printed in London by Berthelet, is found in *RSTC* 10084.7. Wriothesley, *Chronicle*, 1, 54–5.

77 Eyal Poleg, 'The First Bible Printed in England', *JEH*, vol. 67 (2016), 760–80.

78 M. E. James, 'Obedience and Dissent in Henrician England: The Lincolnshire Rebellion of 1536', *Past and Present*, 48 (1970), 3–78.

79 Wriothesley's *Chronicle*, 1, 60; A. G. Dickens, *Lollards and Protestants in the Diocese of York 1509–1558* (London, 1972), 53–113.

80 Wriothesley's *Chronicle*, 1, 65.

81 Wriothesley's *Chronicle*, 1, 61–5.

82 Cranmer to Cromwell, 21 July 1537, *Miscellaneous*, no. 190.

83 Wriothesley's *Chronicle*, 1, 64.

84 Cranmer to Cromwell, August 1537, *Miscellaneous*, nos. 194, 197–8; Matthew Bible: *The Byble, which is all the holy scripture*, trans. Thomas Matthew [pseud. for William Tyndale and Miles Coverdale] (Antwerp, 1537, *RSTC* 2066).

85 Wriothesley's *Chronicle*, 1, 65.

86 *The Institvtion of a Christen Man* (London: Thomas Berthelet, 1537, *RSTC* 5164), sig. a2r.

87 Wriothesley's *Chronicle*, 1, 65–8.

6   Invincible Henry, 1538–1540

'Almighty GOD, which has instructed thy Holy Church, with the heavenly doctrine of thy holy Evangelist Saint Mark: Give us grace to be established by thy holy Gospel, that we be not like children, carried away by every vain Doctrine, Through Jesus Christ our Lord.'[1]

A Lutheran England?

Thomas Cromwell, as England's lord privy seal and vicegerent, reached the pinnacle of his powers over Church and state in mid-1538. He pressed forward reforms that changed the landscape and culture of England for all time, in part by taking preeminence over Archbishop Thomas Cranmer. In that year, the next phase of the suppression of the religious houses began as the convents of the mendicant friars were dismantled in towns across the country. Despite the oaths that they had taken to accept the royal supremacy, the friars remained under heavy suspicion for their covert support of the papacy. They were forbidden to wear their habits in public. Their houses and goods were seized, and their properties were gradually redistributed to civic leaders. In the spring and summer, at the king's order, religious statues that had been revered for centuries were brought to the capital to be destroyed. Bishop John Stokesley of London, then the most powerful opponent of reform, was accused of *praemunire* and marked for destruction. The long-awaited embassy of Lutheran theologians arrived in England. In September, Cromwell ordered every church in England to set up a copy of the English Bible where parishioners could read it. Many of these achievements represented victories that Cranmer shared.

But paradoxically, 1538 was also a watershed year for Cromwell. Within two years he became the victim of the same kind of collision of imperatives that had unseated Anne Boleyn, destroyed by his enemies as a result of the policies he had worked so hard to achieve. He was overshadowed first by the passage of the Act of Six Articles in 1539, and then by his failure to draw England into an alliance with the League of Schmalkalden. Like Thomas Cardinal Wolsey, Katherine of Aragon and Anne, Cromwell was discarded because he too failed to give Henry what the king wanted. Paradoxically, although Cranmer sometimes challenged Henry, he managed to survive the disasters that overtook the others.

Formal contact with the League of Schmalkalden was interrupted in 1536 because of the destruction of Queen Anne, as well as by the risings. Although they had always endorsed Katherine's marriage, the Lutherans were dismayed by the fall of the Boleyns. Anne had been closely associated with evangelicalism, and they feared that her execution signalled the end of Henry's grudging support for the gospel. The king was intrigued by what he had learned from Bishop Edward Fox's negotiations in Wittenberg, but Henry remained profoundly suspicious of Martin Luther's motives.[2] From late 1536 until mid-1537, the king was preoccupied with suppressing unrest in the north, and temporarily, conservatives were disadvantaged. New security for the regime arrived in October 1537 with Prince Edward's birth.

Cranmer and Cromwell continued to hope that an alliance with the League would permit them to introduce real Lutheran reforms, beyond any that had already been achieved for the English Church. In 1537 Pope Paul III called a General Council at Mantua, and the king feared that the combined forces of the emperor, pope, and the king of France would be pitted against him. Within days of Edward's christening, Cranmer wrote Martin Bucer of Strasbourg to re-establish their association.[3] Cranmer had already written Heinrich Bullinger of Zürich to reassure him that the uprisings were over.[4] In Basel, Simon Grynaeus reprinted Hugh Latimer's Convocation sermon of 1536, and he praised Henry for bringing the Reformation to England.[5]

Early in 1538, and without Henry's knowledge, Cromwell approached Landgrave Philip of Hesse and begged him to send an embassy so that England could be won for Christ and the gospel. Relations between the League and England now entered an intense phase. Henry agreed to exchange ambassadors, and he signalled that he was still interested in entering an alliance with the League.[6]

As relations between England and the Lutherans warmed, Cranmer began to revise the liturgy. He planned to redraft the Breviary, the book that set out for each day the worship services, or 'offices', that all those who were in holy orders were required to recite.[7] In his deanery of Hadleigh in Suffolk, curates said the Mass in English.[8]

In anticipation of an agreement with the Lutherans, many of Cranmer's friends who were in holy orders married secretly in the 1530s, even though it was still illegal for priests to take wives. His brother Edmund married so quietly that we have no record of his wife's name. Others included Cranmer's chaplain Rowland Taylor and his friend Henry Holbeach, the future bishop of Lincoln. At some unrecorded time, Cranmer sent to Nuremberg for his wife Margaret.

A dangerous set of doctrinal problems called for Cromwell and Cranmer's attention, especially with a possible alliance in the offing. The first was residual loyalty to the pope and the teachings of the Roman Church, which threatened the stability of the realm and Henry's throne. Another problem was that of heretics who denied the full humanity of Christ in a kind of radical Protestantism known as Anabaptism. A third was the danger posed by those referred to as 'sacramentaries' who rejected the real presence of Christ in the Eucharist. Lutherans defended the real presence against criticism, as Cranmer did at this period of his life. Sacramentaries and especially Anabaptists went far beyond anything that the Lutherans would be willing to countenance in their own regions or in their negotiations with England.

In spring 1538, the archbishop received word that there were heretics in his outpost jurisdiction of Calais. His chief officer there was his commissary John Butler. Cranmer instructed Butler and his chaplain Richard Champion (d. 1543) to investigate. They answered that the rumours were untrue, and whoever had started them should be punished. Nevertheless, within a few weeks similar rumours reached the court, and Cromwell notified the governor of Calais, Arthur Plantagenet, Viscount Lisle (d. 1542).[9] In July 1538 Butler sent Cranmer the preacher Adam Damplip (d. 1543), whose sermons had caused disruptions. Cranmer examined him, and wrote Cromwell that Damplip 'utterly denieth that ever he taught or said that the very body and blood of Christ was not presently in the sacrament of the altar'. When pressed, Damplip confessed that he believed in the real presence, but in his sermons he 'confuted the opinion of transubstantiation'. For the time being, Cranmer was willing to shield Damplip because he did not think his opinions were heretical. Cranmer concluded in his letter to Cromwell, 'I think he taught but the truth'.[10]

The Damplip episode is one the best pieces of evidence that Cranmer continued to believe in the real presence in the mid-1530s, even as he rejected the tenet of transubstantiation. His opinion is also revealed in the letter he wrote in 1537 to the Swiss Reformer Joachim Vadian (1584–1551) of St Gallen in Switzerland, another theologian who had been introduced to him by Grynaeus. The Swiss hoped to coax Cranmer away from his Lutheran opinions, and Vadian sent Cranmer a copy of his recent treatise against the real presence. In response, Cranmer wrote that he was familiar with everything Oecolampadius and Huldrych Zwingli had written, and he found Vadian's *Aphorisms* 'altogether displeasing'. Cranmer told him that ancient authors were not on his side, because the real presence had been taught in the Primitive Church by the earliest ecclesiastical writers. Cranmer wished neither to approve nor to contribute to further divisions among Protestants. Rather, he recommended Vadian join him in promoting Christian concord.[11]

Towards the beginning of 1538, in a series of staged events, Cromwell unleashed a wave of iconoclasm against England's most famous religious statues and relics to impress, persuade, and frighten the king's subjects into acquiescence. The statue of the Virgin Mary was removed from the eleventh-century shrine at Walsingham in Norfolk, and it was burnt at Chelsea, near Sir Thomas More's residence. The Rood of Grace, which Cranmer had removed from Boxley Abbey in 1533, was exposed as a fraud by Bishop John Hilsey of Rochester at Paul's Cross. At the end of his sermon, the boys in the audience were encouraged to smash it to pieces. The great golden shrine of St Thomas Becket was pulled out of Canterbury Cathedral, and it was carried by the wagonload to the royal treasury. According to rumours current in London, at Cromwell's orders, the saint's bones were burned.[12]

The most sensational event of the early summer was the execution at Smithfield on 22 May 1538 of the Observant Franciscan Friar John Forest, who was burnt with a wooden statue from Wales known as Dderfel Gadarn. At Lambeth Palace, Cranmer and Latimer examined Forest, using the same kind of pressures that had been brought to bear against the Nun of Kent. Forest was accused of believing that the Church of Rome was the one, only Catholic Church and that the fourth-century Council of Nicaea had lacked sufficient authority because it had been summoned by the Emperor Constantine the Great (d. 337), rather than by the pope. Forest at first seemed willing to submit. Then it became apparent that he had been using mental reservation to protect his conscience by leaving his real beliefs unsaid. Unlike Elizabeth Barton, he refused to retract his opinions openly, even though Latimer preached against him at Paul's Cross. Under the new and rather vague heresy law that was passed in 1534, Forest was condemned as a traitor and a heretic.[13] Barton had admitted her impostures, and therefore she had been hanged as a gesture of mercy, but Forest was adamant, so Cromwell decided to make his execution a spectacle. Latimer reluctantly presided from a pulpit set up at the place of execution. A special viewing gallery was built so that the mayor and aldermen and the lords of the king's Council could lend their authority to the proceedings. Cromwell, Cranmer, and Stokesley attended. Forest was hanged in chains on a gallows, and alternately raised and lowered into the flames. As thousands watched, he suffered in slow agonies.[14]

Cranmer specially endorsed the idea that in maintaining the authority of the papacy, Forest was both a traitor disloyal to his king as well as a heretical traitor to God, and therefore he deserved his death. We have already noted that Cranmer had first begun to make this argument in 1533 when he exposed Barton as a fraud. As the ecclesiastical historian Peter Marshall has explained, Cranmer defended the idea that the English Church was 'Catholic' and orthodox in its teachings. Associating treason with heresy was a powerful weapon that was also used to denounce Reginald Pole, now a cardinal living in Rome, who had written extensively against the royal supremacy and thereby earned the king's lasting hatred. Although the ferocity of Forest's execution was unprecedented and it was not repeated, Cranmer never completely relinquished the idea that a papist was an enemy of God's word who must have 'a traitorous heart'.[15] Ten years later, when the rebels of Devon and Cornwall rose against the first *Book of Common Prayer*, Cranmer maintained that 'a papist is also both a heretic and a traitor'.[16] Forest's fate was a potent warning against all who secretly disavowed the king's authority over the Church. A week after his execution, Stokesley was accused of *praemunire* for accepting a papal bull at a recent profession of a nun and monks at Syon Abbey.[17]

The spectacle of Forest's burning had long-term consequences that Cromwell and Cranmer did not anticipate. In its aftermath Henry showed renewed favour to conservatives. The League's ambassadors, Friedrich Myconius of Gotha and Franz Burchard, the vice-chancellor to Duke John Frederick of Saxony, arrived in the wake of Forest's execution. They were received with such kindness that they became optimistic that England would now fully embrace the Lutheran Reformation under the terms of the Confession of Augsburg. But at their first meeting, the king expressed disappointment that Philip Melanchthon had not been sent with them, and he indicated that he would prefer to compromise on points of doctrine that he did not want to accept. In presiding over the negotiations at Lambeth, Cranmer found himself seriously disadvantaged by Henry's involvement.[18]

Henry chose those who would participate in the negotiations, and he closely monitored the discussions even though he took Cromwell and the summer court away on a strenuous progress to the south of England. Cromwell had no real opportunity to influence the directions that the discussions took at Lambeth because a new crisis was breaking. In late summer 1538, Henry began to suspect designs upon his throne that implicated Cardinal Pole's brother and his mother, the countess of Salisbury. The resulting investigations, known to historians as the Exeter conspiracy, absorbed most of Cromwell's attention. Latimer was not included in the negotiations, perhaps as a sign of Henry's disapproval of his role in Forest's execution, and he spent the summer out of the way in his diocese, where he could offer Cranmer little support. Bishop Fox's presence at the negotiations would have been essential. However, he died in May, and his loss, especially at such a key moment, hurt Cranmer badly.

In the talks, Cranmer was supported by Robert Barnes and Nicholas Heath, who had also gone on embassy to the Lutheran princes, but the king's other choices were all conservatives: Richard Sampson, bishop of Chichester and dean of St Paul's; George Daye of St John's College, Cambridge; and Nicholas Wilson. In 1534 Wilson had refused to take the oath of succession, for which he had been pardoned only the previous year. Completing the group was Bishop Stokesley. Immediately upon Cromwell's accusation of *praemunire*, Stokesley threw himself on king's mercy, who was 'better to him then he deserved'. His rehabilitation was a signal that Cromwell lacked sufficient support from Henry to topple the most powerful opponent of the reformation of the English Church.[19]

The discussions at Lambeth were difficult. Despite Cranmer's best efforts, the participants disagreed in front of their guests. Too often he was forced to make concessions to conservatives that disappointed and confused the Lutherans. In heated debates, they eventually came to an agreement on justification by faith that was a victory for Cranmer and the Lutherans. Yet, the conservatives insisted on the necessity of confession, and Cranmer struggled without success to find an accommodation with which the Lutherans could agree.[20]

The discussions lasted much longer than the ambassadors anticipated. Eager to return home, on 5 August 1538 they wrote the king to ask about the doctrines that had not been agreed upon during Fox's negotiations in Wittenberg in 1536: private Masses for souls departed, communion in one kind, clerical celibacy, and monastic vows. The Lutherans considered them lingering abuses, and they asked the king for his immediate attention. This turned out to be a serious misstep, for Henry was far less accommodating to their points of view than they had been led to realize.[21]

In the south of England, while Cromwell was immersed in the details of the Exeter conspiracy, the king turned for advice to Sir Thomas More's old friend Bishop Cuthbert Tunstall of Durham.

At the end of 1537, Cranmer sent Henry the Bishops' Book, *The Institution of a Christian Man*, for his belated attention. The king made annotations and corrections which Cranmer commented on in his turn.[22] Now, for the negotiations with the Lutherans, bundles of documents were sent to the king on his progress and returned to Lambeth with his comments and Tunstall's. Henry defended the celebration of private Masses for the souls of the dead, an idea the Lutherans had long since rejected. He refuted their insistence that communion be administered to the laity in both kinds, the wine as well as the bread. He also argued that celibacy was an essential requirement for the priesthood, whose demands were so heavy that they were incompatible with married life.[23]

This marked a dramatic setback. The cautious measures that Cromwell and Cranmer had been using to turn the king little by little had served them well enough to make some limited progress, but now the king's exchanges with the Lutherans intensified his natural conservatism. By the end of August, with nothing decided and the king still out of London, the ambassadors were ready to return to the continent. Cranmer begged them to stay another month to get good answers from the king. He asked them to consider the many thousands of souls that could be saved if they delayed their departure. Cromwell suggested that the king was on the point of agreeing with them. But they refused to write any more position papers, and they left England as soon as they made their farewells to the king at the beginning of October.[24]

The Schmalkaldic embassy of 1538 was disappointing because a lasting commitment was not made with England, although negotiations were not broken off. Henry still hoped that Melanchthon would come to England for the next round of discussions. Cromwell also began an enormous gamble when he suggested that an alliance with the League could be concluded if the king made a marriage with one of the sisters of John Fredrick's wife, Sibylle of Cleves (1512–1554).

The second *Royal Injunctions* of 1538

Perhaps as a consequence of the uneasy intermission in the negotiations with the Lutherans, the second set of *Royal Injunctions* that Cromwell released at the end of September

1538 was not really a new document. Rather than promote fresh changes in the Church that reflected further reforms in a Lutheran direction, they reiterated most of the points that had already been made in the *Injunctions* of 1536. In its most famous proviso, the Second *Injunctions* called for 'a book of the whole Bible' (in Latin and in English) to be set up in the choir of every parish church before 1 August 1539 where anyone could read it.[25]

John Lambert

But even as Cromwell issued the Second *Injunctions*, an unexpected blow came from the Schmalkaldic League as their ambassadors left England. Philip and John Frederick warned Henry in late September 1538 that they had seized a heretic who had in his possession letters that mentioned the spread of Anabaptism in England.

Hesse was experiencing its own disturbing rise in the number of Anabaptists, and the way Philip dealt with the problem was to invite Bucer to Marburg where he engaged in a disputation with Anabaptist leaders. Compared with England's response, Philip's was restrained. The Lutheran princes worried about Henry's reaction to their letter, because their ambassadors were startled by the severity of the measures that were taken against heretics in England. They probably heard how Forest had been killed. Cromwell and lord chancellor Thomas Audley endorsed the burning of the eccentric heretic William Cowbridge at Oxford while the ambassadors were still in England.[26] When the case of a London man accused of heresy came to his attention, ambassador Burchard urged Cranmer and Sampson to permit him to make his submission at his own parish church, rather than in front of great crowds at St. Paul's. But they told him that because error concerning the sacrament of the altar was 'daily increasing', it was important that he did his penance where more people might see him punished. Although Burchard's request was probably granted, the Lutherans were disturbed by the harsh measures they observed in England. In their letter, the princes advised that the best remedy against Anabaptism was to have the word of God truly preached.[27]

The news from the Lutheran princes about the spread of Anabaptism in England created a sensation at court. The efforts Cromwell and Cranmer had already taken to suppress heresies seemed inadequate in the present crisis, which allowed Henry to fuse Anabaptism and disrespect for the sacrament of the altar into one problem of heresy. Immediately Cromwell named a commission to search out Anabaptists. The commissioners included Cranmer, Barnes, Heath, and Edward Crome among the reformers, and Stokesley and Sampson as the conservatives. Although the full committee was evenly divided, they were united in their disdain for Anabaptists.[28] At the end of November, a man and a woman, probably foreign refugees, were burnt at Smithfield for heresy. Another man associated with them was burnt at Colchester.[29]

Among those who were swept up in the arrests was John Lambert (alias Nicholson), who was already well known as a stubborn and awkward figure of contention. In 1531, Stokesley and Archbishop William Warham had examined him in Convocation for holding heretical opinions.[30] In February 1536 Lambert was accused by the duke of Norfolk of saying that it was a sin to pray to saints. Cranmer and Latimer wrestled with him over several days then, and they decided that although they could not say if it was necessary to pray to saints, Lambert had been wrong to say that praying to them was sinful. Latimer was especially astringent in his criticisms, but Lambert refused to give way, and he was imprisoned briefly.[31]

The trial of John Lambert on 16 November 1538, like Forest's execution, became one of the greatest pieces of political theatre of Henry's reign. Clad in white, enthroned in Westminster Hall as 'the perfect image of kingly majesty', Henry conducted Lambert's trial assisted by his bishops. At the same time, Pope Paul was preparing to issue Henry's long-delayed excommunication, this time for his destruction of Becket's shrine. Lambert's trial was meant to enhance Henry's prestige as the supreme arbiter of orthodoxy in defending Christendom against heresy.[32]

Lambert was asked if he believed in infant baptism, if Christ was present in the sacrament of the altar, and if Christ was incarnated by the Virgin Mary. He was questioned by Cranmer, Gardiner, Tunstall, and Stokesley, but first and with great harshness by the king, who hectored him for a long time. When Lambert refused to renounce his opinions, Henry condemned him to death. Appalled by the role Henry had forced him to play at Lambert's trial, Cromwell had the condemned man brought to his house before his execution on 22 November, so that he could ask Lambert's forgiveness.[33]

In time for Lambert's execution, a proclamation drafted by the king denounced both Anabaptists and sacramentaries. The days celebrating Becket's martyrdom were stricken out of England's Kalendar of saints. The proclamation also contained a clause warning against clerical marriages, an early indication of a conservatism that would define the rest of the king's reign.[34]

Before the end of the year, Tunstall succeeded to Fox's place in the Council. In late September, after an absence of three years, Bishop Stephen Gardiner returned to England from his embassy to France.[35] For the rest of Henry's reign, Tunstall and Gardiner were able to rally conservatives to their side, and they opposed Cranmer's plans for the Church.

Act of Six Articles

As the historian Rory McEntegart has noted, when the Lutheran ambassadors asked the king for his immediate attention in their letter of 5 August 1538, they inadvertently focused the king's mind on the issues he decided were the most pressing for the English Church. They were the genesis of the Act of Six Articles that was passed by the Parliament in June 1539. The Lutherans may not have realized the importance that Henry attached to their letter, and when Burchard returned to England in April 1539 without Melanchthon, they were able to offer the king little in fresh negotiations. The first edition of the Great Bible was completed in time for their arrival. Its title page portrayed Henry enthroned under Christ as the embodiment of the heroic safeguard of his people, and perhaps it was inspired by the king's appearance at Lambeth's trial. Cranmer was shown at his right hand, with his gem-encrusted mitre at his feet, as he received from the king a thick volume labelled '*Verbum Dei*'. On the king's left, Cromwell accepted a similar book. Further down the page, Cranmer was shown again, handing the Bible to a learned preacher. The king's subjects appeared along the bottom of the page listening to the sermon gratefully as they repeated '*Vivat rex*' and 'God save the king'.[36]

However, England was not permitted to enter the League of Schmalkalden for the time being. Nor were the Lutherans interested in engaging in further theological discussions. Compromise with the king was out of the question because he would not accept the terms of the Augsburg Confession. Henry was deeply disappointed.[37]

At the same time, fresh revelations reached the king about heresy in Calais. When Henry complained to Audley about the spread of 'the detestable heresy against the Sacrament of the Altar', the lord chancellor suggested that an Act of Parliament should be made against it. Because Cranmer had defended the tenet of the real presence during Lambert's trial, inadvertently he also prepared the way for the Six Articles, which at its inception may have been aimed simply at that most elusive of goals, unity in religion.[38] But as Parliament prepared to meet in May 1539, Cromwell fell seriously ill, and he could not control the direction that the new settlement in religion was taking. Once Henry realized that the Lutherans were not willing to negotiate further, he expanded the discussion in Parliament to the issues that remained unresolved in their negotiations: the Real Presence (and transubstantiation): communion in both kinds, private Masses, clerical marriage, vows of chastity, and auricular confession. A draft of the Six Articles was introduced in the House of Lords by the duke of Norfolk. The doctrinal questions that they raised were complex, and Henry received conflicting advice as they were discussed. The proposals for the new Act represented a step back towards positions that had been rejected by the *Ten Articles* of 1536 and the Bishops' Book.

In one of the most dangerous episodes in Cranmer's career, the archbishop led the counterarguments against the proposals, first in the House of Lords, and then in the Upper House of the Synod. In the beginning, Cranmer was assisted by the men he had raised to bishoprics: Thomas Goodrich, Nicholas Shaxton, Hugh Latimer, and John Hilsey. Cranmer made 'an earnest defense of God's truth' over three days. Twice Henry was present in the Lords on 19 and 21 May. Cranmer openly resisted the very doctrinal positions that Henry himself now promoted.[39]

In an unusual procedure, Parliament was prorogued for a week on 23 May so that the Synod could deliberate. Here too, in the Upper House, Cranmer spoke against the proposed articles in front of the king. Cranmer was able to persuade him and most of his listeners that auricular confession was not required by God in Scripture, which was a small victory. However, the most important articles under discussion concerned the Eucharist. Henry maintained that it was not necessary under God's law for the laity to receive the chalice with the consecrated bread. The draft also defined transubstantiation as an essential dogma. Cranmer opposed the use of the word 'transubstantiation', and he succeeded in having it removed from the final statute. The evangelicals were also able to mitigate slightly the article on Masses for the dead. As we shall see in the next chapter, this article triggered a crisis at the end of Henry's reign, when Cranmer's friend Crome denounced the illogic of closing the religious houses, whose main purpose was to say Masses for departed souls. In the Lower House, almost alone, Crome refused to support the Six Articles.[40]

Cranmer argued that the marriage of priests was allowed by Scripture, although Henry insisted that the law of God categorically forbade such marriages. This was an extreme position that the king seems to have developed by his own eccentric study of the Bible. Similarly, the king argued that vows of chastity or widowhood were forever binding. No pope had ruled that the marriage of priests was inhibited by divine law, but rather, celibacy in the western Church was considered a matter that related to ecclesiastical discipline. Henry, however, refused to be persuaded otherwise.

By the time Parliament reassembled at the end of May 1539, the king had frightened almost all the bishops into acquiescence. According to Morice, Cranmer was deserted by his friends. He stood 'post alone' in opposition to the Six Articles.[41] Foxe recorded that Henry gave Cranmer permission to spare his conscience, and to stay away from the House of Lords by stepping into the Council chamber so he need not be seen to support the measures he so strongly opposed. But Cranmer did not take advantage of Henry's offer. With 'humble protestation' Cranmer refused to leave. Anyone who had witnessed the debates in the Lords or the Upper House would know how bitterly Cranmer opposed the

Six Articles. Yet he chose to obey the will of the king as the supreme head of the Church as the measure passed. Later Cranmer noted that the Six Articles would never have become law if the king had not intervened.[42]

The penalties that the Six Articles would impose were drafted by Gardiner and the conservative bishops. Anyone who denied the real presence was liable to be burnt as a heretic. To break a vow of chastity was a felony, punishable by hanging. Former nuns were severely disadvantaged under the new law. Although most of them no longer had houses or communities to live in, their marriages were forbidden under pain of death. For married priests, the new law threatened their lives and their families. As Lutheran leaders observed developments in England, the penalties for married priests and their wives seemed the most arbitrary and cruel portion of the new law, which struck at the Cranmers and all evangelical priests who had married quietly. Cranmer sent Margaret back to her family in Nuremberg.

Immediately after the passage of the Six Articles, Cranmer feared imminent arrest and he worried that a widespread attack against evangelicals would ensue. Because Latimer and Shaxton had been particularly outspoken against the Six Articles in the Lords, they were deprived of their bishoprics and imprisoned. Secretly Cranmer sent for Alexander Alesius and advised him to flee. Cranmer told him that he wished he could leave England as well, and he would not mind being deprived, as Latimer had been, if that was the only punishment he was likely to face. Cranmer said he had assented to the new law purely out of fear, and he was sorry that he done so. And because he had no ready money, he gave Alesius as a sign of his friendship, a ring that had once belonged to Wolsey, the same ring that the king had given him when he agreed to accept the archbishopric.[43]

Bishop Hilsey surrendered the privilege of appointing the Paul's Cross preachers. He asked Cromwell to return it to Stokesley. All of Hilsey's preachers no longer dared to speak there for fear of being accused of heresy. He told Cromwell he was almost too frightened to preach at Paul's Cross himself, and he died in August 1539 only eight days after his last sermon.

The Lutherans felt betrayed by the Act of Six Articles. Alesius arrived in Wittenberg within a month, but the news of the new law had already preceded him. In October 1539, Bucer and Grynaeus wrote Cranmer of their disappointment that the Six Articles had been passed. Luther and Melanchthon warned Duke John Frederick that blindness had fallen on England. In the hope that an international outcry would prevent Henry from killing Cranmer, Crome, Latimer, and Shaxton, Melanchthon denounced the Six Articles and Gardiner in an open letter to the king that reminded Henry of the threat that the pope and Cardinal Pole posed for England.[44]

Despite Cranmer's fears, he was not arrested, and he was not deprived. Nor were Latimer and Shaxton executed. Rather, they were held in ward until they were pensioned as former bishops. Afterwards they lived in relative obscurity under Cranmer's protection. Although Henry unleashed one set of advisors against the others, the king expected amity among members of his Council. During times of unusual stress he sent them to dine together at Lambeth Palace to build fellowship, as he did when the Parliament of 1539 ended, and he instructed the lords to 'cherish' Cranmer and assure him of his continued good will. At the dinner, Morice heard Cromwell address Cranmer with words that have since become famous as the epitome of the archbishop's relationship with the king: 'You were born in a happy hour, I suppose', for 'do or say what you will, the king will always take it well at your hand'. Even when Cromwell had complained against Cranmer to Henry, the king would never believe it. 'And therefore you are most happy, if you can keep you in this estate'.[45]

For a previous generation of historians who were influenced by John Foxe's description of the new statute as the 'whip with six strings',[46] Cranmer had capitulated by attending the Lords at its passage. In 1962, Jasper Ridley wrote that Cranmer had shown great courage by resisting the king in the Lords and Upper House, but then shamefully compromised his conscience by accepting the law 'without further resistance'.[47] However, Alec Ryrie has argued recently that the Six Articles must be understood in the context of Henry's negotiations with the Lutherans. Subtle ambiguities in the Act may have provided the evangelicals with some relief, and the new law did not represent a categorical defeat for them because even after its passage, its terms were still open to further negotiation and correction.[48] In sending the Council to dine at

Lambeth Palace, Henry also indicated that he wished to study the objections that Cranmer had raised. Morice recorded that whenever the king needed advice on difficult questions of doctrine, he would send word to Cranmer overnight, and the next day Henry would have a comprehensive set of 'brief notes' on a spectrum of opinions, concluding with Cranmer's own. No other theologian could answer the king as swiftly as did the archbishop. Such service convinced Henry of Cranmer's unswerving 'fidelity to God and him'. The next day after the Council's dinner the archbishop composed 'a fair book' of his positions that cited Scripture and the early doctors of the Church. This was the book that Morice lost in crossing the Thames in a famous episode related by Foxe, when his wherry was upset near the king's bear baiting at Paul's Wharf. Although the book then fell into hostile hands, Cromwell and Cranmer made certain that a fresh copy reached the king almost immediately.[49]

The fall of Thomas Cromwell

If the passage of the Act of Six Articles was one of the bitterest episodes in Cranmer's career, it proved to be an even a greater disappointment for Cromwell. It revealed once again how limited his influence actually was. By eliminating Anne Boleyn and her brother, Cromwell removed important elements of support that he needed himself to succeed with the king's Council and other people of influence.[50] Like Anne, Cromwell was ruined by the very policies he worked so hard to achieve. So bitter were the struggles that led to the passage of the Six Articles that old enmities between Cromwell and his opponents, like the duke of Norfolk, which before now could be hidden or controlled, flailed into plain sight. The night of the Council's dinner at Lambeth Palace, a furious argument broke out between Cromwell and one of the dukes that Cranmer could not quell. The renowned historian G. R. Elton traced Cromwell's increasing vulnerability to 1539.[51]

In July, under the new law, Cranmer took fresh steps in Calais against Damplip and others who were accused of heresy. Ultimately, Damplip was executed as a traitor for some early contacts he had had with Reginald Pole. Despite the reversal that the Six Articles represented, Cromwell and Cranmer had little choice but to approach the Lutheran princes again in the hope that the conservatives' gains could be stopped. Secret approaches were made to Bucer, who once again conveyed a plea to Philip of Hesse that Melanchthon should be allowed to come to England to persuade the king. But the Lutheran princes were reluctant to deal any further with Henry, and they did not want to send Melanchthon into possible danger.[52]

Cromwell's position was improved in August 1539 when the king agreed to marry Anne, the daughter of the duke of Cleves and John Frederick's sister-in-law, despite misgivings about the match that Cranmer expressed to Cromwell.[53] Then, in an unexpected turn of events, Stokesley died on 8 September, just one month after Hilsey. No bishop had been as relentless in his opposition to reform. His influence had stretched across the entire realm. According to Foxe, on his deathbed Stokesley expressed satisfaction that he had burnt fifty heretics. When Burchard returned to England from Cleves to complete the marriage agreement, Cromwell and Cranmer were now much more confident, and they suggested that the new law was likely to be overturned soon. Cromwell emphasized how great an enemy Stokesley had been to the Gospel.[54] His death permitted them to take steps to strengthen the evangelicals' position again. Gardiner was briefly put out of the Council when he called Barnes a heretic and said it was a disgrace for Cromwell to employ him as an ambassador.[55]

Anne of Cleves arrived at Dover with a large entourage in the last week of 1539 and she was received at Canterbury by Cranmer. She was in Rochester in time to enjoy the revels of the Christmas season, and according to the chronicle recorded by Charles Wriothesley, at New Year's Anne became so fascinated by the bull beating that was going on beneath her window that she took insufficient notice of the king, who had arrived in disguise with members of his privy chamber to surprise her. It was an inauspicious start.[56]

From their first meeting in Rochester, Henry expressed deep reluctance to marry Anne. Although she is best remembered today because Henry announced that he did not find her as attractive as she had been reported to him, many observers noted that the bride had the graceful dignity that befitted a queen. In a brief time she managed to make an excellent impression upon the king's subjects.

In all probability Henry rejected her because he resented being propelled by Cromwell into an alliance that he decided he did not want. At Greenwich on the day before the wedding, he summoned Cromwell, Cranmer, Tunstall, Suffolk, Norfolk, Hertford and the representatives of the duke of Cleves and he inquired about previous agreements for other marriages that had been made on Anne's behalf. But time was short, and the king concluded that her brother would be driven into alliances with the Emperor Charles V and France should she be rejected.[57] Therefore, on the morning of Epiphany, 6 January 1540, the king and Anne were united by Cranmer in a marriage that was already a failure.[58]

Six months elapsed before Henry repudiated this latest wife, and in that time Cromwell's enemies noted that the king had become immediately infatuated by Katherine Howard (d. 1542), another niece of the duke of Norfolk, who was brought to court for the first time to wait on Anne. Not yet out of her teens, she captivated the king with her youth and vivacity. Gardiner opened his house so that, away from prying eyes at court, the king could woo her.[59]

In mid-April 1540, when a new Parliament opened, Cromwell's position was endangered but not yet desperate. Henry created him earl of Essex and High Chamberlain of England.[60] A second edition of the Great Bible appeared with Cranmer's famous prologue that included long instructive quotations from John Chrysostom (d. 407) and Gregory Nazianzene (d. 390). Cranmer concluded that every man who came to the reading of the Great Bible should fear God and learn how to live a godly life.[61]

Suddenly, Cromwell was toppled by a crisis that was triggered by the poisonous rivalry between Barnes and Gardiner, who were old enemies from their Cambridge days. Barnes complained against a recent sermon Gardiner delivered at court. Barnes was offended again when Gardiner at the last moment replaced him as the Paul's Cross preacher on the first Sunday in Lent, when Winchester denounced the essential Protestant doctrine of justification by faith. Two weeks later, Barnes told the audience at Paul's Cross that he and Gardiner were like 'fighting cocks' and he cast down his glove from the pulpit in a challenge. In subsequent weeks, Barnes was followed at Paul's Cross by the preachers Thomas Garrard and William Jerome, who also attacked Gardiner. Gardiner complained to the king, and after lengthy disagreements

Barnes and his friends seemed willing to submit to correction. Barnes, Garrard, and Jerome made highly equivocal recantations during Easter week that were meant to satisfy the king's orders while convincing their audience that they continued to adhere to their original opinions. Barnes again mocked Gardiner from the pulpit. Henry was angered for their sign of disunity, but even now they might have escaped punishment, for Cromwell tried to make peace with Gardiner. Cromwell was again rising in the king's favour, until word leaked out that Barnes had deliberately disobeyed Henry, with Cromwell's secret approval.[62] Now began the attacks against evangelicals that Cranmer had feared, and some of his deputies in Calais were implicated. Several hundred people were arrested in London.

On 10 June 1540, Cromwell was arrested in the Council chamber. Norfolk and other councillors humiliated him by tearing from him the insignia of his many offices, and he was taken to the Tower. Immediately, Audley announced Cromwell's arrest in the House of Lords. Cranmer was now in great danger. Morice wrote that many in London were willing to bet that before the present Synod was ended, Cranmer would be sent to the Tower 'beside his friend'.[63] Foxe recorded that when the archbishop knew he was about to be seized, he shot up a private staircase to the royal apartments where he spoke with the king, who gave him his signet ring with the instructions that he should appear before the Privy Council, listen to the charges against him, and then produce the ring as a sign of Henry's favour and protection.[64]

Paradoxically, Cranmer escaped the disaster that broke over Cromwell, although he had had shared many of the initiatives that the lord privy seal had advanced. A fragment of a letter Cranmer wrote to the king at this difficult juncture survives, though we cannot be certain that it ever reached Henry's hands. Cranmer wrote that he was 'sorrowful and amazed' to hear in the Council that Cromwell was a traitor, 'he who so loved your majesty (as I ever thought) no less than God', who continually set forth Henry's will and pleasure. Cromwell served Henry 'in wisdom, diligence, faithfulness, and experience'. No other prince had such a councillor. 'I loved him as my friend' and loved him for the love which Cromwell seemed to bear towards the king. 'But now, if he be a traitor, I am very sorry that ever I loved or trusted him'.

Cranmer warned that now he did not know for 'whom your grace may trust'.[65]

An important contribution to Cromwell's fall was Henry's decision to marry Katherine Howard. Cromwell was blamed for forcing the king into a marriage with Anne of Cleves that was so abhorrent to him he could not consummate it. Late in June, Anne was sent away from court to Richmond, and Cranmer had to prepare both an annulment, and also make adjustments to the list of impediments that would have prevented the king's marriage to Katherine, who was Anne Boleyn's first cousin. The king's annulment was considered by the Synod and then Parliament. Cromwell was kept alive, Elton suggested, only long enough to ensure that Henry's divorce from Anne of Cleves could be completed. Cromwell was attainted for treason, heresy, and for licensing heretics to preach. On 28 July 1540, the same day that Cromwell was beheaded on Tower Green, Henry married Katherine Howard. Henry lavished on her Cromwell's lands. On 8 August, she was presented at court as Henry's queen.[66]

Two days after Cromwell's execution, on 30 July 1540, Robert Barnes, Thomas Garrard, and William Jerome went to the stake saying that they did not know why they were about to die. They had been exempted from a general pardon. They received no public hearing. In one fire, they died at Smithfield. Their executions were a scandal that was denounced for many years by evangelical writers. Nearby, three Catholic priests, Thomas Abell, Richard Fetherstone, and Edward Powell, who had been long imprisoned as supporters of Katherine of Aragon, were hanged, drawn, and quartered as traitors as a further warning of the king's ruthless even-handedness.[67]

In a further paradox, following the executions, Crome began to preach with greater zeal for reform, and he interceded with the king on behalf of the many others who had been arrested. By Henry's command, at the beginning of August, no further measures were taken against those accused of heresy. Later Parliament adjusted the Six Articles, and removed the death penalty against priests for sexual incontinence.[68]

Emboldened by the news of Cromwell's destruction, John Dantiscus re-established contact with Cranmer. Now prince-bishop of Warmia in Poland, in 1532 they had been ambassadors together at Regensburg. Then Dantiscus had listened 'patiently' as Cranmer denounced the papacy. Now he lashed out in an attempt to bring about Cranmer's destruction. In a letter, Dantiscus criticized Henry's many marriages (he joked that Henry often changed his Helens). Dantiscus denounced the pillaging of the property of the Church in England. He hinted that he knew that Cranmer had married when he was an ambassador. Alluding to the death of Barnes, Dantiscus warned Cranmer to take care lest the same 'fate of the moth' befall him. Cranmer dared not keep the letter secret, should the king hear about its insults from another source, and he enclosed it immediately to the king's secretary, Thomas Wriothesley.[69]

Cromwell fell because he had pushed the king farther towards the Lutherans than Henry wanted to go. Secretly, Cromwell had encouraged Barnes and others to continue when they had been told to pull back. Within a year, Henry lamented that he had lost Cromwell, and he thought briefly of blaming Norfolk and Gardiner for preparing false accusations against him.[70]

In Wittenberg, Luther mourned his friend Robert Barnes.

Notes

1 The collect for St Mark's day, 25 April, written by Thomas Cranmer, for the second prayer book: *The booke of the common praier and administration of the sacramentes, and other rites and ceremonies of the churche: after the vse of the Churche of Englande* (London: Richard Grafton, March 1549, *RSTC* 16268), 106r.

2 R. McEntegart, *Henry VIII, the League of Schmalkalden, and the English Reformation* (London, 2002), 51, 58–61, 66–73.

3 Martin Bucer to Cranmer, 23 October 1538, *OL*, 2, no. 244; McEntegart, *League of Schmalkalden*, 93.

4 Cranmer's letter to Bullinger of 3 April 1537 is printed in Johannes Kessler's *Sabbata: Mit Kleineren Schriften und Briefen*, eds. E. Egli and R. Schoch (St Gallen, 1902), 463–4. Although their correspondence was probably extensive, only two of Cranmer's letters to Bullinger are known. See Chapter 8 for the other.

5 Hugh Latimer, *Oratio apud totum Ecclesiasticorum conventum* (Basel: Robert Winter, September 1537) with a foreword by Simon Grynaeus.

6 MacCulloch, *Cranmer*, 214–19; McEntegart, *League of Schmalkalden*, 74, 83–93, 97–104.

7 G. Cuming, *The Godly Order: Texts and Studies Relating to the Book of Common Prayer,* Alcuin Club, 65 (1983), 1–4; MacCulloch, *Cranmer,* 221–6.

8 Wriothesley, *Chronicle,* 1, 83.

9 *LP,* 13 (1), nos. 813, 833, 936, 1291.

10 Cranmer to Cromwell, 15 August 1538, *Miscellaneous,* no. 235.

11 Cranmer to Vadian, 1537, *Miscellaneous,* no. 193; P. Brooks, *Thomas Cranmer's Doctrine of the Eucharist* (London, 1965), 3–8.

12 *TRP,* 1, 274. Wriothesley, *Chronicle,* 1, 74–6, 82–7; S. Brigden, *London and the Reformation* (Oxford, 1989), 291–2.

13 24 Henry VIII, c. 14.

14 This method of execution had been used earlier in France. See R. J. Knecht, 'Francis I, "Defender of the Faith"?', in *Wealth and Power in Tudor England: Essays Presented to S. T. Bindoff,* eds. E. W. Ives *et al.,* (London, 1978), 107.

15 Richard Morison, *An inuectiue ayenste the great and detestable vice, treason* (London: Thomas Berthelet, 1539, *RSTC* 18112), D1r–E1r, F2r–Fv (quotation).

16 Wriothesley, *Chronicle,* 1, 78–81; P. Marshall, 'Papist as Heretic: The Burning of Friar Forest', *HJ,* 41 (1998), 351–74. Cranmer's answer to the rebels: CCCC MS 102, 337–405 printed in *Miscellaneous,* 163–87, quotation at p. 165. McEntegart, *League of Schmalkalden,* 97–101.

17 Wriothesley, *Chronicle,* 78–81.

18 McEntegart, *League of Schmalkalden,* 97–101.

19 F. Mykonius, *Historia reformationis* (Leipzig, 1718), 57–8; *LP,* 13(1), no. 1096; Wriothesley, *Chronicle,* 81; MacCulloch, *Cranmer,* 214–19; McEntegart, *League of Schmalkalden,* 74, 83–93, 97–104, 116–17; Brigden, *London,* 282–5.

20 Cranmer, *Miscellaneous,* 472–84; McEntegart, *League of Schmalkalden,* 103–14.

21 McEntegart, *League of Schmalkalden,* 115–27.

22 CCCC, MS 104, 241–70; Cranmer, *Miscellaneous,* 83–114, and letters no. 211–12.

23 In *League of Schmalkalden* (pp. 109–127), McEntegart considered a large number of documents that passed between Henry and the Lutherans during the summer of 1538 that can only be summarized here in passing. Some of the king's comments can be read in CCCC, MS 109, especially 13r–17r; MacCulloch, *Cranmer,* 220–1.

24 MacCulloch, *Cranmer,* 220–1; McEntegart, *League of Schmalkalden,* 127–30.

25 The Second Royal *Injunctions* (London: Thomas Berthelet, 1538, *RSTC* 10086); Wriothesley, *Chronicle,* 1, 85–6.

26 T. S. Freeman and S. Royal, 'Stranger than Fiction in the Archives: The Controversial Death of William Cowbridge in 1538', *British Catholic History*, 32 (2015), 451–72.

27 Cranmer, *Miscellaneous*, no. 231 (*LP*, 13 (1), no. 1237); McEntegart, *League of Schmalkalden*, 133; MacCulloch, *Cranmer*, 231–2.

28 LPL, Cranmer's Register, 67r; Wilkins, *Concilia*, 3, 836; McEntegart, *League of Schmalkalden*, 133.

29 Wriothesley, *Chronicle*, 1, 90.

30 Lehmberg, *Reformation Parliament*, 117–18.

31 The details about Lambert were conveyed in Dorset's letter of 13 March 1536: BL, Cotton MS Cleopatra E. IV, 131r–132v (*LP*, 10, no. 462). McEntegart, *League of Schmalkalden*, 133–40.

32 Wilkins, *Concilia*, 3, 840; *LP*, 13 (2) no. 1087; Sir Thomas Elyot, *The Dictionary* (London; Thomas Berthlet, 1538, *RSTC* 7659), A2r–A2v.

33 Wriothesley, *Chronicle*, 1, 88–9; Foxe, *AM*, 5, 227–36; MacCulloch, *Cranmer*, 232–4; McEntegart, *League of Schmalkalden*, 133–40.

34 McEntegart, *League of Schmalkalden*, 138–9; *TRP*, 1, 274.

35 M. E. James, 'Obedience and Dissent in Henrician England: The Lincolnshire Rebellion of 1536', *Past and Present*, n. 48 (1970), 76; MacCulloch, *Cranmer*, 219, 229–30; McEntegart, *League of Schmalkalden*, 131–3.

36 *The Byble in Englyshe* (London: Richard Grafton and Edward Whitchurch, April 1539, *RSTC* 2068).

37 McEntegart, *League of Schmalkalden*, 131–3, 150–3; *The Byble in Englyshe* (London: Richard Grafton and Edward Whitchurch, April 1539, *RSTC* 2068).

38 Gardiner, *Letters*, no. 127 (quotation at 369); McEntegart, *League of Schmalkalden*, 150.

39 Morice, 248–9; Foxe, *AM*, 5, 264–5; 8, 23. For this complicated episode, see Lehmberg, *Later Parliaments*, 55–79; MacCulloch, *Cranmer*, 242–9; McEntegart, *League of Schmalkalden*, 152–7; Glyn Redworth, 'A Study in the Formulation of Policy: The Genesis and Evolution of the Act of Six Articles', *JEH*, 37 (1986), 42–67.

40 Wriothesley, *Chronicle*, 1, 101.

41 Morice, 248.

42 Cranmer, *Miscellaneous*, 168.

43 Alexander Alesius to Elizabeth I: TNA:PRO, SP 70/17, 11v–12r (*Calendar of State Papers Foreign, Elizabeth*, 1, no. 1303).

44 Bucer to Cranmer, 29 October 1539, *OL*, 2, no. 245; *Corpus Reformatorum: Philippi Melanthonis Opera quae supersunt omnia*, ed. Carolus Gottlieb Bretschneider, 3 (Halle, 1836), nos. 1865, 1868.

45 Morice, 258–9.

46 Foxe, *AM*, 5, 262.

47 Ridley, *Cranmer*, 178–98.
48 A. Ryrie, *The Gospel and Henry VIII: Evangelicals in the Early English Reformation* (Cambridge, 2003), 23–39.
49 Morice, 249–50; Foxe, *AM*, 5, 388–91.
50 McEntegart, *League of Schmalkalden*, 103.
51 Foxe, *AM*, 5, 265, 398; 8, 14; G. R. Elton, 'Thomas Cromwell's Decline and Fall', *HJ*, 10 (1951), 150–85.
52 McEntegart, *League of Schmalkalden*, 167–77.
53 MacCulloch, *Cranmer*, 257–8, 271–2.
54 Foxe, *AM*, 5, 232; McEntegart, *League of Schmalkalden*, 180–5.
55 *LP*, 14 (2), no. 750.
56 Wriothesley, *Chronicle*, 1, 109–12, 119–20; Edward Hall, *The Union of the two noble and illustrate famelies of Lancastre and Yorke* (London: Richard Grafton, 1548, *RSTC* 12721), 237v–240v.
57 *LP*, 15, no. 823.
58 Wriothesley, *Chronicle*, 1, 109–12, 119–20; Hall, *Union*, 237v–240v.
59 Scarisbrick, *Henry VIII*, 429–30.
60 Wriothesley, *Chronicle*, 1, 115; Hall, *Union*, 241v.
61 *The Byble in Englyshe, that is to saye the content of all the holy scrypture, both of the olde, and newe testament with a prologe therinto, made by the reuerende father in God, Thomas archbysshop of Cantorbury.* (London: Edward Whitchurch, 1540, *RSTC* 2070). Cranmer's prologue occurs on sigs. ✠1r–✠3v.
62 See the dedicatory epistle to Gardiner's *A declaration of such true articles as George Joye hath gone about to confute as false* (London: John Herford, 1546, *RSTC* 11588), reprinted in his *Letters*.
63 Morice, 249.
64 Foxe, *AM*, 8, 43.
65 Cranmer to Henry VIII, June 1540, *Miscellaneous*, no. 270.
66 H. A. Kelly, *The Matrimonial Trials of Henry VIII* (Stanford, 1976), 261–75; Hall, *Union*, 243v; Elton, 'Decline and Fall', 177–83; MacCulloch, *Cranmer*, 272–4.
67 See Henry Brinkelow's *The complaynt of Roderyck Mors . . . vnto the parliament howse of Ingland* [(Strasbourg, 1542], *RSTC* 3759.5) D2r, F7v.
68 Brigden, *London*, 320–2; Cranmer, *Miscellaneous*, 168; MacCulloch, *Cranmer*, 274.
69 Cranmer, *Miscellaneous*, no. 261, 401–4.
70 *LP*, 16, no. 590 Lehmberg, *Later Parliaments*, 127.

7   The Privy Council, 1540–1547

'Merciful father give us grace, that we never presume to sin through the example of any creature, but if it shall chance us at any time to offend thy divine majesty: that even then we may truly repent and lament the same, after the example of Mary Magdalene, and by lively faith obtain remission of all our sins through the only merits of thy son our saviour Christ.'[1]

After Thomas Cromwell

Thomas Cromwell had no successor as vicegerent in the English Church. Nor was he followed by a chief minister who would direct the king's policy. Rather, the king's Council was now renamed and redefined as the Privy Council, in whom executive authority was invested as a body. Its members served at the pleasure of the king. They included the dukes of Norfolk and Suffolk; Lord Chancellor Thomas Audley; Stephen Gardiner of Winchester; and Edward Seymour, earl of Hertford, the uncle of Prince Edward. Sir William Paget (1506–1563) was appointed clerk of the Privy Council at Cromwell's death. Archbishop Thomas Cranmer had nominal precedence among the privy councillors by virtue of his office, and his attendance at their meetings was recorded from mid-1542.

Until the end of his life, Henry VIII dominated his Privy Council. As a body, or as individual members, the Privy Council had no independence of authority or action. Political parties in the modern sense did not exist, and its members formed loose coalitions, or factions, that responded to specific problems. Ambition and changes in religious policy drove the formation of shifting coalitions. Usually three or more divisions existed amongst the privy councillors at any time, and the rivalries they engendered were intense, sometimes leading to acts of violence and revenge.

John Foxe believed that the period following the passage of the Act of Six Articles was a time of great repression for Protestants, who were living under 'the whip with six strings'. Although, as we will see, Anne Askew and others were sacrificed under the Six Articles, Foxe's view was unduly pessimistic. Some of the harshest provisions of the law were modified by subsequent statutes. Despite his conservatism, Henry never intended to re-embrace the papacy nor undo the suppression of the religious houses. After Cromwell was executed, the king permitted further reforms, though not as many as Cranmer wished. In 1541, Henry ordered his bishops to take away any images or shrines that had not already been removed. The only lights still allowed were those that burned before the sacrament of the altar.[2] In 1543, the Bishops' Book was revised in a new formulary known as the King's Book that was issued with Henry's approval. Bible reading was limited to the uppermost levels of society under the terms of the Act for the Advancement of True Religion and for the Abolishment of the Contrary.[3] At the end of 1545, Parliament began to suppress the chantries, whose purpose (like the monasteries) was to supplement Masses in the parishes on behalf of the souls of their departed founders. Henry needed money to pay for England's wars, and the economy weakened. It remained weak in the new reign. Other changes in religion were slow and faced intense opposition.

Henry's privy councillors were among the most ruthless men ever to serve the king. Some were ready to thwart him, doublecross him, or betray him, if they dared. Many hoped he would die, but they did not say so, for to speak of the king's death was treason. Henry knew that he could not trust most of them, and he was a past master at playing one set of his advisors against the others.

In addition to the Privy Council, Henry also received advice from the gentlemen who waited on him in his private suite of rooms, known as the king's privy chamber. Many of its members were evangelicals, especially once he wed Katherine Parr (1512–1548), his last wife, in 1543. The chief figures of the privy chamber were his physician, Dr William Butts (d. 1545), Sir Anthony Denny

(1501–1549), and Sir William Herbert (1507–1570), who was married to Anne (d. 1552), Katherine's sister. As we have already observed, Butts came from Cambridge to enter the king's service in 1528. He played an instrumental role in protecting Cranmer and other Protestants at court. The members of the privy chamber did their utmost to manage the king and to persuade him to do as they thought best.

From 1540 until the end of the reign, the members of the court and the Privy Council were locked in relentless struggles for power that no one could win. The year 1543 was especially difficult for Cranmer, when he was exposed to his enemies and almost overcome. But Henry refused to give the victory to any side, not until his life ebbed at the close of 1546, when the suggestions and influence of the evangelicals in the king's privy chamber were vital. Rather surprisingly, the balance of the scales turned towards the evangelicals, and towards Cranmer.[4]

The Six Preachers of Canterbury

Among the peculiarities of the Reformation in England was the fact that the Church's administration was not fully changed despite the gradual closure of its greatest intercessory institutions: the monasteries, friaries, and chantries. In contrast, in many Protestant cities on the continent, bishops were demoted. Cathedrals, colleges, and convents were confiscated and they were put to new uses. But in England, cathedrals were preserved and the office of bishop was retained in service to the crown. When the monks were disbanded, the cathedral chapters were refounded for secular canons or prebendaries. Each diocese continued to be important in the administration of the realm. In 1541, several new bishoprics were created as some of the larger dioceses, like Lincoln, were divided into smaller dioceses that were easier to run. When the Benedictines were turned out of their houses, Westminster Abbey, very briefly, became a cathedral and the abbot, Cranmer's friend William Benson, became the dean of the new foundation.

Canterbury's Benedictine Priory of Christ Church was also closed and refounded when the cathedral was given a new chapter. The reorganization gave Cranmer the opportunity to promote plans that he had been forced to relinquish when Anne Boleyn was destroyed. Now he wanted to found a college at the cathedral that included a grammar school and a permanent staff of preachers. The original plan for the school called for schoolmasters, lecturers in Latin, Greek, and Hebrew, as well as sixty students. But Henry intervened, and the new chapter became more elaborate than Cranmer wished. He wrote Cromwell in 1539 that although the proposed college was 'a very substantial and godly foundation', he had his doubts about the advisability of providing for a dozen prebendaries as the cathedral's chapter, each of whom was to have only light duties and a generous salary. Cranmer suspected that they would spend 'their time in much idleness' and their money in 'superfluous belly cheer'.[5] Alongside the prebendaries, a separate staff of preachers was created. Known as the Six Preachers of Canterbury, they formed a college-inside-a-college which continues to the present day, an innovation unique to Canterbury amongst the other cathedral foundations.

Cranmer recommended his friend Edward Crome as dean of the new chapter. Had Crome been appointed, he would have been a staunch protector of Cranmer's interests. Instead, the promotion went to the diplomat Nicholas Wotton (*c.* 1497–1567). Moreover, Henry insisted that in creating the new chapter, his policy be followed of making appointments evenly to conservatives and reformers. Although Cranmer was able to place a few of his own men (including his chaplain Richard Champion), several prebendaries were former monks who bitterly resented the injuries they had already endured at Cranmer's hands. Three of the Six Preachers were evangelicals: John Scory (d. 1585), Michael Drum, and Nicholas Ridley's cousin Lancelot (d. 1576). The other three, including Robert Serles (originally from Oxford), were conservatives. The members of the chapter disagreed amongst themselves from the start. Wotton was often abroad on diplomatic missions and Cranmer never had complete control over the cathedral foundation. From its inception, the conservative members of the new cathedral foundation conspired to destroy him. Angered by their defensive arguments about devotions, in 1541 Cranmer told the conservative prebendaries that he would break them of their old '*mumpsimus*': a byword then for wilful ignorance and the obstruction of reform.[6] When Champion died in May 1543 his colleagues threw hot coals from the thurible into his grave. They considered him, like Cranmer, a heretic worthy of burning.[7]

The end of the king's fifth marriage, 1541

The risings that occurred in Lincolnshire and Yorkshire in 1536–1537 were the greatest domestic disturbances of Henry's reign, and in 1541 the king went on a progress to ensure that the north remained pacified. He travelled with an army of soldiers and horsemen to instil fear. He was also accompanied by a small summer court that included Queen Katherine Howard and her attendants, as well as select members of his Privy Council and privy chamber. They left London at the end of June 1541. On 9 August the king was in Lincoln, and then he proceeded to Stamford and Pontefract. The king spent nearly a week in York because he wanted to hold negotiations with his nephew, King James V of Scotland (1512–1542). Henry was concerned that the Scots might invade England once again in conjunction with their traditional ally France. But Henry was disappointed. James did not join him.

While they were in Yorkshire, the king and his Privy Council were disturbed by the unexpected appearance of Six Preacher Serles, who attempted to present them with a complaint against Cranmer's destruction of religious images in Kent. Serles badly misjudged the king, for Henry could see on his progress that many images still had not been removed, despite many warnings. From Hull, the king sent a letter to the bishops that ordered them to take down any remaining shrines that still received offerings. Serles was sent back to Cranmer, who expelled him from the Six Preachers temporarily and placed him in prison.[8]

While Henry was in the north, Cranmer was approached by John Lascelles (d. 1546), one of Cromwell's many former clients, who made damaging revelations concerning the queen. His sister warned him that Katherine had taken lovers before her marriage, when they had both served in the household of Agnes (d. 1545), the dowager duchess of Norfolk. As a Protestant, Lascelles deeply resented Norfolk and Gardiner for bringing about Cromwell's destruction. To strike at them, however, was fraught with danger. The information Lascelles's sister revealed could be used as a weapon against anyone who told the king, who was obviously happy in his present marriage. But Henry had to be told when he returned at the end of October. All who knew of Katherine's misconduct and did not reveal it were liable to punishment for the crime of misprision of treason.[9]

The problem called for the greatest delicacy and it placed Cranmer in an unenviable position. Ralph Morice described this as one of the most dangerous episodes in Cranmer's career, especially because he could not depend upon the support of members of the Privy Council. When he turned to Hertford for advice, the earl told him that only he would know how to break such news to the king. On All Souls' Day 1541, while the king was at Mass, Cranmer left a letter for him in his seat that conveyed the facts as they were then known.[10]

Henry refused at first to believe the allegations, which were quickly proved. Katherine had given one of her lovers, Francis Dereham (d. 1541), a place at court, and he confessed. Even now, she might have escaped with her life, if her pre-contact with Dereham could be written off as a valid marriage. Cranmer was given the responsibility of questioning Katherine, who broke down completely. Her plight aroused his sympathies. As he informed Henry, 'it would have pitied any man's heart' to see the frenzies she suffered, especially when Cranmer told her that the king was willing to show her mercy.[11] Cranmer tried to convince her that her contact with Dereham constituted a valid marriage, but before he had succeeded in helping her, the disastrous affair she had been conducting since her marriage was revealed. In Lincoln or at other stops on the summer's progress, while Henry was out hunting or meeting with his subjects, Katherine committed adultery with Thomas Culpeper (*c.* 1514–1541), one of the king's favourite members of his privy chamber. Culpeper had been let into the queen's apartments by her attendant, Jane (ex. 1542), the widow of Anne Boleyn's brother Lord Rochford.

Katherine Howard's behaviour was completely exceptional for its time. Most young noblewomen were so carefully taught and chaperoned that they would have no opportunity to take lovers before or after their marriages. The dowager duchess (the stepmother of the present duke) had known about Katherine's affairs. Not only had she failed to stop them, but also she had not given due warning once the king's attraction to Katherine became apparent. Instead, Katherine had been offered to the king as an inducement to destroy Cromwell. Norfolk and Gardiner hastened to protect themselves from implication in the disaster, and paradoxically they emerged from the catastrophe almost unscathed. To decide how to proceed against the queen, the king held all-night meetings with the Privy Council, first at Hampton Court, and then at Gardiner's palace in Southwark. Cranmer remained at Hampton Court, charged with safeguarding the king's coffers and jewels, and he was instructed to interview Katherine again concerning Culpeper.[12]

The king also ordered Cranmer to admonish his niece, Lady Margaret Douglas (1515–1578) for the warm interest she had shown in Katherine's brother Charles. Margaret was the half-sister of King James, as well as a possible heir to the English throne as the daughter of Henry's elder sister, Margaret (1489–1541), the queen of Scotland, who died that autumn. Henry directed Cranmer to tell his niece to beware that she did not to repeat such indiscretions again.[13]

On 13 November 1541, Katherine's household was discharged, and the next day she was sent away to Syon Abbey, which had only recently been closed. After a trial at the Guildhall in London, Culpeper and Dereham were executed at Tyburn on 10 December. A new Parliament was summoned to convict Katherine of high treason. The House of Lords commissioned Cranmer to urge her to speak in her own defence, even though her fate was a foregone conclusion.[14] Once the news spread that Henry had repudiated his latest marriage, the ambassador of the duke of Cleves approached Cranmer to recommend that Henry receive Anne in matrimony again. His request placed the archbishop once more in an awkward position, because Anne's cause was clearly impossible.[15] Katherine and Lady Rochford were beheaded at the Tower on 13 February 1542.[16] At the time of her death, Katherine was no more than twenty-four.

The Canterbury Convocation of 1542

The latest parliament was summoned not only to proceed against Katherine, but to prepare for war. When Convocation began its sessions Cranmer was denied his latest opportunity to take up some of his most cherished plans. The long-delayed revision of canon law was still waiting. The Bishops' Book, *The Institution of a Christian Man*, had been released in 1537 without Henry's full approval. In the intervening years, bishops Nicholas Heath, Thomas Thirlby, John Salcot, and George Daye had prepared the draft of a new version, and Henry took serious interest in their work. Cranmer also wanted to release a new collection of ordinary sermons or homilies that he envisioned would be another collaborative effort that could build consensus and unity in the Church and the realm. He had elicited contributions from a wide spectrum of opinion. From Bishop Edmund Bonner of London (who had succeeded John Stokesley in 1540), he commissioned the homily 'Of Christian love and charity'. Cranmer also invited Gardiner to contribute. Cranmer saved for himself the homilies on the most important topics: salvation, faith, and works.

But Cranmer was trying to make progress despite severe disadvantages. Cromwell may have overshadowed him, but the vicegerent had possessed the forcefulness to move the king's business along. Now he was gone, and Cranmer's greatest allies, Hugh Latimer and Nicholas Shaxton, and also been ejected from the Upper House when they lost their bishoprics. Gardiner and Bonner seized their opportunity to persuade the king that worship services were being disrupted by laypeople as they read the Bible openly in their parish churches, and Henry ordered Convocation to reconsider the matter. When Cranmer asked the members of the Upper House if the Great Bible could be retained, he was told that it could not. Another new translation was needed to correct it. Thereupon Cranmer once again had both testaments divided into parts for fresh attention. Stokesley had hampered Cranmer's efforts to translate the Bible in 1535, as we have already observed. Now the opposition was led by Gardiner, who wanted to reintroduce Greek or Latin words into the English text to defeat the New Testament's intelligibility. In March 1542 Cranmer announced that the work would be taken over at the universities, and we hear little more of any plans to retranslate the Bible then. As Diarmaid MacCulloch noted, Cranmer was able to save the Great Bible, but at a heavy cost.[17] His plan for a book of homilies was also sacrificed in favour of the new King's Book, which came out the following year.

War with France, 1542–1546

Warfare and diplomatic concerns dominated the last three years of Henry's reign. A dangerous flare-up of the Italian Wars convulsed the whole of Europe from 1542. The king's relationship with Cranmer and his other courtiers became even more complicated as a consequence. Renewed warfare meant that Henry encouraged conservative doctrinal positions to ensure peace at home, and once again he entered into an alliance with the Holy Roman Emperor Charles V and his brother Ferdinand, king of Hungary. In June, Henry sent Thirlby (*c.* 1500–1570), the bishop of Westminster, to negotiate. The emperor wanted to attack King Francis I, and Henry suggested that France be caught in a pincer movement between invading imperial armies from the east and English forces moving westward from the coast. To forestall the possibility that his nephew James might attack England, in September 1542 Henry sent Norfolk to make an unprovoked raid against Scotland. But in November, when James died unexpectedly following his defeat at the Battle of Solway Moss, Henry lacked sufficient forces to seize further military advantages. Nor was he successful in gaining the infant Mary Queen of Scots for his son.[18]

Francis renewed his alliance with Suleyman the Magnificent, and the Habsburgs' territories along the Mediterranean and the Danube became vulnerable once again to the superior Turkish navy. In mid-1542, the Privy Council instructed both archbishops to call for processions and to command that special prayers be said in every parish in England for the success of the 'Christian Army' against the Turks. The Anglo-Imperial Treaty was concluded in mid-February 1543, and in June Henry delivered an ultimatum to the French ambassador. Henry sent Charles and Ferdinand a sum amounting to £10,000 to help their defences. To meet part of the costs of the looming 'calamity', on 19 July 1543 Cranmer issued a letter of appeal to every bishop in his province for the relief of Christians in Hungary, with an exhortation that urged parishioners to give freely of their own good will. The respectable sum of more than £1900 was raised by Cranmer's appeal to defend Christendom against the Turk.[19]

The King's Book, 1543

The next sessions of Parliament and Convocation began again at the beginning of 1543. Peace at home was absolutely essential now that England was at war. In February, Cranmer announced in Convocation that Henry once again wanted to remove all references to the bishop of Rome from service books, and those of any saints who were not New Testament figures. Cranmer also ordered that every Sunday, curates should read to parishioners one chapter of the New Testament in English, and when they had finished they should begin again with the Old.[20]

But in this session too, Cranmer's hopes for further reforms were disappointed as the king continued to rely on conservative bishops. Several members of the court were arrested on the suspicion of heresy. Parliament continued to consider the objections that Gardiner and Bonner raised about the disruptions laypeople caused as they read the Bible during worship services in their parish churches. In May, Parliament passed the Act for the Advancement of True Religion and for the Abolishment of the Contrary, which prohibited the reading of the Bible by most members of the laity.[21] The king decided that a collection of homilies, each by a different author, could not convey the consistency in doctrine that he thought essential, and the homilies were sacrificed in favour of the new King's Book.

At the same time, Convocation took up the long-delayed revision of the Bishops' Book. Now, in spring 1543, when Convocation discussed the definition of faith that should appear in the new volume, the prelates rejected Martin Luther's thinking on justification by faith alone. Once more, they endorsed the real presence of Christ in the sacrament of the altar. The new volume, *A necessary doctrine and erudition for any Christen man*, known as the King's Book, opened with a letter in Henry's name that urged his subjects 'to live charitably and quietly together'. They were to conform themselves to the new law because it was 'not so necessary' for all people to read the Bible for themselves. Remarkably, Cranmer's order that curates read the New Testament in church every Sunday now became part of the policy that took the Bible out of the laity's hands. Parishioners were encouraged to accept 'the doctrine of scripture taught by the preachers' and to keep the lessons they were taught 'inwardly in their heart'. They were also warned not to 'grudge' if they were not offered the chalice at communion.

The King's Book also began with a remarkable statement on the meaning of faith that reflected Convocation's rejection of Lutheran doctrine. Daye, who had started his career as chaplain to Bishop John Fisher, drew upon aspects of Fisher's writings when the article on faith was composed. The Christian was justified by faith, but 'neither only nor alone'. Faith was accompanied by hope and charity. Good works, and especially penance, were recommended for salvation, points that were also made in that summer's exhortation against the Turk. Predestination was rejected, for it could not be found in Scripture or in the writings of the doctors of the Church. The perfect faith of a true Christian man included obedience to the whole doctrine and religion of Christ.[22]

In later years, as we will see in the next chapter, Cranmer could denounce the compromises that were made in the King's Book and the ambiguities that encouraged the opponents of reform, but until the end of Henry's reign, the English Bible was withheld from most members of the laity, and the King's Book remained the statement that defined the religious settlement for his Church that all of his subjects were required to believe.[23]

The prebendaries plot, 1543

While the draft of the King's Book was considered by Convocation, Cranmer was endangered by a series of interlocking threats that involved Canterbury Cathedral's chapter and the conservative gentry of Kent that reached to Oxford and to Gardiner. The speaker of the House of Commons, Sir Thomas Moyle (d. 1560) was involved. The most famous episode concerned the attack against Cranmer in the Privy Council, recorded for posterity by Ralph Morice.

The attacks opened when Cranmer was accused in the Commons for his heretical sermons. Henry was told that Cranmer and his 'learned men' had so infected the realm 'with their unsavory doctrine' that three-quarters of the king's subjects had become 'abominable heretics'. Henry was urged to send him to the Tower. According to Morice, the king at first refused to listen to the complaints, and for the time being Cranmer's enemies could not prevail against him. We have already noted that in early 1543 several members of the court were seized at Windsor and they were accused of heresies against the sacrament of the altar. Three were burned.[24] Evangelical presses were closed. Thomas Becon (1515–1567), an influential pamphleteer, and the Protestant preacher Robert Wisdom (d. 1568) recanted at Paul's Cross on 8 July.

At about the same time, the king went rowing on the Thames and Morice recorded that he stopped at Lambeth Palace. Henry received Cranmer into his barge with the words, '"Ah my chaplain, I have news for you: I know now who is the greatest heretic in Kent"'. He pulled out of his sleeve accusations against Cranmer that were made by Kentish gentleman together with the conservative prebendaries of Canterbury's cathedral chapter. Henry was about to marry Katherine Parr, whose second husband Lord Latimer had died only four months earlier. The king asked Cranmer if he was still keeping to all the terms imposed by the Six Articles, or whether the privacy of his bedchamber was exempt. So Henry knew Cranmer was married. Cranmer hastened to reassure the king of his obedience, and he requested that the accusations against him be investigated. To his astonishment, the king told him to conduct the inquiries himself. Cranmer replied that any investigations he made would not look impartial, but Henry insisted that he should conduct them so that 'I may understand how this confederacy came to pass'.[25] At the same time, the king seems to have given Cranmer permission to bring his wife Margaret back.

Some of the results of Cranmer's investigation can be found in a manuscript that survives in the Parker Library at Corpus Christi College, Cambridge.[26] They reveal a diligent and surprisingly even-handed investigation that was aimed at the 'confederacy' as well as suspected excesses among members of the evangelical clergy in Kent. In September, Scory and two other Six Preachers were temporarily imprisoned for their sermons. John Bland (ex. 1555), who was sponsored by Cranmer's commissary Christopher Nevinson, seems to have flirted with radicalism, and he was indicted for heresy. The investigation also revealed how widely hated Nevinson and the Cranmers were for their destruction of religious images. Nevinson later married Cranmer's niece Anne Bingham, the daughter of his sister Jane. The investigation revealed rumours that Jane was supposed to have married her second husband while her first was still alive, which was unlikely, but the story indicated how bitter feelings were against the archbishop's family.[27]

So cautiously had Cranmer proceeded in his investigations that after six weeks Morice began to despair that the full extent of the confederacy would not be revealed. He wrote to Butts and Denny, and they encouraged the king to send Dr Thomas Legh (d. 1545) to help Cranmer. In the 1530s, Legh was one of Cromwell's most implacable visitors who prepared the closure of many religious houses. He brought his servants to Canterbury and Henry's ring as a sign of his authority. Legh unleashed his men in a surprise search of the houses, chests, and papers of the prebendaries and of local gentlemen. Many were exposed, including Richard Thornden (d. 1558), formerly a Benedictine monk who was now one of the Canterbury prebendaries as well as the suffragan bishop of Dover. The letters Legh discovered also revealed Gardiner as the hidden instigator of the plot against Cranmer and the protector of the archbishop's enemies.[28]

Before the investigations were completed, a fresh disaster occurred when Cranmer's palace in Canterbury caught fire. While others ran around in panic, Foxe recorded that Cranmer was calm. He walked up and down and warned members of his household not to take risks. But one of his brothers-in-law died.[29]

In the chaos, as Cranmer's possessions and papers were retrieved from the burning palace, a fresh rumour was born: hidden in one of the great chests was Cranmer's wife Margaret. Probably the box contained only documents,[30] but according to the notorious fiction told later by the Jesuits Robert Parsons and Nicholas Sander, Cranmer pleaded that a particular wooden chest be rescued because (as they said) his 'pretty nobsey' was inside. This story originated after Cranmer's death in Reginald Cardinal Pole's household. Its author was probably Nicholas Harpsfield, who became archdeacon of Canterbury in 1554 when Edmund Cranmer was deprived, and his information seems to have come from the family of Archbishop Warham, and the nephew who was pensioned to enable Edmund to take his office. The story was often repeated in Elizabeth's reign.[31] It may be the first (or perhaps the only) story that is told about Margaret. Despite the story's inherent implausibility, it epitomized the deep repugnance with which Harpsfield, Parsons, and Sander regarded the abandonment of Cranmer's vow of celibacy, which represented for them an outrageous desecration of the office of the priesthood.[32]

Just before Christmas, Cranmer was suddenly summoned to court, because the conservatives had marshalled themselves against him once more. Members of the Privy Council persuaded the king that Cranmer would likely make damaging admissions if he were sent to the Tower. In the most famous of all of Morice's stories, Henry sent for the archbishop and spoke with him privately in the gallery at the Palace of Whitehall. When told of the accusations, Cranmer thanked the king for warning him, and he asked to be heard impartially, as the king no doubt intended. But Henry told him that once he was imprisoned, false witnesses would be procured against him to obtain his condemnation. Then the king gave him his ring as a sign of his protection.

The next day, Cranmer discovered that he was locked out of the Privy Council chamber, and he had to sit among the serving men for nearly an hour while others went freely in and out. Morice was with him. Deeply worried, he went to Butts, who told the king of the 'strange sight' of the archbishop of Canterbury, shut out of the very body where he presided as one of its most important members. When Cranmer at last was called in, his colleagues accused him of infecting the realm with heresy, and that it was the king's pleasure that he should be sent to the Tower. Then Cranmer showed them Henry's ring. Defeated, together they went to the king, who told them that Cranmer 'was as faithful a man towards me as ever was prelate in this realm'. Henry said he felt in indebted to Cranmer for the many services he had rendered him. The king warned them against further examples of 'malice' aimed against Cranmer or against each other. Afterwards, Gardiner was nearly arrested, but he too escaped by submitting himself to the king. Morice noted that Cranmer 'delighted not in revenging'.[33]

Foxe made Morice's story of the Privy Council a centrepiece in his account of Cranmer's life in the *Actes and Monuments*.

In the early seventeenth century, Foxe's account was incorporated into *King Henry VIII* (or *All is True*), the last history play that William Shakespeare wrote in 1613 collaboration with John Fletcher, whose grandfather was one of Foxe's friends. The Shakespeare play presented Cranmer as an uncomplicated figure of heroism, the mild-mannered victim of the king's wicked councillors. His character is ennobled by his self-effacing loyalty and his faith, as a tacit allusion to his eventual martyrdom, which Shakespeare and Fletcher developed further in the final scene of the play. As Cranmer holds the infant Elizabeth in his arms at her baptism, he declares that England is promised in 'this royal princess...a thousand thousand blessings'. She will be the 'pattern to all princes' living, and the virtuous exemplar to those who those follow her. She is a phoenix from whose ashes new kings will rise, just as, by implication, a new Church will rise from Cranmer's ashes. *All is True* established Cranmer as the prophet of England's future greatness.[34]

The English litany, 1544

As Henry prepared to leave for France in 1544, Cranmer wrote an English litany to be used everywhere in his province. The litany and public processions played prominent roles in English devotional life before the Reformation, when the laity followed their priests as they carried a cross or monstrance with the consecrated host as they petitioned heaven for blessings. Cranmer was well acquainted with the elaborate processions that were a feature of the University of Cambridge's religious life in the early part of the century. Now he revised the litany to encourage the English people to pray for their king and to avoid rebellion in his absence. Cranmer acknowledged that he used 'more than the liberty of a translator' in revising the litany because the Latin seemed 'barren' and 'little fruitful', and he seized the opportunity to severely reduce the petitions to the saints which had been one of the great defining features of processions in the medieval Church. Although the litany was only a short piece of text, it marked the true start of Cranmer's *Book of Common Prayer*, and it was incorporated into both editions.[35]

Henry invaded France in mid-1544 at the head of forty thousand men. Cranmer contributed to the war effort, especially in the defence of coastal Kent. In August 1545 he came to Dover armed and helmeted, leading one hundred horsemen.[36] At his palace at Bekesbourne, he maintained a hospital for wounded soldiers, staffed with a physician and a surgeon. The wounded were fed from Cranmer's own kitchens, and when they were well enough to travel, they were given enough money to reach home.[37]

Henry returned in triumph, but with little in the way of real results to show for his heavy expenditures. Over the next two years his health gradually deteriorated. As he visibly weakened, conservatives and reformers fought to give themselves the best advantage should the king die. The last months of Henry's life were marked by some of the bloodiest contests of his reign.

The crisis of the sacrament of the altar, 1546

Cranmer was at risk once more when a crisis concerning the Mass developed during Lent 1546, provoked by his old Cambridge friend, Edward Crome. We have already seen that in 1539 Crome supported Cranmer in opposing the passage of the Act of Six Articles in the Lower House of Convocation. Crome was a daring preacher, and he had been in trouble frequently during a turbulent career. Twice before now he was accused of heresy, in the early 1530s and again in 1541, when he became famous for his slippery recantations at Paul's Cross, made (he always said) with the king's approval. Each time he equivocated, and he managed to evade a complete retraction of the opinions he habitually expressed. In 1541, he told his listeners that it was superstitious to say Masses for the dead. He taunted his enemies by saying that if the Mass was as important as they said it was, then the king had done wrong when he put down the abbeys. Now in 1546, as the chantries were scheduled for suppression, Crome returned to the same themes. Parliament had done well to bestow chantries as well as the monasteries on the king, he preached, because private Masses did not relieve souls in purgatory. Christ was the only sufficient sacrifice for the sins of the world. The Mass was not a sacrifice, but rather it was a commemoration of the death of Christ. Thus Crome impugned the doctrine of the real presence, which meant that again he was in violation of the Six Articles.

Conservatives used the outcry that followed Crome's sermon to purge reformers at court and in many parts of the country. Cranmer was not at Lambeth during Lent 1546. Rather, he was in Kent seeing to coastal defences as part of the war effort, because England was still under imminent threat from the French fleet.[38] New commissions were authorized to hunt for offences against the Six Articles. Pursued by Bishop Bonner, on 20 April Crome promised to appear at Paul's Cross in three weeks' time, when he was to declare that he believed that the words of consecration turned the bread and wine into the very body and blood of Christ, and that the Mass was profitable to both the living and the dead. In the interval he was visited by many friends, including members of the court, who encouraged him not to recant. Only one of them warned him to do as the king expected.

On 9 May 1546, Crome entered the pulpit at Paul's Cross. The royal chaplains Nicholas Ridley and Richard Cox (c. 1500–1581) were assigned to assess his performance. Emboldened by the private advice he had received, Crome refused to recant. He said that he had not been commanded to recant, although that was indeed the king's expectation. The next day, he was brought before the Privy Council to explain himself before bishops Bonner and Nicholas Heath as well as Gardiner and Cuthbert Tunstall. Eventually he was induced to tell the names of those who had advised him to stick to his own views. In mid-May, when two men and a woman from Essex were found guilty of holding opinions against the real presence, the king approved their executions 'for the example and terror of others'.[39] When peace with France was declared on Whitsunday, Bonner processed through the streets of London when he displayed the consecrated host.[40]

On 27 June Crome returned to Paul's Cross to satisfy the king and to endorse the law without further evasions. Under the watchful eyes of the duke of Norfolk and other privy councillors, he told the enormous audience that 'we have in this Church of England the very true sacrament which is the very body and blood of our Saviour Christ under the form of bread and wine'.[41] Crome now did as he was told to do, but there was every reason to doubt his sincerity.

The controversy that Crome aroused in 1546 was one of the key turning points for Cranmer and for the Reformation in England. It led to the burning of Anne Askew in July, and Gardiner's attempt to destroy Katherine Parr, which are some of the most famous episodes of the end of Henry's reign. More than a score were investigated for their association with Crome, and nearly one hundred fled abroad. The archbishop was an obvious target for Gardiner and Bonner, especially because many of those who had counselled Crome not to submit were under Cranmer's protection, including the former bishops Latimer and Shaxton. Since their disgrace, Latimer frequented Cranmer's library at Lambeth Palace. Shaxton was living in Hadleigh in Suffolk, one of Cranmer's peculiar jurisdictions, where he was able to hide his illegal wife and children. At the beginning of June, Shaxton came on a mission to London to preach in Crome's defence, and he also openly rejected the real presence. Ralph Morice's brother William was questioned by the Privy Council. Cranmer's chaplain Rowland Taylor was troubled for a sermon he preached in Bury St Edmunds. John Lascelles, who had revealed Katherine Howard's indiscretions, was sent to the Tower. Arrested also was Anne Askew, the daughter of a Lincolnshire knight, an occasional visitor to the ladies of Queen Katherine Parr's court, whose brother Edward had been a member of Cranmer's household.[42]

The attack on Askew was used as an attempt to purge the most important evangelical members of the king's privy chamber, including Sir Anthony Denny, and William Herbert, whose wife Anne was the queen's sister. Askew was told that Lady Joan Denny and Lady Herbert sent money to her in prison. Lord Chancellor Thomas Wriothesley racked Askew in the Tower after she was condemned and Gardiner tried unsuccessfully to implicate the queen in the heresies.

On 16 July, Askew, Lascelles, and two other sacramentaries were burned at Smithfield. Shaxton escaped because he submitted and was pardoned. He preached at their executions, and then again at the beginning of August, weeping for his offence. In late September, books by Frith, Tyndale, and Barnes were burned at Paul's Cross.[43]

Some difficult aspects of Cranmer's opinion about the Eucharist were revealed as a result of the crisis. Crome, Shaxton, and Ridley were among Cranmer's oldest Cambridge friends, and they had all preceded him in rejecting the real presence. Although Ridley had to testify before the Privy Council about Crome's stubbornness, in actuality his opinions may have been dangerously close to Crome's. For several years, Ridley had studied the early fathers of the Church, as well as the writings of the ninth-century monk 'Bertram' or Ratramnus of Corbie (d. *c.* 870), who embraced a mystical understanding of the Eucharist. At some time in the first half of the 1540s, Ridley had also rejected what theologians term a 'realist' opinion about the presence of Christ in the Eucharist in favour of the idea that the Mass is a commemoration of the death of Christ.

Cranmer and his colleagues also would have been well aware that John Calvin was making important statements about the nature of the Eucharist in his *Short Treatise on the Lord's Supper* (1544), as well as in his provocative dedications to King Francis in his *Institutes*, which became more critical of traditional doctrine in every new edition. Calvin joined Huldrych Zwingli and Heinrich Bullinger's side of the arguments, and he denounced the idea that Christ's body could be 'locally' enclosed in the bread of the Eucharist, because the body of Christ has ascended into heaven, and resides there. Calvin argued that it was just as mistaken for canon law to rule that the presence of Christ was limited to the bread as it was to deny marriage to the clergy. In the third edition of the *Institutes* (1543), Calvin wrote that those who imagined that the substance of the bread and wine was transformed when the Lord's words were spoken over them were mistaken. Rather, Christ was spiritually present in the Supper he had instituted on the night that he was betrayed. The Eucharist was indeed miraculous, but the miracle occurred through the agency of God in the transformation of the souls of those who worthily ate the bread and drank the wine of the Lord's Supper.[44]

Luther had died at the beginning of 1546, and although Philip Melanchthon continued to be a strong and well-respected figure, over the next decades, the Lutherans became isolated among Protestants in their own understanding of the Eucharist. In coming years, as the *Consensus Tigurinus* (or the Consensus of

Zürich) was framed from late 1548, a figurative understanding of the Eucharist emerged as the new agreement for Reformed Protestants, if not all Lutherans. Before the crisis of the summer, Ridley, Crome, and Shaxton probably already believed that Christ was present in the Eucharist 'truly' and spiritually, but not 'really' or bodily as the Six Articles insisted. Shaxton was so shaken by the dangerous events of 1546 that he abandoned his wife and children and returned to traditional opinions. In contrast, Ridley continued to rise and he became one of the great men of the next reign.

Crome's predicament was that he carried the logic of the dissolution of the monasteries and chantries further than the king approved. He may have meant to disturb the Six Articles, but instead the immediate advantage went to his opponents. In addition to sending Askew, Lascelles, and the others to the stake, the conservatives printed several powerful defences of the sacrament of the altar in 1546. Most notable among them was Gardiner's *Detection of the Devil's Sophistry* that denounced Luther, Frith, Bucer, Bale, and all the authors of the 'crooked arguments and counterfeit contradictions' that robbed the laity of their confidence in the real presence.[45] As a royal chaplain, even if Ridley secretly shared Crome's opinion, he could not be seen to condone Crome's challenge to the law and the king's authority. As archbishop, Cranmer also could not condone Crome, especially because he still believed in the real presence. In 1546, Cranmer's belief in the real presence was his best defence against his enemies.

But as a result of the crisis, Ridley and Cranmer embarked upon the discussions that ultimately persuaded the archbishop to relinquish his Lutheran ideas about the real presence. In that 'extraordinary' year 1546, Ridley began to draw Cranmer away from his former opinions.[46] Some of Cranmer's working papers that explore Bertram's opinions have been preserved.[47] Gradually, over the next three years, Cranmer embraced the opinion of a 'true' or spiritual presence of Christ in the bread and wine of the Lord's Supper.[48]

The sacramentary crisis of 1546 also highlights the fact that Cranmer was slower to endorse change than were many of his closest colleagues. As archbishop he had to be seen to conform to the law, even if he disagreed with it, just as Crome was forced to subscribe to doctrines that he did not truly believe. Cranmer had made his courageous stand against the Six Articles at the time they were passed, and since then he had not challenged them in any constructive manner. He believed in the value of obedience, as we will see again in the next reign when he and Ridley confronted John Hooper's objections against oaths and vestments. There were those who believed that Crome should have been willing to die, as Anne Askew and John Lascelles were. The courage with which they went to their deaths brought about new perceptions about the meanings of the Eucharist as well as martyrdom. After they died for the tenet of a spiritual presence of Christ in the Lord's Supper, it was harder for English evangelicals to maintain the Lutheran idea that Christ's body and blood were really present in the consecrated bread and wine. From this time forth, Luther's opinions were surpassed by Swiss Reformers and their allies, who began to dominate theological thinking in England. The sacrifices of 1546 spelled what the historian Alec Ryrie has called the 'death' of Lutheran England.[49]

The death of Henry VIII, January 1547

When Henry concluded peace with France in mid-1546, the Anglo-Imperial alliance was still intact. England was reconciled with both of its greatest rivals simultaneously. For the first time since Henry repudiated his first marriage, rapprochement with the papacy became a possibility, and a papal agent met Henry in early August to invite English theologians to the Council of Trent.[50] Gardiner's tract defending the real presence was perhaps meant to prepare for the great reversal that would have led England back to Rome.

But for reasons that are not altogether clear, Henry did not heal the breach with the papacy. In addition to Cranmer, the end of the war brought other men of influence back to regular attendance at the Privy Council and the court. John Dudley, Lord Lisle, and Edward Seymour, the Earl of Hertford, acted as counterweights against Gardiner and the duke of Norfolk, and the campaign against heretics stopped.

During his recent embassy to the imperial court, Gardiner had sent Sir William Paget many letters why he thought it was unwise for England to engage with the Lutheran princes. Gardiner's *Detection of the Devil's Sophistry* was so contentious that it unleashed an angry series of exchanges with Cranmer and others in the next reign. Now, in a fresh attack against heretics, Gardiner released an account of the measures he had taken against Barnes in 1540. Barnes's burning had never been sufficiently explained, and now, for the first time, part of the mechanism that had also destroyed Cromwell was revealed. Although Gardiner said that he had not acted against Barnes out of any sense of revenge, he catalogued the insults he said Barnes had offered him since their days in Cambridge.[51] Emotions ran high among members of the Privy Council as they began to position themselves to the best advantage as the king's health failed. In one of their meetings, Lisle struck Gardiner. Gardiner also offended the king when he refused to exchange some of his property at Henry's request. In contrast, Cranmer lost both Knole and Otford to the king, even though he would have preferred to keep them for himself.[52]

In the middle of August, the French admiral, Claude d'Annebaut (1495–1552), arrived with an entourage of over one thousand men to sign the treaty of peace. Henry prepared elaborate receptions that involved the building of new banqueting houses at Hampton Court for the entertainment of the visitors. Anne of Cleves and both of his daughters attended the celebrations. The king was now fifty-five years of age, and so ill and swollen that he had to be moved from room to room in a chair. On the first or second evening, the king made an appearance, leaning with one arm on the admiral, and the other on Cranmer. Henry made an extraordinary suggestion that evening: that the Mass should be abolished in both England and France in favour of a communion service. Francis should banish the bishop of Rome from his realm, and then he should persuade Charles to do the same in Flanders and in all his other territories. The king also told Cranmer to write a memorandum of his suggestion for Francis to consider.[53]

This episode raises many complicated problems that have been difficult for historians to reconcile. It seems very strange that Henry could have said something of the sort to d'Annebaut and Cranmer in August, while in the previous month he had countenanced the burning of several people who rejected the Mass. Askew and Lascelles would have welcomed his suggestion. The main source for this information was an additional account that Morice gave to Foxe that was not part of his main biographical information about Cranmer. Cranmer seems to have told Morice this story for the first time in 1549.

In the chaotic diplomatic scene of August 1546, Henry may have considered every possible diplomatic feint. At the end of the month, desperately worried ambassadors from the League of Schmalkalden arrived again. Following the Diet at Regensburg in January, Charles decided that the time had arrived at long last to crush the Protestants of central Europe. If he succeeded, Henry feared that the emperor would then attack England, and therefore his suggestion to the admiral was a serious ploy to hold Francis close as the means to prevent England's isolation. The League could serve as a buffer between England and the emperor, even though, as Henry's biographer J. J. Scarisbrick observed, 'Henry wanted troops, not theologians'. Henry offered Landgrave Philip a large pension if he would serve him alone. He told the ambassadors that he was willing to enter an alliance with the Protestants, and that they should have their own theological conference to rival the Council of Trent. But he also suggested that France be permitted to enter the League, which was unlikely to happen quickly.[54]

The king made his final appearance before Parliament on 24 December 1545, and he delivered a tour-de-force performance that repudiated any return to the papacy. He also attacked excesses on every side of the doctrinal issues: the old stiff '*mumpsimus*' of the traditionalist and the alarming new '*sumpsimus*' of those who sowed doubts.[55]

Henry's speech was one of the very last times he was seen by anyone except the members of his privy chamber. As his health failed, in the final weeks of his life he was cut off from almost everyone else, including Queen Katherine Parr and Cranmer. Access to his bedside was controlled by Denny. Only a few privy councillors, like Hertford and Herbert, were admitted.[56]

As he moved towards death, Henry became anxious to control the men he chose to be Edward's guardians, who would rule England during the minority of his son.[57] Henry began to fear that the duke of Norfolk and his son Henry Howard, earl of Surrey (d. 1547) would seize Edward and the throne. In mid-December, Surrey was arrested and charged with quartering the royal arms with his own. Surrey was an evangelical and a poet, but he was also a rash and dangerous man. His adoption of the royal arms for his own use became the evidence of his treason. Probably the real target was his father, just as two years earlier an effort was made to topple Winchester that resulted in the execution of his nephew Germaine Gardiner.[58]

The day after Christmas, Henry lay ill, he called for his will and had it read to him. The last time Henry had prepared his will was before he left for France in 1544. Then Henry had chosen a mixed group of conservatives and reformers as his executors who would rule England, in essence, as a council of regency for his young son. Cranmer's name was at the head of the list that included Edward's uncle Edward Seymour, earl of Hertford, with Gardiner, Tunstall, Wriothesley, John Dudley, Viscount Lisle (1540–1553), Paget, Denny, and Sir Anthony Browne (*c.* 1500–1548), master of the horse. The executors were as evenly balanced between conservatives and reformers as those that Henry insisted to Cranmer were essential to guarantee the peace and unity of the realm.

But now, at the end of his life, Henry ordered that Gardiner's name be stricken from his new will, along with that of his close associate, Bishop Thirlby of Westminster. We are indebted for our account of what happened next to Foxe, who was told by Morice from information he received from Cranmer, through Sir Anthony Denny, who was in constant attendance at Henry's bedside. Browne was one of Gardiner's great friends, and he was alarmed by the directions the king was giving. Kneeling beside Henry's bed, he spoke of Gardiner's long service and worthiness to be included in the next government. Henry told him that he intended to leave Gardiner out, for if he were an executor 'you should never rule him, he is of so troublesome a nature'. When Browne persisted, the king threatened to remove him from the list as well. In the context of Norfolk's arrest and pending execution, Gardiner's exclusion meant that for the first time the evangelicals would have a clear advantage in the government that was to come.[59]

Parliament reopened on 14 January 1547. Cranmer was present when the vote was taken in the Lords to attaint Surrey, who was beheaded on 21 January 1547. His father was to follow him to the block a week later.

But Henry moved against Norfolk too late. He grew steadily weaker at Whitehall, and no one dared to suggest to him he was failing until Denny told him on 27 January that his physicians and the members of the privy chamber all thought that he had not much longer to live. He warned the king to prepare for death and to call upon God in Christ for grace and mercy. When asked if he wanted to open his mind to any learned man, Henry replied that if he wanted anyone, he would want Cranmer, but first he wished to take some sleep and then decide. Still weaker when he awoke, he asked for Cranmer.

The archbishop was staying a dozen miles away at Croydon. By the time he arrived, Henry could no longer speak and he was almost unconscious. But he gave his hand to Cranmer and held him fast. Cranmer exhorted him to put his trust in Christ and call upon his mercy, and he asked him to give some sign with his eyes or hand that he trusted in the Lord. Henry wrung Cranmer's hand as hard as he could, and shortly afterwards, in the early hours of Friday, 28 January 1547, the king died.[60]

Immediately Hertford brought Edward into safekeeping at Enfield, where Elizabeth was living. Not until 31 January did a tearful Lord Chancellor Wriothesley break the news of Henry's death to Parliament. With a fanfare of trumpets, the new reign was proclaimed at the Palace of Westminster and in the City of London. Edward was escorted to the Tower, where Cranmer met him at the head of Privy Council, and their first meeting was held that afternoon. As they swore loyalty to Edward, they pledged to 'stand to and maintain' the provisions of Henry's will to the utmost of their power.

However, in less than two months the evangelicals subverted the old king's intent to provide for a council of regency to rule until Edward reached adulthood. In his will, the old king insisted that none of his son's privy councillors should do anything 'alone', but rather they should always act with the written consent of the majority. For six-and-a-half years, governance at the highest levels had been effectively stalemated by the rivalries that Henry had energetically encouraged between his privy councillors. Now Cranmer helped to bring that system to an end. The king's executors chose one 'special man' to be 'preferred in name and place' above the rest. They made Edward Seymour, the earl of Hertford, the new king's uncle, Protector of the realm and governor of his nephew's person.[61]

The next day, Henry's will was read in the Privy Council and Edward's consent was obtained to have Hertford as Lord Protector. Norfolk was spared execution by Henry's death, and he was kept prisoner in the Tower through Edward's reign, thus silencing for the time being one of the most powerful voices against the Protestants. The executors divided Norfolk's and Surrey's honours and lands between them. They also gave themselves new promotions that they said had always been Henry's intent, but in reality were a division of the spoils of their rivals' defeat. Hertford now became duke of Somerset with extraordinary powers as Lord Protector. As an evangelical, he was willing to follow Cranmer's desires and to introduce further reforms into the English Church.[62]

On 9 February a requiem Mass was celebrated for Henry's soul in every parish church in England. Official mourning for the king lasted until after his funeral at Windsor, when Gardiner presided. On 16 February the king's body was buried in the choir of St George's Chapel, next to Queen Jane's.[63]

Cromwell told Cranmer that the king trusted him, and that he would take well anything Cranmer told him. Henry turned to Cranmer in his final agony. But Cranmer's private opinion of Henry is less easy to know. He grew a beard, he said, as a sign of mourning for his old master. But Cranmer's beard may have also been a symbol of his liberation. In time, it reached to his waist, which placed him visually in the company of Heinrich Bullinger and John Calvin, whose beards expressed the patriarchal authority they aspired to wield in succession to Old Testament prophets. Cranmer's beard was the symbol of the new directions he intended to take for the English Church.

The coronation of Edward VI

For the second time in his life, Cranmer presided at a coronation when he crowned the nine-year-old Edward at Westminster Abbey on 20 February 1547. Until recently, historians believed that Cranmer delivered an address then that praised the king as appearing in succession to King Josiah in the Old Testament, who restored Scripture and smashed idols. The sole piece of evidence for his address came from the papers that his biographer John Styrpe assembled in the eighteenth century. Cranmer's 'address' was reprinted in the Parker Society's collection of Cranmer's works in 1844, and it obtained a wide currency among historians. It seemed to signal the sharp change in direction, at the dawn of Edward's reign, towards the reforms that Cranmer intended to lead. However, Diarmaid MacCulloch has recently established that Strype was betrayed by his source, which was a forged document. In actuality, Cranmer made no such clarion call at Edward's coronation. Moreover, both Gardiner and Tunstall played prominent roles in the ceremonies as the young king was crowned. Only after Gardiner was removed from his positions of influence from mid-1547 could Cranmer and Somerset embark upon substantial reforms of the English Church.[64] For the first months of 1547, Henry VIII cast a long shadow over his son's reign.

Notes

1 Cranmer's collect for the feast of St Mary Magdalen on 22 July from the 1549 Prayer Book: *The booke of the common praier and administration of the sacramentes, and other rites and ceremonies of the churche: after the vse of the Churche of Englande* (London: Richard Grafton, March 1549, *RSTC* 16268), 113.

2 *AM*, 5, 463; *LP*, 16, no. 1262.

3 34 and 35 Henry VIII, c. 1.

4 E. W. Ives, 'Henry VIII's Will—A Forensic Conundrum', *HJ*, 35 (1992), 779–804; Scarisbrick, *Henry VIII*, 482.

5 Cranmer, *Miscellaneous*, letter to Cromwell, 29 November 1539, no. 265.

6 P. Marshall, 'Mumpsimus and Sumpsimus', in *Religious Identities in Henry VIII's England*. (Aldershot, 2006), 157–65, and *LP*, vol. 18, pt. 2, no. 546, 322, 349, 378.

7 CCCC, MS 128, p. 31 (*LP*, 18, pt. 2, no. 546, 300–1).

8 M. L. Zell, 'The Prebendaries Plot of 1543: A Reconsideration', *JEH*, vol. 27 (1976), 241–53; Duffy, *Altars*, 431–7; MacCulloch, *Cranmer*, 283–6.

9 Scarisbrick, *Henry VIII*, 427–33.

10 Morice, 259–60; H. A. Kelly, *The Matrimonial Trials of Henry VIII* (Stanford, 1976), 275–8.

11 Cranmer, *Miscellaneous*, letter to Henry VIII, November 1541, no. 273.

12 S. E. Lehmberg, *The Later Parliaments of Henry VIII 1536–1547* (Cambridge, 1977), 127–9.

13 Chapuys to the Queen of Hungary, 10 November, 1541 (*LP*, 16, nos. 1328, 1331, 1333, 1366). Through the marriage Henry arranged for her in 1544, Lady Margaret Douglas became the mother of Lord Darnley and the grandmother of King James VI & I.

14 Lehmberg, *The Later Parliaments*, 128, 141–8.

15 Cranmer, *Miscellaneous*, letter to Henry VIII, 13 January 1542, no. 274.

16 Wriothesley, *Chronicle*, 1, 130–4.

17 Lehmberg, *Later Parliaments*, 163–5; MacCulloch, *Cranmer*, 289–94; S. Wabuda, '"A Day after Doomsday": Cranmer and the Bible Translations of the 1530s', in *The Oxford Handbook of the Bible in Early Modern England, c. 1530–1700*, eds. K. Killeen, H. Smith, and R. Willie (Oxford, 2015), 23–37.

18 Lehmberg, *Later Parliaments*, 172; Scarisbrick, *Henry VIII*, 434–44, 452–7.

19 *APC*, vol. 1, 15; P. Ayris, 'Preaching the Last Crusade: Thomas Cranmer and the "Devotion" Money of 1543', *JEH*, 49 (1998), 683–701.

20 Wilkins, *Concilia*, 863; Lehmberg, *Later Parliaments*, 184.

21 34 and 35 Henry VIII, c. 1; Lehmberg, *Later Parliaments*, 184–8; S. Wabuda, 'The Woman with the Rock: The Controversy on Women and Bible Reading' in *Belief and Practice in Reformation England*, eds. S. Wabuda and C. Litzenberger (Aldershot, 1998), 40–59.

22 *A necessary doctrine and erudition for any Christen man* (London: Thomas Berthelet, 1543, *RSTC* 5168), especially A2r–A4r, B1r–B3v, D1r–E5r, K1r; the Act for the Advancement of True Religion: 34 and 35 Henry VIII, c. 1; Ayris, 'Last Crusade', 683–701; Lehmberg, *Later Parliaments*, 184–5; Duffy, *Altars*, 441–4. See also the article on Day in the *ODNB*.

23 Gardiner, *Letters*, nos. 122, 123, 124.

24 Morice, 251–2; D. Starkey, *Six Wives: the Queens of Henry VIII* (New York, 2003), 723–5.

25 Morice, 252; Parker, 392–3.

26 CCCC, MS 128, calendared in *LP*, vol. 18 (2), no. 546.

27 *FOR*, 27.

28 Morice, 253, Foxe, *AM*, 8, 28–31; Starkey, *Six Wives*, 727–8.

29 Foxe, *AM*, 8, 41. The brother-in-law who died was not Harold Rosell (married to Dorothy Cranmer) or Edmund Cartwright (the husband of Agnes), as MacCulloch suggested in *Cranmer*, 322. They were still alive in the mid-1550s, as Cartwright's will attests.

30 MacCulloch, *Cranmer*, 322.

31 *A treatise on the pretended divorce between Henry VIII and Catharine of Aragon, by Nicholas Harpsfield*, ed. N. Pocock, *Camden Society*, 2nd series, 21 (London 1878), 178, 275, 290–1; E. Duffy, *Saints, Sacrilege and Sedition: Religion and Conflict in the Tudor Reformations* (London, 2012), chapter 8. A man named Warham was questioned by the Privy Council in 1550 at the same time Gardiner was suppressed, *APC*, 3, 83.

32 Ridley, *Cranmer*, 148–151; MacCulloch, *Cranmer*, 250–1, 322.

33 Morice, 251–8; Parker, 291–6; Starkey, *Six Wives*, 728–31.

34 *King Henry VIII (All is True)*, act five, scene four.

35 Cranmer's letter of 7 October 1544, printed in *Miscellaneous*, no. 276. See the perceptive comments of B. Cummings in *The Book of Common Prayer: The Texts of 1549, 1559, and 1662*, (Oxford, 2011), xxiii. Also, Duffy, *Altars*, 443, 452. In the 1549 *Book of Common Prayer* the 'Letany and Suffrages' appears before the section on Public Baptism. It is not mentioned on the Contents page of the first Prayer Book, whose pagination in every printing is unreliable.

36 MacCulloch, *Cranmer*, 323.

37 Foxe, *AM*, 8, 22.

38 Scarisbrick, *Henry VIII*, 455.

39 *APC*, 1, 414, 417–19, 467. Other references for Crome will be found in my article 'Equivocation and Recantation during the English Reformation: The "Subtle Shadows" of Dr Edward Crome', *JEH*, 44 (1993), 224–42. See also Foxe, *AM*, 5, appx. xvi, document 6.

40 Wriothesley, *Chronicle*, 1, 163–5.

41 Foxe, *AM*, vol. 5, appx. xvi, document 6; Wriothesley, *Chronicle*, 1, 167–70.

42 MacCulloch, *Cranmer*, 352–5.

43 Wriothesley, *Chronicle*, 1, 167–70, 175.

44 'Locally' appeared in the second edition of the *Institutes*: John Calvin *Institution de la Religion Chrestienne* (Generva: Michel de Bois, 1541), C4v–D1r; *A faythful and moste godly treatyse concernynye the most sacred sacrament of the blessed body and bloude of our Sauiour Christ* (London: William Hill, 1548?, RSTC 4410); B. A Gerrish, *Grace and Gratitude: the Eucharistic Theology of John Calvin* (Eugene, 1971), 9–10; and the same author's 'The Reformation and the Eucharist', in *Thinking with the Church: Essays in Historical Theology* (Cambridge, 2010), 229–58.

45 Stephen Gardiner, *A detection of the Deuils sophistrie wherwith he robbeth the vnlearned people, of the true byleef, in the most blessed sacrament of the aulter* (London: John Herford for Robert Toye, 1546, RSTC 11591), 5r, 69v, 71v, 91v. Also, William Peryn, *Thre godly and notable sermons, of the sacrament of the aulter* (London, 1546, RSTC 19786); Richard Smith, *The assertion and defence of the*

sacramente of the aulter (London, 1546, RSTC 22815); Ryrie, 'Death of Lutheran England', 77–8.

46 The letter to the reader attributed to Cheke in Cranmer's *Defensio Verae et Catholicae Doctrinae de Sacramento corporis et sanguinis Christi* (Emden: Egidius van der Erve, 1557, *RSTC* 6005), A5r–A5v referred to the extraordinary year 1546 ('nimirum anno 46'); Cranmer, *Miscellaneous*, 218; P. Brooks, *Thomas Cranmer's Doctrine of the Eucharist* (London, 1965), 38–43; MacCulloch, *Cranmer*, 354–5.

47 CCCC MS 102, fol. 159v.

48 B. A. Gerrish, 'The Reformation and the Eucharist', in *Thinking with the Church: Essays in Historical Theology* (Cambridge, 2010), 229–58; P. Brooks, *Thomas Cranmer's Doctrine of the Eucharist* (London, 1965).

49 A. Ryrie, 'The Strange Death of Lutheran England', *JEH*, vol. 53 (2002), 64–92.

50 Scarisbrick, *Henry VIII*, 464–78; MacCulloch, *Cranmer*, 355–8.

51 Stephen Gardiner, *A declaration of such true articles as George Joye hath gone about to confute as false* (London: John Herford, 1546, *RSTC* 11588, reprinted in *Letters*, no. 81.

52 Morice, 266–7.

53 Foxe (1570), 1426–7; *AM*, vol. 5, 562–4; Wriothesley, *Chronicle*, 1, 171–3.

54 Scarisbrick, *Henry VIII*, 466–78 (quotation at 466); R. McEntegart, *Henry VIII, the League of Schmalkalden, and the English Reformation* (London, 2002), 212–13.

55 Scarisbrick, *Henry VIII*, 470–1; Marshall, 'Mumpsimus and Sumpsimus', 157–65.

56 H. Miller, 'Henry VIII's Unwritten Will: Grants of Lands and Honours in 1547', in *Wealth and Power in Tudor England: Essays Presented to S. T. Bindoff*, eds. E. W. Ives *et al.* (London, 1978), 87–105.

57 Ives, 'Henry VIII's Will', 779–804.

58 Wriothesley, *Chronicle*, 1, 176–7.

59 Ives, 'Henry VIII's Will', 779–804; Miller, 'Henry VIII's Unwritten Will', 87–105.

60 Foxe, *AM*, vol. 5, 689–96; Scarisbrick, *Henry VIII*, 495–6.

61 Wriothesley, *Chronicle*, 1, 178–9, 182; *APC*, 2, 3–22.

62 Ryrie, 'Death of Lutheran England', 68.

63 Wriothesley, *Chronicle*, 1, 181–2.

64 Cranmer, Miscellaneous, 126–7. See MacCulloch's 'Forging Reformation History: A Cautionary Tale', in *All Things Made New: Writings on the Reformation* (London, 2016), 321–58.

8   Edward VI and the *Book of Common Prayer*, 1547–1552

'Stir up we beseech thee, O Lord, the wills of thy faithful people, that they plenteously bringing forth the fruit of good works: may of thee, be plenteously rewarded: through Jesus Christ our Lord.'[1]

The purge

The opening salvos of Edward VI's reformation were fired not at his coronation, but in sermons that were delivered in the days that followed it. On Ash Wednesday, 23 February 1547, Nicholas Ridley denounced as papistical the use of holy water and the images of saints when he preached before the king at court. His themes were taken up again on the following Sunday at Paul's Cross. The first important sermons that were delivered in the young king's reign indicated that further reforms would be encouraged now.[2]

The Lord Protector Somerset had already assured Gardiner that there would be no substantial alterations in religion until the king reached full age. Disquieted by Ridley's sermon, and chafing from his exclusion from the council of executors, Gardiner wrote Somerset to warn him that no changes should take place in the realm, not in its religion, laws, lands, or decrees, until Edward reached his majority.[3] But Gardiner was on the wrong side of the decisions that were being made at the beginning of the reign.

On Sunday 6 March 1547, Thomas Wriothesley was over-thrown as lord chancellor, and the Great Seal was taken away from him.[4] His demotion was a successful coup mounted by the evangelicals in the new king's government. The council of exec-utors that Henry VIII had established in his will to rule England during the minority of his son lasted only six weeks. Now Somerset emerged as the initial strong man of Edward's government, with more powers than the dead king had wanted any single person to enjoy.

The last occasion in Edward's reign when all London parishes were asked to celebrate requiem Masses was in June 1547 to mark the death of the king of France. Francis I had died at the end of March, only two months after Henry. Although their reigns had been marked by the bitter wars they waged against each other, stories were told that the French king was never happy again once he learned of Henry's death. The international perspective worsened dramatically. On 24 April, at the Battle of Mühlberg, the Emperor Charles V won a decisive victory against the League of Schmalkalden. Duke John Frederick of Saxony was wounded and taken prisoner. Briefly condemned to death, he capitulated and surrendered his government into the hands of a cousin. Landgrave Philip of Hesse was held captive until 1552. Charles imposed a series of restrictions in Lutheran regions, known as the Interim, which threatened the cradle of Protestantism.

Against this troubling backdrop, Archbishop Thomas Cranmer presided over a sumptuous requiem for Francis at St Paul's, partly as an act of defiance aimed at Charles. Arrayed in full pontificals, he was assisted by the archbishop of York and eight other bishops. King Edward led the French ambassadors and English noblemen in mourning. London's mayor and aldermen attended at the head of two hundred members of the livery companies. In the funeral sermon, Bishop Henry Holbeach of Lincoln promoted an evangelical message when he praised Francis for releasing a French Bible for all of his subjects to read, which was also meant as an implicit criticism of the late king Henry, who had often withheld the Bible from his own people.[5] The requiem for King Francis marked an end of the Henrician era in the English Church.

Within six months of Henry's death, his memory was insulted by a series of books that praised the courage of those who had gone to the stake in the summer of 1546. John Bale printed Anne Askew's account of her ordeals, in which he articulated a new understanding of Protestant martyrdom that became the standard for the rest of the century and beyond, especially as it was developed further by John Foxe in his *Actes and Monuments*.

The conservatives who brought about their deaths were also attacked. The open letter Philip Melanchthon had written in 1539 to castigate Henry was printed in an English translation in mid-1547 to insult the 'shameless bishops', like the 'wicked Stephen Gardiner bishop of Winchester' who used the Act of Six Articles 'to deceive the eyes of Christian people'.[6] Gardiner wrote Somerset in protest that Bale's books were spreading lies.

Another early target for suppression for his association with the old king was the conservative Regius Professor of Divinity at Oxford, Dr Richard Smyth (1500–1563). When Askew was burnt, Smyth denounced heresy in a book he ostentatiously dedicated to Henry.[7] Now in changed circumstances, Smyth became the pursued. In mid-May 1547, the Privy Council ordered him to burn his books at Paul's Cross, where he made an ironical 'retraction' of his opinions of the sacrament of the altar that took as his text Paul's commentary from Romans, *Omnia homo mendax*: every man is a liar. This was so unsatisfactory that he had to recant again in Oxford in July. Moreover, he was deprived of his professorship.[8] Smyth was the earliest of the stumbling blocks that were removed to make way for Edward's Church.

The *Book of Homilies*, 1547

In May 1547, a royal proclamation announced that the entire English Church in both provinces would be visited. Although all current religious legislation was ordered to be obeyed, the proclamation signalled that changes to the Henrician laws should be expected. Gradually, many of the laws and policies that had inhibited further reforms were dismantled. In June, Gardiner was shocked when Cranmer informed him that he was reviving his project for the homilies. In the previous chapter, we observed that Cranmer had spent years of unrewarded effort in preparing a collection of homilies which was sacrificed in favour of the King's Book of 1543. Now, Cranmer wrote Gardiner in the strongest terms that the King's Book contained many errors, especially in its article on faith. The letter Cranmer wrote no longer exists, but according to the portions Winchester quoted in his response, Cranmer said that Henry had been deluded or 'seduced' when he approved the King's Book. Cranmer intended to discard the deliberate obscurity that had been made as concessions to traditionalists in the King's Book. He denigrated its definition of faith as one of its misleading 'amphibologies': a dubious ambiguity that was capable of being interpreted in more than one sense. The King's Book was objectionable, Cranmer told him, because it was 'such a fountain' from which 'both sides may fetch water'.[9] Despite Gardiner's protests, in August, *Certain sermons or homilies* was released. It was the first of Cranmer's definitive statements on faith for Edward's Church.

The *Book of Homilies* was a collection of twelve sacred addresses that were 'appointed by the King's Majesty' to be read in every parish church in England.[10] No individual contribution was signed, but the portions that Cranmer probably wrote were the preface; the first homily, 'A fruitful exhortation, to the reading and knowledge of holy scripture'; and the three homilies that addressed the most controversial subjects: salvation, faith, and works.[11] The preface denounced the 'manifold enormities' that had crept into the realm through 'the false usurped power of the bishop of Rome, and the ungodly doctrine of his adherents' which led to the destruction of innumerable souls. King Edward, with the advice of his uncle Somerset, now commissioned the *Book of Homilies* to deliver his subjects 'from all errors and superstitions, and to be truly and faithfully instructed in the very word of God'. The homilies would teach them how to honour God and to serve the king 'with all humility and subjection'.[12]

A homily is a sermon that is read to an audience by a clergyman from a fixed text. The origins of the homily are found in the teachings of the Fathers in the early Church, including Chrysostom and Basil (d. 379). Homilies on a rich variety of subjects survive from the middle ages. The Augustinian canon John Mirk (d. *c.* 1414) developed an important homiliary known as the *Festial* which he drew from the famous thirteenth-century collection of saints' lives, the *Legenda aurea*. But Cranmer wanted his *Book of Homilies* to replace the pulpit fare that conservative clergy still used to teach their audiences. He wanted to prevent clergymen in Edward's reign from preaching the kind of '"foolish lying legends"' that he argued was the staple of Mirk's *Festial*.[13] The purpose of the *Book of Homilies* was to provide standardized direction to the laity concerning belief and behaviour that was consistent with the Protestant doctrines that Somerset and Cranmer were putting in place in Edward's Church.

The first homily in the volume was Cranmer's 'A fruitful exhortation, to the reading and knowledge of holy scripture' which marked an implicit repudiation of the restrictions against Bible reading that had been imposed on the lower social orders and women in 1543. Like his introduction to the 1540 Great Bible, the homily cited as its authority St John Chrysostom: '"whatsoever is required to salvation is fully contained in the Scripture of God"'. There could be nothing more necessary for a Christian man than the knowledge of God's true Word. To 'them that be desirous to know God or themselves', the 'reading, hearing, searching, and studying of Holy Scripture' is 'as drink is pleasant to them that be dry, and meat to them that be hungry'. Holy Scripture 'is the food of the soul'. For our justification and salvation, we should search the New and Old Testaments, which are the 'well of life', and we should 'not run to the stinking puddles of men's traditions'.[14]

It was followed by 'Of the misery of all mankind', written by the conservative John Harpsfield (the brother of Nicholas), Oxford's first Regius Professor of Greek, and it was perhaps prepared for the intended earlier edition of the *Homilies*. 'Of the misery of all mankind' was a powerful warning that 'from the first infection' of 'our great grandfather Adam', all people should know 'their vile, corrupt, frail nature' which was nothing more than 'dust, earth and ashes'. Humankind was lost when Adam fell. Vainglory and pride should be pulled down whenever they appeared. 'Let us look upon our feet, and then down peacocks' feathers, down proud heart, down vile clay, frail and brittle vessels'.[15]

'Of the misery of all mankind' prepared the listeners for Cranmer's homilies on salvation, faith, and works. They were deeply related to each other and their themes were completely intertwined. Cranmer taught that one depended upon another: Salvation was the gift of God. Faith flowed out of salvation. Good works flowed out of faith. Good works were insufficient in themselves as the means to salvation, but rather they were pleasing to God as the product and sign of a lively faith.

In the 'Homily of the salvation of mankind, by only Christ our savior', Cranmer drew from Paul to argue all men are sinners and offenders against God. No man may be justified by his own acts, works, or deeds, no matter how worthy they might seem. Rather, remission, pardon, and forgiveness must be sought and received from God. Man was not justified by works, but rather, 'freely by faith in Christ'. Justification, or the salvation of the soul, was made possible 'by God's mercy and Christ's merits, embraced by faith'. When 'all the world' was 'wrapped in sin' for the breaking of the law, God sent his only Son to make a satisfaction for our sins by the shedding of his most precious blood. Out of his great mercy, God delivered us, through the sacrifice of his own Son. Justification comes freely by the mercy of God to those who truly believe in him. A true and lively faith is the gift of God, as St Paul declared. Cranmer wrote that 'we be justified by faith only, freely, and without works'. Our works are insufficient to deserve salvation at God's hands. Only Christ and his most precious blood-shedding obtained our justification. Unmerited grace was God's greatest gift. We must trust only in God's mercy and in the sacrifice of Christ Jesus, once offered for us upon the cross.[16]

Faith, as Cranmer defined it in the Homily of Salvation, is to believe that Holy Scripture and the Creed are true; and moreover, faith is to have a sure trust and confidence in God's merciful promises of salvation from everlasting damnation by Christ, and with a loving heart to obey his commandments.[17]

The two homilies that followed continued to explore the inter-dynamic between faith and works. In 'A short declaration of the true, lively and Christian faith', Cranmer explained that wicked Christians who confess God with their mouths but deny him in their deeds were without the right faith. Faith that was dead was not the 'sure and substantial faith which saveth sinners'. Rather, quick and lively faith is 'a sure trust and confidence of the mercy of God, through our lord Jesus Christ' upon whom we commit ourselves wholly, ready to obey and serve only him. This faith brings forth good works. Without it, no good works shall be acceptable to God. God is pleased by this faith, and its reward was the salvation of the soul.[18]

In 'An homily or sermon of good works annexed unto faith', Cranmer wrote that true faith gives life to the works, and out of such faith come works that are very good indeed. No good work could be acceptable to God without faith. Like Jacques Lefèvre, Cranmer used the example of the penitent thief who was crucified alongside Jesus as an illustration that it was possible to be saved only by faith without any good works at all. '"The thief that was hanged when Christ suffered did believe only, and the most merciful God did justify him"'.[19]

The rest of the homilies, starting with Bishop Edmund Bonner's 'Homily of Christian love and charity', explored the kind of good works that were acceptable to God. The homilies also warned 'Against swearing and perjury' and 'Against Whoredom and Adultery'. They counselled against 'Declining from God' and 'The fear of death'. 'An exhortation concerning good order and obedience to rulers and magistrates' and 'Against Strife and Contention' were mature statements that argued that obedience was necessary for peace in the kingdom.

The *Book of Homilies* did not address the nature of the sacrament of the altar, which had to wait until the first Prayer Book of 1549. Cranmer anticipated that 'the Nativity, Passion, Resurrection, and Ascension of our Saviour Christ, of the due receiving of his blessed body and blood, under the form of bread and wine' would appear in the next collection of homilies. A second *Book of Homilies* would also take up other topics including fasting, praying, alms deeds, and denunciations against idleness; gluttony and drunkenness; covetousness; envy, ire, and malice. Martin Bucer, in his response to the 1549 *Book of Common Prayer*, also encouraged Cranmer to commission homilies on the worthy reception of each sacrament; the lawful care for the needy; holy wedlock; and the education of children.[20] Cranmer probably anticipated the release of a second *Book of Homilies* at some later time, after the 1552 Prayer Book, but in this, as well as much else, he was interrupted by the young king's untimely death.

At the beginning of Edward's reign, only a strictly limited number of licensed clergymen were allowed to preach,[21] and therefore the homilies were the only approved addresses that were sounded from most pulpits. Bishops were forbidden to preach except in their own cathedrals, a prohibition that especially offended Gardiner.[22] Sunday by Sunday, the *Homilies* were to be read in every parish in England. When the end of the book was reached, they were to be begun again. Bucer complained that in too many parishes only a portion of a single homily was read each Sunday. Short though they were, the laity did not have the patience to listen to an entire address, he thought, but his observation means that the *Homilies* were indeed being read from parish pulpits.[23] In some parishes the full *Book of Homilies* may have been read through five or six times before the king died in mid-1553. Gardiner admitted that laypeople obtained copies of the *Homilies* and read them aloud in their households 'as well as the priest, or better'. He thought they should be instructed to come to church to hear them, but more to the point, the *Book of Homilies* was so well received that many people wanted to own the volume for themselves.[24] The *Book of Homilies* was more successful than the first *Book of Common Prayer* in gaining acceptance for the reforms Cranmer wanted to encourage and for instilling in hearts and minds a Protestant understanding of faith.

Gardiner reacted with defiance when the *Book of Homilies* was released in August 1547. In recently discovered letters, he disparaged the definition of faith that was presented in the Homily of Salvation. Gardiner argued that justification by faith alone was not confirmed in Scripture or by the early Church authors. Faith without hope and charity was imperfect. He maintained that 'the Homilies be over far out of the way', and in good conscience he was unwilling to preach them.[25]

Gardiner was also offended by the royal visitation that started at the end of the summer. Many of the visitors were Cranmer's closest associates: Ralph Morice, Christopher Nevinson, Nicholas Ridley, Rowland Taylor, and William Benson; and for the northern province, his friend Sir John Markham. The injunctions for the royal visitation were unusually long and stringent. In addition to requiring that every parish church should be supplied with a copy of the newly translated *Paraphrases* of the Gospels by Erasmus, they also called for all images to be removed from every parish church. Across England, lights were extinguished, crosses were taken down from rood lofts, statutes of the saints were broken into pieces, and holy pictures were openly burnt.[26]

Gardiner insisted in letters to Somerset that Henry had opposed innovation, and that the doctrines of the Church as they were expressed in the *King's Book* should not be changed until Edward reached the age of majority in 1555, a day so distant that Gardiner thought that by then Cranmer might be dead. In September 1547, the Privy Council summoned Gardiner to appear and he was sent to the Fleet Prison for intransigence. After a brief period of release, he was required to preach an examination sermon at court in mid-1548, when he was expected to endorse the idea that Edward's authority (and thus Somerset's government) was just as great as if the king had been of full age. But Gardiner evaded many of the subjects that Somerset wanted him to set out in his sermon, and he was committed to the Tower.

Towards the first *Book of Common Prayer*

While the *Book of Homilies* moved towards the press, Cranmer and Ridley continued to discuss the meaning of the Eucharist, which (as we have already noted) was a central problem for Cranmer's career. At the opening of Parliament in November 1547, the Mass was sung in English for the first time.[27]

As we have observed, the sermons that were delivered at Paul's Cross, especially when Parliament and Convocation were in session, were important political statements. Ridley was made bishop of Rochester in September, and when he preached at Paul's Cross at the end of the year, he rebuked 'evil disposed persons' who were spreading 'railing' handbills that insulted the Eucharist. He had to be careful not to run afoul of the Act of Six Articles, which had not yet been repealed, and yet find a balance that would distance the English Church from the radical views of the Anabaptists, who continued to cause Cranmer regular concern through Edwards's reign. Ridley tried to summarize the new positions that were still under discussion: that the sacrament of the altar was 'truly and verily the body and blood of Christ, effectually by grace and spirit'. However, his sermon was not well received, because the doctrine of a spiritual presence was still so new and abstruse that members of his audience fastened upon the novel and shocking aspects of what he said rather than on the substance of his meaning. When he attempted to deflect questions on the nature of the presence of Christ in the sacrament, he left his audience confused. Anyone who asked after sacred things in crude terms, he said, was 'worse than dogs and hogs'.[28]

At the end of the year, Parliament abolished the Act of Six Articles and voted to allow the laity to take communion in both kinds, which meant that parishioners were to receive the wine as well as the bread. This was a striking change from traditional practice, because until now, in both the medieval Church and at Henry's insistence, the chalice had been withheld from laypeople.[29] On 8 March 1548, an *Order of the Communion* was released, an important forerunner of the *Book of Common Prayer*. It provided a liturgy in English for April's Easter communion service. Priests were to let parishioners drink once from the chalice 'and no more'. For the first time, Cranmer's 'general confession' appeared: 'Almighty God, father of our Lord Jesus Christ, maker of all things, judge of all men: We knowledge and bewail our manifold sins and wickedness, which we from time to time, most grievously have committed by thought, word, and deed, against thy divine majesty, provoking most justly, thy wrath and indignation against us: We do earnestly repent'. Like the General Confession, for the first time the *Order* also included the Prayer of Humble Access. In due course, they became some most familiar passages of the *Book of Common Prayer*.[30]

However, after Easter, Cranmer's actual intentions for the English Church became confused when he released a *Catechism* for the instruction of children. The *Catechism* had begun as a book that Andreas Osiander prepared in Nuremberg during the brief period in 1532 when Cranmer visited him. First printed there in 1533, it was issued again in 1539 by Martin Luther's friend Justus Jonas (1493–1555), and it was brought to England by his son, one of the refugees who arrived at the end of 1547. In summer 1548 it was translated, revised, and issued under Cranmer's name, although it conflicted with the clear instructions just released in the *Order of the Communion*, as well as with the new law just passed by Parliament. The *Catechism* assumed the laity would not be given the cup, and it taught children, as the Lutherans did, that 'we ought to believe, that in the sacrament we receive truly the body and blood of Christ'.[31]

The *Catechism* of 1548 marked almost the last time that Cranmer could be said to endorse what might be considered a Lutheran position concerning the presence of Christ in the Eucharist. Immediately he was criticized, and the *Catechism* was revised and then revised again into the autumn. Still, a realist position of the presence in the sacrament was not completely removed from the book. Later Cranmer complained that many 'ignorant persons' who were unused to reading 'old ancient authors', did 'carp' against the *Catechism*. Cranmer's positions on the Eucharist were not always clearly expressed for the English Church at the same time that his own private opinions were moving far beyond the new standards he released so gradually.[32]

Deeply concerned about the repressions that the Emperor Charles unleashed in the Interim, Cranmer extended warm invitations to many Protestant leaders to find refuge in England. Arriving from Strasbourg at the end of 1547 were Peter Martyr Vermigli and Bernardino Ochino (*c.* 1487–1565). Vermigli rapidly became an important advisor to Somerset's government, and he was given Smyth's Regius Chair of Divinity at Oxford in 1548, which he held until the end of the reign despite persistent opposition from Smyth's friends. Vermigli brought with him a manuscript version of an epistle by John Chrysostom that he had discovered in Italy, which conveyed fresh evidence that the saint had thought that bread in the sacrament remained after the consecration. The new evidence confirmed Ridley's readings in Ratramnus of Corbie. That, as well as the embarrassment of the problematic *Catechism*, may indicate that Cranmer was now ready to relinquish his endorsement of the real presence.[33]

In December 1548, the meaning of the Eucharist was debated over four days in the House of Lords. Ridley spoke vigorously. For the first time, Cranmer openly embraced the doctrine of the spiritual presence. He declared that Christ's body was taken up into heaven at his ascension when he 'left the world', which meant that his body could not be locally present in the consecrated bread and wine. To observers, like the friends of Heinrich Bullinger of Zűrich, who had long hoped to persuade Cranmer to accept their opinions, their delight was unbounded. They said, perhaps optimistically, that at last Cranmer was coming over to Zűrich's side of the controversies. 'It is all over with Lutheranism'.[34]

Dame Margaret Cranmer

Early in 1549, when the laws that prohibited the marriage of priests were repealed, for the first time, Margaret could appear openly as Cranmer's wife.[35] She had lived in eclipse for so long that many assumed that they had married only recently. When Cranmer acknowledged their two adolescent children, Margaret and Thomas, suddenly his enemies perceived that he had been married secretly for many years.

Some modest provisions were made to safeguard Margaret's future. As long ago as the 1540s, Sir William Butts had made a private appeal to Henry on behalf of Cranmer's family. As we have already noted, Cranmer had been forced to grant or sell to the king many manors belonging to the archbishopric. Henry promised to grant him properties in exchange, and in early 1547 the rectories of Whatton and Aslockton at his birthplace were made over to him. Cranmer also received lands formerly belonging to Kirkstall Abbey and Arthington Priory in Yorkshire, which were granted to him and to his heirs. They provided Margaret with the only real security she enjoyed in her widowhood.[36]

The wives of bishops were not readily accepted as ladies of rank, and we know from his will that Holbeach insisted that his wife be called by the title Dame Joan. Margaret did not live at Lambeth Palace, nor did she assume the impressive role that Katarina von Bora enjoyed when she presided as hostess at Luther's table. Instead, Margaret's position as the archbishop of Canterbury's wife remained almost completely undefined, as Matthew Parker and his wife discovered for themselves during the reign of Elizabeth. A married primate remained anomalous well into the seventeenth century. Not until after the Restoration did the wives of the archbishops of Canterbury attain a permanent position in English society.[37]

The 1549 *Book of Common Prayer*

At the conclusion of the debate on the Eucharist in the Lords, Parliament appointed a committee to make a new English liturgy. In Chapter 3, we observed that as he arrived in Nuremberg in March 1532, Cranmer was immediately fascinated when he observed Osiander's liturgy. The Epistle and Gospel lessons were read in German, and every day the congregation was taught a chapter from the New Testament.[38] For most of his tenure as archbishop, Cranmer yearned to provide a vernacular liturgy for the English Church, and he had spent years of preparation for his opportunity. We have already noted that his revision of the litany in 1544 marks the true start of the Prayer Book.[39]

The *Book of Common Prayer* was a crowning achievement in Cranmer's career. It is one of the supreme religious and literary masterpieces of sixteenth-century England.

Until recently, it was so familiar to generations of English church-goers that its contents seemed reassuring and uncontroversial. But at its introduction in 1549, Cranmer meant the *Book of Common Prayer* to be what the Renaissance scholar Brian Cummings has called 'an engine of change'. The Prayer Book was not supposed to be set or fixed, but rather, it was an adaptation that was in step with the emerging patterns of worship that Protestant Churches elsewhere had adopted. Like the *Homilies*, the language of the *Book of Common Prayer* was full of nervous energy and vivid, urgent expressions. But the *Book of Homilies* was well received. In contrast, very largely the English people did not want an English Prayer Book, and they resented its imposition.[40]

Cranmer drew upon an impressive array of sources for the *Book of Common Prayer*. Several Latin liturgies, or 'uses', were current in England at the beginning of the sixteenth century. The most common was the use of Sarum (or Salisbury), but there were others, including for York. A revised Sarum breviary with the psalms, collects, and readings for the Divine Office was printed in 1541, and it may be seen as an early step towards Cranmer's greater goal. Large portions of the Sarum Missal were translated for the *Book of Common Prayer*, and the other English uses were compared. A translation of *A Consultation*, Archbishop Hermann von Wied's extensive program to reform the administration of the sacraments in Cologne, was sponsored in 1548 by the godly Katherine, dowager duchess of Suffolk (1519–1580), and it too informed Cranmer's new Prayer Book.[41]

The 1549 *Book of Common Prayer* established the rituals of the English Church.[42] It set out a table and calendar for the readings of the psalms and lessons; the order for the services of matins and evensong for the entire year; the introits, collects, Gospels, and Epistles to be used at the celebration of the Lord's Supper, Holy Communion; the communion service itself; the litany; baptism; confirmation (with a catechism for children); the service for matrimony; a service for the visitation of the sick, for burial, and for the 'purification' of women (the special service of thanksgiving to be used after a woman gave birth); a service for Ash Wednesday; a list of ceremonies 'omitted or retained'; and notes of an explanation concerning the 'decent ministration of things contained in this book'. As we have already noted, the *Order of the Communion* introduced some of the most important passages that Cranmer used again in the Prayer Book. Much could be said about its contents, but here we will limit our discussion mainly to two topics with which Cranmer was most intimately associated: the collects, and Holy Communion.

A collect is a short petitioning prayer that was recited by the priest on behalf of the people, most notably before the lessons of the communion service. In general, they follow a fivefold pattern: the address or invocation to God the Father; an acknowledgement of God's power, or of human weakness; the actual petition concerning a specific urgent need; an aspiration of some higher purpose; and a plea. About one hundred collects appear in the 1549 Prayer Book. Most were close translations of the original Latin prayers from the Sarum Missal. Others were adaptations. About two dozen collects were Cranmer's own unique compositions.

The collects are the best and most emotive examples of Cranmer's prose. Many of them have become deeply embedded in English cultural life. In adapting them from the Sarum Missal, Cranmer was careful to eliminate any suggestion that good works merited salvation. Thus he replaced almost all of the original collects for saints' days with his own creations that emphasized the merits of Christ's sacrifice. Selections from his collects appear at the head of each chapter in this book.[43]

The most famous of all Cranmer's collects is part of the communion service, and in the 1549 Prayer Book it occurred after the institution. Known as the Prayer of Humble Access, it was said by the priest in the name of all who were about to receive communion:

> We do not presume to come to this thy table (O merciful lord) trusting in our own righteousness, but in thy manifold and great mercies: we be not worthy so much as to gather up the crumbs under thy table, but thou art the same lord whose property is always to have mercy: Grant us therefore

(gracious lord) so to eat the flesh of thy dear son Jesus Christ, and to drink his blood in these holy Mysteries, that we may continually dwell in him, and he in us, that our sinful bodies may be made clean by his body, and our souls washed through his most precious blood.[44]

The 1549 Prayer Book called the Eucharist 'the Supper or the Lord, and the Holy Communion, commonly called the Mass'. The service marked a dramatic departure from the medieval Mass as well as a fundamental break from the teaching of the Lutherans.

The service of Holy Communion was not a sacrifice. Christ made his one oblation on the cross, but at the Last Supper on the night before he suffered, he commanded that a perpetual memory of his death be celebrated in the Eucharist. The dogmas of transubstantiation and the real presence were implicitly rejected, even as Christ was truly present spiritually. In a long exhortation following the homily, the officiant was to remind the people that 'the benefit is great, if with a truly penitent heart and lively faith' they received the holy sacrament, when they 'spiritually' ate the flesh of Christ and drank his blood, for 'then we dwell in Christ and Christ in us'. The Host was not to be elevated or shown to be gazed upon, which, until the *Order of the Communion* was released in 1548, had been one of the most common acts of devotion. The bread and wine were no longer the focus themselves, but rather, the emphasis of the service was on their reception and on the benefits to the souls of those who received them worthily.[45]

Just as the new Prayer Book was to provide uniformity for the entire realm by replacing the Sarum and other uses, the *Book of Common Prayer* was also designed to replace the psalters, primers, and books of hours that still enjoyed flourishing interest among laypeople at every level of society, whose devotions to the saints Cranmer thought distracted their readers from the full meaning of the sacrifice of Christ. In the *Book of Homilies*, the 'homily of good works' ended with a long denunciation of the 'papistical superstition and abuses' of traditional devotions, including the recitation of the rosary and the prayers of the psalter of Our Lady, which were still cherished by many people. By removing shrines, Cranmer eliminated numberless objects of local devotion. He intended to reduce the shock of the new especially by his sensitive attention to language, but many people were disturbed by the suppression of the Latin Mass in the Prayer Book. In effect, the appeal to a wide spectrum of opinion that Henry thought essential for the peace of his realm was cautiously abandoned by Somerset's government.[46]

The *Prayer Book* risings, 1549

The *Book of Common Prayer* was ordered to be placed in all parish churches by Whitsunday, 9 June 1549. It arrived on the heels of the destruction of images and the removal of crosses in churches across England, as well as the dissolution of the chantries, which had begun in 1547. Silver and gold ornaments were confiscated from parish churches to pay for the government's wars in Scotland and France as England's currency was devalued. So much land had been diverted into the hands of the gentry from the closure of the religious houses that the economy still had not had time to adapt.

Dissatisfaction was already widespread, and now the new *Book of Common Prayer*, with its unfamiliar English liturgy, triggered immediate resistance. Risings began first in Cornwall and then spread to Devon. They were the most dangerous domestic threat to the realm since the Lincolnshire Rebellion and Pilgrimage of Grace of 1536–1537. In June 1549, Exeter was besieged, but Somerset was slow to respond. Fleeing Oxford, Vermigli took refuge at Lambeth Palace. Londoners were alarmed. On 21 July 1549, Cranmer came in great state to St Paul's to pray for an end to the commotions, which he said went against God's commandments and the true obedience King Edward was owed as the supreme head of the English Church.[47] At the end of the summer the risings in the west were suppressed with great violence by soldiers acting under the direction of the Lord Privy Seal, Lord John Russell (d. 1555), whose victory that Cranmer celebrated at St Paul's. The village of Clyst St Mary near Exeter was burned, and many hundreds were killed.[48]

Further resistance broke out in East Anglia towards harvest time, where the discontent had been fuelled by Somerset's agrarian policies. The rebellion was led by Robert Kett (ex. 1549), whose forces occupied Norwich. Here too Somerset's response left much to be desired, especially as he offered pardons to the insurgents before he secured their submission. Compared with Henry's energetic repression of the north in 1536, Somerset did not seem sufficiently interested in quelling the revolts. Although he had seen battle in Scotland and France during the last reign, he refused to lead an army into the field now. An initial attempt to retake Norwich failed dismally. In August 1549, John Dudley, now earl of Warwick, led a sizeable force into Norfolk, and he defeated Kett. At least two thousand rebels were killed. The new king of France, Henri II (1519–1559), took advantage of the risings to attack Boulogne, which was in English hands. Thus the threat to the young king's government intensified.

In the midst of the crisis, Sir Anthony Denny and Cranmer's friend William Benson (the dean of Westminster) both died.[49] By early October 1549, Somerset lost the confidence of many members of the nobility and gentry, and a coup was planned against him by Warwick and other members of the Privy Council. Somerset feared that Edward was at risk, and he issued a summons for the king's subjects to protect the king from a dangerous plot against his rule. In one of the most dramatic episodes of the reign, on the evening of 5–6 October, Cranmer rode with Edward under the protection of a heavy guard when Somerset suddenly moved the king from Hampton Court to greater safety at Windsor Castle.[50] Probably Edward was in no real danger, but he was kept close, almost as a hostage, to protect his uncle Somerset, whose appeal for assistance failed to attract serious support. A few days later, Cranmer, with William Lord Paget, persuaded Somerset to surrender, and on 11 October the Lord Protector was arrested and removed to the Tower. The Protectorship was at an end.[51]

The king's privy chamber was reorganized, and the Privy Council began to rule as a body. By the end of the year, out of a period of dangerous disarray, Warwick emerged as England's real leader on the strength of the military support he enjoyed. In February 1550, he assumed the title of lord president of the Privy Council, and he was made duke of Northumberland the following year. Northumberland was willing to continue the religious reforms that Somerset had sponsored, but as we will see, Cranmer's relationship with him was difficult. In 1550, Somerset was briefly rehabilitated, but Northumberland saw him as a threat, and in early 1552 he was executed. Northumberland dominated the government until the end of the reign.

Martin Bucer in England

Cranmer invited Martin Bucer to take refuge in England in October 1548, and he arrived with Paul Fagius (*c.* 1504–1549) the following April, as the Prayer Book disturbances began. Of all the theologians who arrived in England at Cranmer's invitation, Bucer was undoubtedly the most eminent.[52]

We have already observed that Bucer had played a major role in the Reformation from its earliest years. In 1518, as a Dominican friar, he had attended Luther's disputation in Heidelberg. Deeply moved by his message, Bucer left his religious order, and he was among the first of the reformers to marry. From 1523 he was a tireless preacher and writer. Working closely with Wolfgang Capito and other civic leaders, Bucer brought about the abolition of the Catholic Mass in Strasbourg in 1529. At the same time, Bucer became attracted to Zwingli's thinking, and he accepted Zwingli's opinion that the Lord's Supper was a memorial of Christ's death.[53]

Through much of his career, Bucer endeavoured to find common doctrinal ground that would lead the Lutherans and the Zwinglians to agree on the meaning of the Eucharist. He took part in a number of colloquies in the hope of building consensus. In February 1536, five years after Zwingli's death, Bucer and Capito met in Basel to hold discussions with Simon Grynaeus and Heinrich Bullinger, which resulted in the First Helvetic Confession. When they agreed that Christ's natural body could not be locally present in the Eucharist, they subtly modified Zwingli's original opinion. Instead, they agreed that the bread and wine were holy and true 'signs', offered to believers by the Lord himself, as nourishing food for spiritual and eternal life. Three months later, on the strength of the First Helvetic Confession, Bucer and Capito signed the Wittenberg Concord with Luther and Melanchthon. However, the ultimate prize of Protestant consensus was lost when the Wittenberg Concord was subsequently rejected by Swiss Reformers.[54] Undeterred, in the 1540s, Bucer redoubled his efforts by holding talks with Catholic leaders, including Luther's old foe Johannes Eck. Bucer also assisted Archbishop Hermann with the reformation in Cologne, and we have already noted the influence his *Consultation* had on the *Book of Common Prayer*.[55] After the *Consensus Tigurinus* (or the Consensus of Zürich) was framed from late 1548, a figurative understanding of the Eucharist emerged as the new agreement for Reformed Protestants. However, Bucer earned Bullinger's lasting enmity for his willingness to compromise, and Swiss Reformers observed his arrival in England with deep suspicion.

Bucer and Fagius spend their first six months with Cranmer at Lambeth and Croydon. Cranmer and Bucer were inseparable, which caused Bullinger's friends to fear that Cranmer was being unduly led by him. He was given the Regius chair in Divinity at Cambridge, the corresponding professorship that Vermigli already occupied at Oxford.[56]

Before the Prayer Book risings occurred, in early 1549 Vermigli led a formal debate on the meaning of the Eucharist at Oxford, and he summarized his positions in his *Treatise on the Sacrament of the Eucharist*. Like other Protestants, he rejected transubstantiation, but he was also critical of the views of both Luther and Zwingli. The disagreements between them encouraged 'contention and strife', which Vermigli (like Bucer) wanted to avoid.

For Vermigli, Christ reigned in heaven, where he was bodily present at the right hand of the Father, as the Creed taught. Christ did not descend corporally into the consecrated Host and wine. Instead, the presence of Christ in the Eucharist was spiritual in nature. Vermigli compared the Eucharist with baptism, the one other true sacrament that was established by Christ in the Gospels. In baptism, the nature or the substance of the water did not change, Vermigli argued. Nor did the bread and wine change into a different substance. Rather, change occurred in the souls of those who worthily received communion. Through Christ's institution, the priest's pronouncement of the word of Holy Scripture, and the operation of the Holy Spirit, the sacraments had their strength and efficacy. Baptism was a spiritual birth and a nativity for the soul. Just as the soul of the person being baptized was changed, so too were the souls of those who worthily ate the bread and wine of the Lord's Supper, which was spiritual food. Christ's flesh fed the soul. The bread of the Eucharist was spiritual bread and an allegory of Christ's unique sacrifice on the cross for humankind.[57]

Vermigli's and Bucer's work provided Cranmer with valuable support in the strides he was making to reform the English Church, and he was able to make more overt statements about the Lord's Supper in his book, *A Defence of the True and Catholic Doctrine*, which appeared in 1550. All sides of the Eucharistic controversies claimed the power of the word 'Catholic' for themselves. Using stark language, Cranmer denounced transubstantiation and the idea that the Mass is a sacrifice as the 'weeds' of 'popish doctrine' that had been sown in the Lord's vineyard by his adversaries, the devil and Antichrist. 'Christ is the true and perfect nourishment, both of body and soul'. Our souls are fed by Christ. We feed 'upon him to our spiritual strength and perfection'. Christ's body and blood are 'received with a pure heart, and a sincere faith'. Our sins are forgiven by his sacrifice on the cross.[58]

Cranmer's *Defence* also attacked Gardiner's belief in the real presence, which he had expressed in his 1546 book, the *Detection of the devil's sophistry*. Cranmer noted that Bucer's idea of a 'true' presence of Christ in the Eucharist disagreed with Gardiner's. As Cranmer described it, Bucer 'denieth utterly that Christ is really and substantially present in the bread, either by conversion or inclusion'. Bucer's opinion 'dissenteth in nothing' from the views expressed by Oecolampadius or Zwingli. But in the ministration of the Lord's Supper, 'he affirmeth Christ to be present, and so do I also'.[59]

Reading the *Defence* in the Tower, Gardiner was amazed by the directions that Cranmer's opinions had taken. They had long been enemies, but a belief in the real presence was one of the few points of seeming agreement that had existed between them. Now Gardiner believed that Cranmer had fallen headlong into heresy. For the rest of their lives, Cranmer and Gardiner were locked in bitter contention about the Eucharist. Gardiner's response, an *Assertion of the true Catholic faith*, was smuggled out of the Tower and printed in Rouen in 1551. We have already noted that Gardiner had no theoretical framework beyond obedience to the king as supreme head of the Church for the directions the English Church had taken under Henry VIII. Implacably opposed to the decisions that had been made since the old king's death, Gardiner began to prepare for his own return to the papacy.[60]

Cranmer responded to Gardiner's *Assertion* immediately in his *Answer* of 1551, which he also aimed at Smyth, who had fled to Louvain rather than debate Vermigli at Oxford. Cranmer's *Answer* conveys some of the direct statements concerning the Eucharist that he ever committed to paper. No one should 'grossly' think that we eat Christ with our mouth, but rather we eat him 'with our faith'. Bodily, Christ is 'in the eternal life and glory with his father' in heaven, and 'we are made partakers with him of his nature, to be immortal, and have eternal life and glory with him'. Christ was not bound to one locality or to a single era, for even before the Incarnation, faithful people had shared in his Supper. Christ is fully present spiritually in his Supper. Christ is present fully in his life, in his sacrifice, and in his resurrection. We 'are made partakers with him of his nature, to be immortal, and have eternal life and glory with him'.[61]

In the words of the Church historian Alec Ryrie, the Reformed doctrine of the Eucharist was late in coming to England, but upon arrival in the reign of the young King Edward it 'seized the reins' under Cranmer's leadership.[62] During the debate on the Eucharist in the House of Lords in 1548, several bishops had revealed themselves resistant to further change. One by one, Cranmer deprived and imprisoned them. Gardiner remained a prisoner until the end of the reign. In February 1551, after a lengthy process that involved interminable hearings and depositions, Gardiner was deprived of his bishopric. Winchester was given to Cranmer's protégé John Ponet (c. 1514–1556). Ridley was translated to London to replace Edmund Bonner in early 1550.[63] Encouraged by Bucer's views that a table was more suitable than an altar in calling communicants to the Lord's Supper (because altars had been misused by the Mass to re-enact Christ's sacrifice), Ridley ordered that altars be removed from every church throughout his diocese. By the end of the year the Privy Council extended the mandate to the entire realm.[64] Altars were replaced by simple tables.

The execution of Joan Bocher, 1550

Waves of refugees continued to come to England as the Interim was imposed, and among them were Anabaptists, whose presence caused the government renewed alarm. In April and May 1549, Cranmer examined several Anabaptists at St Paul's and at Lambeth. Three men were exposed to humiliation at Paul's Cross.[65]

The most notable of those accused was Joan Bocher of Kent, who already had a long history as a heretic. In 1528, she had been questioned, perhaps for Lollard beliefs, by Cuthbert Tunstall when he was bishop of London. In the early 1540s, she had spoken against the sacrament of the altar, but Christopher Nevinson, the archbishop's commissary, released her without punishment, a fact that was used against Cranmer in the Prebendaries' Plot in 1543. Now she had been persuaded by Anabaptist refugees that Christ's flesh was celestial in nature, which meant she denied Jesus' full humanity. She was condemned before Cranmer on 29 April 1549, and she was held in the Newgate Prison, where many divines, including Bishop Ridley and Hugh Latimer, tried to persuade her to retract her opinions. In her examinations, she associated herself with the same ideas that Anne Askew had expressed in 1546, although it was obvious that her views had become much more radical than Askew's. Bocher refused to submit, and after a full year in prison, she was burnt at Smithfield on 2 May 1550.[66]

The Stranger churches and the crisis of non-conformity, 1550–1551

The refugees from the continent joined a substantial number of foreign merchants and workmen who, since the middle ages, had taken up residence in London's Steelyard. In 1549 Bucer petitioned the Privy Council on their behalf, and in mid-1550, two 'Stranger' congregations for French and Dutch refugees were given the extraordinary privilege to found their own churches and to worship by their own liturgies. They were served by John à Lasco (or Jan Laski, 1499–1560). Cranmer wrote to invite him and Melanchthon to England in mid-1548.[67] Originally from Poland, Lasco had been acquainted in the 1520s with Jacques Lefèvre in Paris and Erasmus in Basel. More recently, he had been the superintendent of churches in Emden and throughout East Friesland. Upon his arrival in England in 1549, he lived at Lambeth, and in mid-1550 he was made superintendent over the Stranger Churches in London. Lasco was instrumental in gaining the grant of the former house of the Austin friars as a church for the strangers.[68]

Working closely with him was John Hooper (d. 1555), one of the most dynamic of the English Protestants who had gone into exile during Henry's reign. Hooper had travelled first to Strasbourg and then to Zürich, where he studied with Bullinger. There he wrote a denunciation of Gardiner's *Detection of the devil's sophistry*, in which he accused Winchester of manipulations that would blind the laity from the truth.[69] Upon his return to England in May 1549, Hooper's rise was spectacular. He immediately gained Somerset's favour, and he became an energetic leader among the foreigners. Nothing seemed to impede his progress. In Lent 1550 he delivered a series of sermons at court that stirred Edward to offer him the bishopric of Gloucester, even though Hooper took strong exception to the new *Ordinal* Cranmer had just released.

Although Cranmer had simplified clerical dress, he considered the surplice and the cope to be essential emblems of the office of a bishop. They were required by the Prayer Book and the *Ordinal*. Bishops-elect were to present themselves for consecration wearing surplices and copes. The *Ordinal* also required candidates to take the supremacy oath.[70] Provocatively, Hooper argued in his court sermons that clerical dress belonged to the contested category of *adiaphora* or 'things indifferent' that were not required for Church discipline, and he refused to accept the bishopric.

For his recalcitrance, Hooper was summoned before the Privy Council on Ascension Day 1550, when Cranmer spoke against him severely, especially because he criticized the supremacy oath as 'shameful and impious' for its reference to the saints. Rather surprisingly, Hooper was granted permission to be consecrated without the vestments, and for a brief moment it seemed as if, against Cranmer's wishes, he would be the catalyst for an immediate revision of the Prayer Book that would strip away the last vestiges of traditional doctrine.[71]

But despite the instructions of the Privy Council, Ridley refused to consecrate Hooper except by the ritual approved by Parliament in the *Ordinal*. A long controversy about Hooper's ordination ensued. Vermigli and Bucer were canvassed for their opinions, and although they disliked vestments *per se*, they decided that clerical dress could be defined by the government. Warwick insisted that the king must be obeyed and Hooper must conform. After a period of imprisonment at Lambeth Palace, Hooper submitted. In 1551 he was consecrated wearing the garments he hated.[72] Hooper was brought into line because conformity to ecclesiastical rules was essential in the state Church that Cranmer built, though his opposition to clerical vestments opened a controversy whose repercussions would cause trouble to Archbishop Parker and the Elizabethan Church in the Vestiarian controversy in the 1560s.[73]

Lasco tirelessly supported Hooper even though he risked hurting the cause of the Stranger churches. Like Hooper, the Stranger Churches were aligned with Zűrich, and they worried Cranmer and Ridley for the potential disunity they could encourage when the regime was already faced with unrest. Lasco was more an organizer than a theologian, and while he was in London, he was developing forms of worship that implicitly challenged the Prayer Book. He stressed the performance of the Eucharistic rite as a participatory action, and he did not believe that Christ was present spiritually in the bread and wine. Following the practice of the apostles in the Primitive Church, each congregation was to elect its own elders, deacons, and ministers. The role of the superintendent, as Lasco envisioned it, was even more powerful than the office of a bishop in encouraging strict discipline. Lasco fled England after Edward's death. In the mid-1550s, first in Emden and then in Frankfort, he was able to bring his vision for ecclesiastical organization to fruition in his book, the *Forma ac ratio*, which proved to be enormously influential.[74] But in the meantime, Ridley kept a watchful eye on the Stranger Churches. In early 1551, George van Parris was excommunicated by the Dutch Stranger Church, and in March at Lambeth he was condemned by Cranmer. He was burnt at Smithfield on 24 April 1551.[75] The executions of Joan Bocher and George van Parris, like Hooper's submission, defined the furthest boundaries of England's 'broad Church' in Edward's reign under Cranmer.

The 1552 *Book of Common Prayer*

Another disputation on matters of doctrine was held at Cambridge from June to August 1550, when Bucer defended justification by faith and the sufficiency of Scripture against three conservative fellows, that included Andrew Perne (d. 1589) and John Young. In September, Lasco visited Bucer, and they came to an agreement in every subject except the presence of Christ in the Lord's Supper. Bucer never conceded his position on the true presence.[76]

Before Bucer died at Cambridge in March 1551, he gave Bishop Thomas Goodrich of Ely a detailed commentary on the first Prayer Book, which Vermigli later saw and approved. The removal of altars from parish churches meant that the communion service had to be adapted once again, and it intensified the understanding of the Eucharist as a memorial of Christ's death and sacrifice. Now the priest was also a minister, and at the Lord's Supper, he advised the people to 'Take and eat this, in remembrance that Christ died for thee, and feed on him in thy heart by faith with thanksgiving'.[77]

The new Prayer Book was scheduled to be released at All Hallows Day, 1 November 1552, but in a sermon delivered at Windsor in late September, after the book went to the press, the royal chaplain John Knox (d. 1572) raised strenuous objections against its directions that the people kneel at communion. He complained that kneeling was offensive and reminiscent of Roman practice. Sitting, rather than kneeling, was the correct way to take communion, he said. The Privy Council halted the printing until the matter could be reconsidered. Deeply angered, Cranmer objected that the text had already been approved by Parliament and the king, and therefore the Privy Council had no authority to order changes. He denounced Knox as an 'unquiet spirit' and a troublemaker who had to be brought into line. Cranmer drafted an additional rubric that explained that kneeling did not imply adoration of any real presence in the bread and wine. It was hurriedly printed, but not in red, as it should have been, and the 'black rubric' was tipped into the Prayer Book as an authorized afterthought.[78]

On All Hallows Day, Bishop Ridley conducted the first service from the new Prayer Book in St Paul's Cathedral, and he preached that afternoon at the Cross before the assembled mayor and alderman in a show of authority. The high altar in the cathedral was broken down, and a communion table was set up in the lower choir. The next round of confiscations began in the following spring, and commissioners removed any remaining jewels, plate, candlesticks, chalices, and embroidered vestments from churches across the country.[79]

A Protestant answer to the Council of Trent

At the beginning of 1552, Cranmer probably occupied the most advantageous position among the Protestant leaders of western Europe. Hermann von Wied of Cologne died in August, and although he had been deprived in 1547, he and Cranmer were in contact until the end of his life. Unlike the misfortunes suffered by so many of his friends on the continent, Cranmer's place seemed secure and his prince was encouraging. At last he was in position to be able to work towards the realization of his greatest goal: to encourage all Protestant leaders to reconcile their disagreements about doctrine, especially the Eucharist. Cranmer wanted to hold a summit meeting, a 'godly synod', to be held in England or in some other safe place, that he envisioned would be the Protestant answer to the Roman Church's Council of Trent. The *Consensus Tigurinus* was agreed between Bullinger and Calvin in 1549. Now Cranmer yearned to heal the painful breach that continued to divide the Swiss Reformers from the Lutherans. Once again Cranmer invited Philip Melanchthon to England, now to succeed Bucer in the Regius Chair of Divinity at Cambridge.[80]

Calvin responded to Cranmer's invitation immediately with approbation and encouragement. He warned Cranmer about being influenced further by Osiander, with whom Calvin had recently had serious disagreements about justification. Osiander had continued to defend the role of private penance in salvation, which caused Calvin to denounce him in the *Institutes*.[81] Calvin urged Cranmer to persevere with his reforms until something was achieved, even if at first 'things do not turn out according to your wish'.[82]

Had a Protestant version of Trent taken place under Cranmer's leadership, his reputation would have been assured for all time. He was on the threshold of his greatest achievements. His rivals in England had been sidelined. In late 1552, Cuthbert Tunstall was deprived of the bishopric of Durham, and he was sent to join Norfolk and Gardiner in the Tower. Goodrich, one of his oldest friends, was lord chancellor. His ally Sir John Cheke was one of the Privy Council's principal secretaries. Conformity was upheld in the submission of Bishop Hooper and the defeat of Knox. The doctrines of the English Church were defined in the *Forty-Two Articles*. The second edition of the *Book of Common Prayer* was issued, and Cranmer had already begun work on the third. The long-desired revision of the canons of the English Church was approaching completion. Cranmer was recognized across Europe as one of the greatest defenders of the Protestant Church, and he anticipated a meeting among its leaders that would heal the disagreements concerning the Eucharist that had haunted them for the past quarter century. Moreover, his marriage was successful and his daughter and son were nearly grown.

But in a little more than six months, suddenly the hopes and achievements of a lifetime were snatched away.

Notes

1 One of the most famous collects Cranmer prepared for the first prayer book, which is read for the twenty-fifth Sunday after Trinity. Associated with the beginning of Advent, for generations it has served as a reminder to 'stir up' for the Christmas feast. *The booke of the common prayer and administracion of the sacramentes and other rites and ceremonies of the Churche: after the vse of the Churche of England* (London: Edward Whitchurch, March 1549, *RSTC* 16267), 97–8.
2 Gardiner, *Letters*, no. 117; Duffy, *Altars*, 449–50.
3 Gardiner, *Letters*, no. 117.
4 Wriothesley, *Chronicle*, 1, 183.
5 Wriothesley, *Chronicle*, 1, 184–5, MacCulloch, *Cranmer*, 370.
6 *The epistle of the famous and great clerke Philip Melancton made vnto oure late Souereygne Lorde Kynge Henry the eight, for the reuoking and abolishing of the six articles*, trans. John Careless? (Wesel [Antwerp], May 1547, *RSTC* 17789).
7 Richard Smyth, *The assertion and defence of the sacramente of the aulter* (London: John Herford, 1546, *RSTC* 22815), and *A defence of the blessed masse, and the sacrifice therof* (London: John Hertford, 22 July 1546, *RSTC* 22820).
8 Psalm 116:2; Romans 3:4; Richard Smyth, *A godly and faythfull retractation* (London: Reginald Wolfe, 1547, *RSTC* 22822), and *A playne declaration made at Oxforde the 24. daye of July* (London: Rayner Wolfe, 1547, *RSTC* 22824); Wriothesley, *Chronicle*, 1, p. 184; T. Kirby, 'Public Conversion: Richard Smyth's "Retraction" at Paul's Cross in 1547', in *Paul's Cross and the Culture of Persuasion in England, 1520–1640*, eds. T. Kirby and P. G. Stanwood, Studies in the History of Christian Tradition Series, 171 (Leiden, 2014), 161–73.
9 Gardiner, *Letters*, nos. 122, 123, 124.
10 *Certayne sermons or homilies appoynted by the kynges Maiestie, to be declared and redde, by all persones, Uycars, or Curates, euery*

   Sonday in their churches, where they haue cure (London: Edward
   Whitchurch, 20 August 1547, RSTC 13641).
11 Gardiner attributed to Cranmer the Homily of Salvation: *Letters*,
   no. 124.
12 *Certayne sermons or homilies*, sig. ✠2r.
13 Gardiner, quoting Cranmer, in *Letters*, no. 124, at p. 311. See
   R. B. Bond, ed., *Certain Sermons or Homilies (1547) and a
   Homily Against Disobedience and Wilful Rebellion: A Critical
   Edition* (Toronto, 1987); S. Wabuda, *Preaching during the English
   Reformation* (Cambridge, 2002), 27–33, and also my 'Bishops and
   the Provision of Homilies, 1520 to 1547', SCJ, 25, 551–66.
14 *Certayne sermons or homilies*, sigs. ¶1r–¶6v, quotations at sigs.
   ¶1r–¶2r.
15 *Certayne sermons or homilies*, sigs. ¶¶1r–¶¶¶2v, quotations at sigs.
   ¶¶1r–¶¶4r, citing (among other texts) Psalm 13:3; Romans 3:11–28.
16 *Certayne sermons or homilies*, sigs. ¶¶¶3r–¶¶¶¶¶3r.
17 *Certayne sermons or homilies*, sigs. ¶¶¶¶¶2r; Bond, Certain *Sermons
   or Homilies (1547)*, p. 86.
18 *Certayne sermons or homilies*, A1r–C1r.
19 *Certayne sermons or homilies*, C2r–E3v, quotation at sig. C4r, and
   Bond, *Certain Sermons or Homilies (1547)*, 105. For Lefèvre, see
   Chapter 2.
20 *Certayne sermons or homilies*, U2v; *Martin Bucer and the Book of
   Common Prayer*, ed. E. C. Whitaker, Alcuin Club, 55 (1974), 46–9.
21 TNA: PRO, SP 10/2, 122r–v.
22 Gardiner, *Letters*, nos. 121, 289; 124, 306.
23 *Martin Bucer and the Book of Common Prayer*, 46–7.
24 Gardiner, *Letters*, no. 135; Foxe (1563), 803–4; AM, 6, 217, 140–2.
25 S. J. Weinreich, 'Two unpublished letters of Stephen Gardiner, August–
   September 1547 (Bodleian Library, Oxford, MS Eng. th. b. 2)', *JEH*,
   67 (2016), 819–33 (quote 833).
26 Wriothesley, *Chronicle*, 2, 1; Duffy, *Altars*, 453–4; MacCulloch,
   Cranmer, 371–2.
27 Wriothesley, *Chronicle*, 1, 187.
28 *The works of Nicholas Ridley, sometime lord bishop of London, martyr,
   1555*, ed. H. Christmas, PS (1843), 265; MacCulloch, *Cranmer*, 378–9.
29 Wriothesley, *Chronicle*, 1, 187; Diarmaid MacCulloch, 'Parliament
   and the Reformation of Edward VI', *Parliamentary History*, 34
   (2015), 383–400.
30 *The Order of the Communion* (London: Richard Grafton, 8 March
   1548, RSTC 16456.5), sigs. B4r (General Confession), C1v (chalice).
31 *Cathechismvs That is to say a shorte instruction into Christian religion for the synguler commoditie and profyte of children and yong
   people* (London: Nicholas Hill, 1548, RSTC 5992.5), 235r.

32 Cranmer, *Lord's Supper*, p. 226; D. G. Selwyn, 'A Neglected Edition of Cranmer's Catechism', *Journal of Theological Studies*, 15 (1965), 76–91; P. Wilson-Kastner, 'Andreas Osiander's Probable Influence on Thomas Cranmer's Eucharistic Theology', *SCJ*, 14 (1983), 411–25; P. Collinson, 'Thomas Cranmer and the Truth' in *From Cranmer to Sancroft*. (London, 2006), 1–14; MacCulloch, *Cranmer*, 384–92; B. A. Gerrish, 'The Reformation and the Eucharist', in *Thinking with the Church: Essays in Historical Theology* (Cambridge, 2010), 229–58.

33 MacCulloch, *Cranmer*, 391–2.

34 *OL*, 1, no. 152, 2, no. 186; B. Hall, 'Martin Bucer in England', in *Martin Bucer: Reforming Church and Community*, ed. D. F. Wright (Cambridge, 1994), 144–75, especially, 149; MacCulloch, *Cranmer*, 382–3; A. Ryrie, 'The Strange Death of Lutheran England', *JEH*, 53 (2002), 64–92.

35 2 & 3 Edward VI, c. 21.

36 Morice, 263; F. R. H. Du Boulay, 'Archbishop Cranmer and the Canterbury Temporalities', *EHR*, vol. 67 (1952), 19–36.

37 Ridley, *Cranmer*, 146–7; P. Collinson, *Religion of Protestants: The Church in English Society 1559–1625* (Oxford, 1982), 37; Collinson, 'Thomas Cranmer and the Truth', 16; E. J. Carlson, *Marriage and the English Reformation* (Oxford: Blackwell, 1994), 57–65. See Holbeach's 1551 will: TNA:PRO, PROB 11/34, 212r–213r at 212v.

38 Sir Thomas Elyot to the Duke of Norfolk, 14 March 1532, BL, Cotton MS Vitellius B/XXI, 59r (*LP*, 5, no. 869).

39 Cranmer's letter of 7 October 1544, printed in *Miscellaneous*, no. 276. See the perceptive comments of B. Cummings in *The Book of Common Prayer: The Texts of 1549, 1559, and 1662*, (Oxford, 2011), xxiii. Also, Duffy, *Altars*, 443, 452. In the 1549 *Book of Common Prayer* the 'Letany and Suffrages' appears before the section on Public Baptism. It is not mentioned on the Contents page of the first Prayer Book, whose pagination in every printing is unreliable.

40 For much of my discussion here, I am indebted to Cummings's recent edition of *The Book of Common Prayer: The Texts of 1549, 1559, and 1662*, xi–xiv; Bond, *Certain Sermons or Homilies (1547)*, 33.

41 Hermann von Wied, *A simple, and religious Consultation* (London: John Daye and William Seres, 1548, *RSTC* 13214). Katherine's arms are printed at the beginning of the book.

42 Of the many printings of the 1549 Book of Common Prayer, I have used the following for my references: *The booke of the common prayer and administracion of the sacramentes and other rites and ceremonies of the Churche: after the vse of the Churche of England* (London: Edward Whitchurch, March 1549, *RSTC* 16267); and *The*

booke of the common praier and administration of the sacramentes, and other rites and ceremonies of the churche: after the vse of the Churche of Englande (London: Richard Grafton, March 1549, RSTC 16268). See also *The Book of Common Prayer*, ed. Cummings.

43 G. Cuming, *The Godly Order: Texts and Studies Relating to the Book of Common Prayer*, Alcuin Club, 65 (1983), 56–62; J. A. Devereux, 'Reformed Doctrine in the Collects of the First *Book of Common Prayer*', *Harvard Theological Review*, 58 (1965), 49–68; *The Collects of Thomas Cranmer*, comps. C. F. Barbee and P. F. M. Zahl (Cambridge, 1999), x–xi (which does not, however, reproduce any of Cranmer's collects for saints' days).

44 *The booke of the common praier* (*RSTC* 16268), 130r–130v.

45 Duffy, *Altars*, 91–130, 448–503; Gerrish, 'The Reformation and the Eucharist', 252; Hall, 'Bucer', 151.

46 Bond, *Certain Sermons or Homilies*, 104; Devereux, 'The Collects', 67–8; Duffy, *Stripping of the Altars*, 450–4.

47 Wriothesley, *Chronicle*, 2, 16–18.

48 Wriothesley, *Chronicle*, 2, 20; Duffy, *Altars*, 467–8; E. H. Shagan, 'Protector Somerset and the 1549 Rebellions: New Sources and New Perspectives', *EHR*, 114 (1999), 34–63. Somerset's brother, Thomas Seymour, Baron Seymour of Sudeley, was executed in early 1549, after he was accused for attempting to gain control of the king.

49 Benson's will was made 10 September 1549 and proved 23 September 1549, TNA:PRO, PROB 11/32, 290r–291v.

50 Hooper to Bullinger, 5 February 1550, *OL*, 1, no. 37.

51 Wriothesley, *Chronicle*, 2, 25–8.

52 Cranmer to Bucer, 2 October 1548, *Miscellaneous*, letter no. 287; Hall, 'Bucer', 145.

53 See especially the entry on Bucer in the *ODNB* by N. S. Amos.

54 The First Helvetic Confession of 1536, printed in A. C. Cochrane, *Reformed Confessions of the Sixteenth Century* (Louisville, 2003), article 22; B. A. Gerrish, 'The Reformation and the Eucharist', 229–58.

55 See the entry on Bucer in the *ODNB* by N. S. Amos.

56 Hall, 'Bucer', 145–50.

57 Peter Martyr Vermigli, *Tractatio de sacramento eucharistiae* (London: Rayner Wolfe, 1549, *RSTC* 24673) translated by Nicholas Udall as Vermigli's *A discourse or traictise . . . wherein he openly declared his whole and determinate iudgemente concernynge the sacrament of the Lordes supper* (London: Robert Stoughton [Edward Whitchurch], 1550, *RSTC* 24665), especially 19v–21r, 45v, 47r, 68v, 91v–92r, 106r.

58 Thomas Cranmer, *A Defence of the True and Catholique Doctrine* (London: Reginald Wolfe 1550, *RSTC* 6000), *3v, 9v, 11r, 13r, 14r.

59 Cranmer, *Lord's Supper*, 225; P. Brooks, *Thomas Cranmer's Doctrine of the Eucharist* (London, 1965), 72–111; Gerrish, 'The Reformation and the Eucharist', 239.

60 Stephen Gardiner, *A detection of the Deuils sophistrie* (London: John Herford, 1546, *RSTC* 11591), and *An explication and assertion of the true Catholique fayth, touchyng the moost blessed sacrament of the aulter with confutacion of a booke written agaynst the same* ([Rouen]: 1551, *RSTC* 11592).

61 *An answer of the Most Reuerend Father in God Thomas Archebyshop of Canterburye, primate of all Englande and metropolitane vnto a crafty and sophisticall cauillation deuised by Stephen Gardiner doctour of law, late byshop of Winchester, agaynst the trewe and godly doctrine of the moste holy sacrament of the body and bloud of our sauiour Iesu Christe Wherein is also, as occasion serueth, answered such places of the booke of D. Rich. Smyth, as may seeme any thing woorthy the aunsweryng.* (London: Raynold Wolfe, 1551, *RSTC* 5991), reprinted in *Lord's Supper.*

62 Ryrie, 'Death of Lutheran England', 68.

63 Wriothesley, *Chronicle*, 2, 24, 33–4.

64 Hall, 'Bucer', 158; MacCulloch, 'Parliament and the Reformation of Edward VI', 391–6.

65 Wriothesley, *Chronicle*, 2, 10–13.

66 LPL, Cranmer's Register, 74r–79r, Wriothesley, *Chronicle*, 2, 37–8.

67 Cranmer to Lasco 6 July, 1548, *Miscellaneous*, letter no. 285.

68 Andrew Pettegree, *Foreign Protestant Communities in Sixteenth-Century London* (Oxford, 1986), 9–31.

69 John Hooper, *An answer vnto my lord of Wynchesters booke intytlyd a detection of the deuyls Sophistrye* (Zürich: Augustine Fries, 1547, *RSTC* 13741), sig. X3r.

70 *The forme and maner of makyng and consecratyng of Archebishoppes Bishoppes, Priestes and Deacons* (London: Richard Grafton, March [1550], *RSTC* 16462), especially I2r.

71 *APC*, vol. 3, 30–1, 42–4; Hooper to Bullinger, *OL*, 1, nos. 37, 39; Micronius to Bullinger, *OL* 2, nos. 260, 263–4, 267, 270; Hall, 'Bucer', 151–2; Pettegree, *Foreign Protestant Communities*, 31–4.

72 Hooper to Bullinger, *OL*, 1, no. 39; Micronius to Bullinger, 2, nos. 260, 263–4, 267, 270; Pettegree, *Foreign Protestant Communities*, 37–40.

73 Karl Gunther, *Reformation Unbound: Protestant Visions of Reform in England, 1525–1590* (Cambridge, 2014), especially Chapter 6.

74 Pettegree, *Foreign Protestant Communities*, 73–6; Hall, 'Bucer', 153–4; John à Lasco, *Forma ac ratio tota ecclesiastici ministerij, in peregrinorum, potissimùm uerò Germanorum Ecclesia instituta*

Londini in Anglia, per pientissimum principem Angliae &c. Regem Eduardum, eius nominis sextu[m]: anno post Christum natum 1550. (Frankfort and Emden, 1554?, *RSTC* 16571), among other editions. See also the entry on Lasco in the *ODNB*.

75 See Andrew Pettegree's entry for van Parris in the *ODNB*.

76 *OL, 2, no. 264;* Hall, 'Bucer; 158–9; P. Collinson, 'Andrew Perne and His Times', in P. Collinson, D. McKitterick, and E. Leedham-Green, eds., *Andrew Perne: Quatercentenary Studies* (Cambridge, 1991), 1–34.

77 For the second Prayer Book, I have referred to *The boke of common praier, and administracion of the sacramentes, and other rites and ceremonies in the Churche of Englande* (London: Richard Grafton, August 1552, *RSTC* 16285). The Litany appears on 9v–13r.

78 J. Dawson, *John Knox* (New Haven, 2015), 72–8; Gerrish, 'The Reformation and the Eucharist', 252

79 Wriothesley, *Chronicle*, 2, 78–9, 82–3.

80 MacCulloch, *Cranmer*, 539–40.

81 Calvin, *Institutes*, Book 1, chapter 15, 3–5; Book 2, chapter 12, 6–7; Book 3, chapter 11, 5–11.

82 Cranmer's letters to Bullinger, 20 March 1552, printed in *OL*, 1, no. 13; to Calvin on the same date, no. 14; to Melanchthon, 27 March 1552, no. 15; Calvin's reply, April 1552, *OL*, 2, no. 337.

9   Oxford, 1553–1556

'O Lord, which for our sake didst fast forty days and forty nights: Give us grace to use such abstinence, that our flesh being subdued to the spirit, we may ever obey thy Godly motion, in righteousness and true holiness, to thy honour and glory: which livest and reignest with thee and the Holy Spirit, one God, now and forever.'[1]

The *Forty-Two Articles*, 1552–1553

In the same intense period in which the second Prayer Book was produced, Archbishop Thomas Cranmer and his commissioners prepared the *Forty-Two Articles* from the same eclectic selection of sources that he used for all of his compositions. With the *Book of Homilies* and the *Book of Common Prayer*, the *Forty-Two Articles* provided the essential character of the reformed Church that Cranmer built for England.

The *Forty-Two Articles* began with unusually strong statements on the Trinity. Christ truly rose from the dead, and took again his body, complete with flesh and bones, and he ascended into heaven (article four). Holy Scripture contained all things necessary for salvation (article five). The Creed was warranted by Scripture. In article eleven, Cranmer referred to the homilies as 'wholesome doctrine' that explained justification by faith. They were to be read to the people 'diligently, distinctly, and plainly' (article thirty-four). Purgatory was denounced as 'repugnant to the word of God' in article twenty-three. Similarly, transubstantiation was rejected in article twenty-nine. No faithful man should believe in the real and bodily presence in the sacrament of the

Lord's Supper. The new Prayer Book was 'in no point repugnant to the wholesome doctrine of the Gospel', and indeed it was meant to further and beautify the biblical message (article thirty-five).[2]

Cranmer sent the final text of the articles (originally there were forty-five) to William Cecil and John Cheke, the secretaries of the Privy Council, in September 1552. On their recommendation, the draft was given to the king. The articles were reconsidered by a panel that was once again drawn from across a spectrum of opinion that included John à Lasco, Andrew Perne; Edmund Grindal (1520–1583), one of Bishop Nicholas Ridley's chaplains; and John Knox (who remained under heavy scrutiny for the objections he raised about kneeling in the second Prayer Book). The articles were approved and returned to Cranmer. Over the course of the considerations, the number of articles in the final version became forty-two.[3] They were released hurriedly in 1553, without the approval of Convocation, in the midst of the crisis that was occasioned by Edward's failing health.

The *Reformatio Legum Ecclesiasticarum*

At the same time, Cranmer completed another new revision of canon law. We have already mentioned that his predecessor Archbishop William Warham had begun a reconsideration of the laws of the Church. However, his efforts met with disaster in 1532 at the time of the Submission of the Clergy. Cranmer resumed that endeavour early in his archiepiscopate, and in the mid-1530s, his efforts produced a body of new laws known as the Henrician Canons. It consisted of some three-hundred-sixty laws that were revised from the large standing corpus of existing legislation, a substantial portion of which had been produced by Cranmer's predecessors from the thirteenth century. But the Henrician Canons never received approval from Henry VIII, and they were not implemented.

After a long hiatus, in late 1551, Cranmer began a fresh attempt. The Henrician Canons were redrafted into a fresh document, later named by John Foxe as the *Reformatio Legum Ecclesiasticarum* (the reformation of the ecclesiastical laws). Gerald Bray, who edited a recent study edition of the *Reformatio*, noted that the new set of laws maintained considerable continuity with medieval legal matters. At the same time Protestant concepts were introduced, especially as the laws' titles. The text of the *Reformatio* was conservative, but its purpose was to improve the speed and fairness of administration in the English Church.[4]

Cranmer presented the *Reformatio* for approval in the House of Lords in March 1553, where it was rejected by John Dudley, duke of Northumberland. Bray has suggested that Northumberland realized that there were too many risks in letting the Church control its own affairs without oversight by Parliament. It is not completely clear whether the *Reformatio*, if passed, could have meant that the Church would have regained relative independence from parliamentary control, or whether it would have created a new relationship between the Church and Parliament that had not yet been defined. In either case, Northumberland did not wish to risk giving the Church the kind of legislative autonomy that would have meant that the bishops could take decisions and pursue policies that affected the laity without parliamentary approval. The royal supremacy may have put the Church under the direct control of the king, but some of the tensions between Parliament and Convocation continued to be so difficult as to be almost irreconcilable.

The rejection of the *Reformatio* was a bitter disappointment. Later Cranmer told Queen Mary that Northumberland long sought 'my destruction'.[5] Cranmer may have hoped that he could try again for its passage at some future time. However, within a few months he was interrupted and then destroyed by the disaster that overtook him at Edward's death in July 1553.

Edward's death and the succession

Edward turned fifteen as the 1552 *Book of Common Prayer* was released. For some considerable time his health was the cause of concern. In the winter of 1552–1553, he was so ill that observers did not think that he would be able to regain strength easily once the weather improved. Probably the cause of his fatal malady was tuberculosis.[6] He was obviously unwell when he opened the next session of Parliament on 1 March 1553, and his health continued to worsen. In May his doctors suggested that he would probably not live into the autumn.[7]

The king's precarious health may explain the urgency with which another new catechism, in Latin and English editions, was prepared by Bishop John Ponet (Gardiner's replacement at Winchester) and issued in May 1553. Ponet's *Short Catechism* replaced its disappointing predecessor of 1548, and it was accompanied by the text of the *Forty-Two Articles*. In June the *Forty-Two Articles* were printed on their own with the words 'Articles published by the King's Majesty' at the top of every page. The title page proclaimed that the *Forty-Two Articles* had been agreed upon 'in the Synod at London' although they had not, in fact, been approved by Convocation at all. Rather, the endorsements were audacious efforts to strengthen the position of the Church as Edward's health failed.[8]

In his weakening condition, as his life and his prospects for all he had hoped to achieve were seeping away, Edward began to brood about the succession. Its terms had been established by the Third Henrician Act of Succession, passed in the 1544 session of Parliament, as well as by the will Henry had prepared at the end of 1546. The statute, which had been written to clarify the succession before Henry went to war in France, stipulated that the crown should pass first to Edward and then to the lawfully begotten children he might one day have. Failing them, the crown would pass to Edward's half-sister Mary and her children, and in default of them, to his half-sister Elizabeth and her children, subject to certain conditions that Henry specified in his will. As we have seen, his will expanded the succession beyond his three children to his nieces Frances and Eleanor, the daughters of his sister Mary, the French Queen.[9]

Edward was dissatisfied with the arrangements his father had made. Because Mary and Elizabeth were illegitimate, he believed that they were disqualified from the crown. He feared that either of his sisters could make a marriage with a foreign prince that would undermine the laws of England (Hugh Latimer had made this explicit point in a sermon he preached before the king in 1549). Moreover, Edward preferred that the crown pass to a man, as soon as feasible, though through an accident of fate, all possible heirs happened to be female.

Edward decided to divert the succession away from his sisters in favour of an eccentric plan that would give a type of regency to his cousin Frances, duchess of Suffolk. She would rule with a council until the crown could pass to an adult male heir who was born to one of her daughters. As his health worsened, Edward changed his mind. He decided to give the crown to Frances's eldest daughter Lady Jane Grey (1537–1554), and her 'heirs male'. Jane was impeccably Protestant and an eager scholar. She was esteemed for her learning by Heinrich Bullinger of Zűrich, with whom she corresponded. There had once been plans that Edward and Jane should wed. Edward was probably encouraged to make Jane his heir by Northumberland, whose son Guildford married Jane on 21 May 1553.

Edward, although king, was still a minor, and he probably had no right to change his father's succession without the approval of the Privy Council and without a new act of Parliament. Historians disagree about the motives of most of those to whom Edward confided his wishes, but he seems to have wanted Jane's male descendants to occupy the throne forever. Cranmer does not seem to have been involved in the king's plans, but for many of the Protestants who served the king, the plan to subvert the succession to Jane was a desperate attempt to keep Mary from inheriting the throne. According to the Third Henrician Act of Succession, there was to be no return to 'the long usurped power authority and jurisdiction of the bishops of Rome'.

Edward spent his waning strength persuading and ordering his officers to accept his wishes, and Cranmer was probably not told of the king's intentions until mid-June 1553, after many members of the Privy Council had already assented to the plan. Cranmer was surprised by the king's wishes, and he tried to persuade Edward out of them. At first Cranmer refused to sign the new device of the succession because he had already sworn to obey the terms of Henry's will, which meant he thought that Mary was Edward's lawful heir. To do otherwise Cranmer believed would be 'manifest perjury'. He said he would have to give an account of his own conscience and not those of other men's. He refused to sign until the dying king spoke with him privately and implored him to give his assent. Edward signed the device of his succession on 21 June, followed by Cranmer, lord chancellor, Bishop Thomas Goodrich of Ely, and other councillors. Signatures were also collected from the mayor and aldermen of London. More than one hundred men of influence signed.[10]

Edward's plan to leave the crown to Jane without first obtaining the approval of Parliament was certainly incomplete, if not exactly illegal, as Cranmer and the other members of his government were only too well aware. Writs were prepared to summon Parliament for mid-September. Had a new Act of Succession been passed, and had Edward lived long enough to endorse his cousin publicly, in time, Jane may have been accepted as the next heir. But in mid-1553, Mary's right to succeed her brother under the law and Henry's will was common knowledge. She enjoyed a large measure of popularity, especially in East Anglia, where she had been given extensive lands since her father's death. More than two-and-one-half years of concerted effort by Cranmer and the members of the Privy Council had been required to deprive Stephen Gardiner of the bishopric of Winchester. To detain Mary while her brother was still alive would have required even greater measures, and would have given offense to the considerable affinity she had cultivated ever since her father's death. Edward's government lacked enough resources and time to move against her.

Edward's death came suddenly, before anyone was fully prepared. He was attended at the end by his physicians and by his lord chancellor, Bishop Goodrich, who heard his last confession. He died at Greenwich on the evening of 6 July 1553. Two days later the mayor and aldermen of London were informed secretly. On 10 July, Jane and Guilford Dudley were received in the Tower to prepare for a coronation, and Edward's death was proclaimed. Jane was not yet sixteen, and it is unlikely that she understood the full import of what she was being asked to do. At the Tower, Jane's Privy Council opened with Cranmer at its head.

The failure to secure Mary at the time of Edward's death spelt disaster for Jane's government. Probably everyone underestimated Mary's resolve and resourcefulness. She had visited her brother in February, when she was warned that she might be detained if she came to court again. Initially she stayed close enough to London to hear reports of the king's health, and as his death approached, she withdrew into Suffolk. From Kenninghall she wrote the Privy Council immediately upon her brother's death demanding that she be recognized as queen. In response, Cranmer and the other councillors informed her that in light of the invalidity of her parents' marriage, she was illegitimate and therefore ineligible for the crown. Jane was the rightful queen, and they instructed Mary to show herself 'quiet and obedient' to the new government.[11] On 16 July, Ridley entered the pulpit at Paul's Cross, and he preached that Mary and Elizabeth were illegitimate by God's law and by acts of Parliament made in the days of their father, 'which the people murmured sore at'.[12]

Within ten days, Mary mounted a successful coup against Queen Jane. Not even the Protestants who had the most reasons to be concerned should Mary become queen were certain that Jane had the right to succeed. Bishop John Hooper rallied local gentlemen in Gloucestershire and Worcestershire to turn out their tenants in support of Queen Mary.

Cranmer sent troops northward against Mary, and he held steady for Jane until her government collapsed. Towns across the country proclaimed Mary queen. The conservative gentry rose for her. As Jane's biographer Eric Ives demonstrated, at Edward's death, the government sent warships to defend the Suffolk coast. The sailors mutinied, and they delivered their weapons to Mary at Kenninghall. Once it was known that Mary had artillery, Northumberland turned his fighting men back to Cambridge, because it was plain she had invincible support. On 19 July, only thirteen days after Edward's death, Mary was proclaimed queen in London. The next day, Jane's Privy Council capitulated. Jane remained in the Tower, now as a prisoner. On 3 August 1553, Mary arrived in the capital in triumph.[13]

Cranmer's arrest

Edward's death and the failure to exclude Mary from the throne were disasters that destroyed Cranmer and threatened the survival of his Church. Mary abominated Cranmer for invalidating the marriage of her mother, as well as for the changes in religion that he had led under her father and brother. But such was the influence of the archbishop of Canterbury that Mary could not afford to proceed against Cranmer hastily. She took no immediate efforts against him. Once she reached London, Cranmer wrote her an abject apology for consenting to Edward's wishes, and he begged to know her mind concerning 'the estate of religion, as it is used in this realm of England at this present'.[14] Mary refused to see him.

Cranmer was under no illusions about the future. For the time being, the 1552 Prayer Book was the only liturgy that was legal in England. On 8 August, he presided over Edward's funeral at Westminster Abbey according to its rites. However, at her entry into London, Mary released from the Tower the duke of Norfolk, Stephen Gardiner, and Cuthbert Tunstall. They were restored to their former dignities and admitted to her Privy Council. On the day of the king's funeral, Gardiner celebrated a requiem Latin Mass for the repose of Edward's soul in the Tower in the presence of the queen. Before the end of August, Gardiner was made lord chancellor and he was restored to the bishopric of Winchester. Edmund Bonner was also freed from prison, and he was reinstated as bishop of London at Ridley's arrest. Already it was plain that the queen intended to reverse her brother's Reformation.

Cranmer knew that his arrest was also likely. In the few weeks of freedom that remained to him, he paid all his creditors. He forgave the many large debts that Sir John Markham and others owed to him. Cranmer also prepared an inventory of his possessions, and his name and title was written onto the first pages of his books.[15] His family was in turmoil. At the beginning of September, his brother-in-law Edmund Cartwright of Nottinghamshire, who was married to his sister Agnes, retracted his old will, and he prepared a new one that would protect the leases of his property from the dissolved monastery of East Malling, near Maidstone in Kent, which had been confirmed by the 'now' archbishop of Canterbury as well as by the cathedral corporation. Just as Cranmer advised Alexander Alesius to flee in 1539 following the passage of the Act of Six Articles, now he begged his friends take flight 'into some place where God is most truly served' to avoid falling 'into the persecutors' hands'.[16]

For several weeks following the king's death, Edmund Cranmer remained in place as archdeacon of Canterbury. Although it is difficult to know the details, at some time soon, Edmund fled to the continent with his brother's wife and two children. We do not know if their sister Alice, the former nun, was still alive and if she accompanied Edmund into exile. The arrangements for their journey were made by Reyner Wolfe (d. *c.* 1574), who was Cranmer's printer. Margaret could not return to Nuremberg because her uncle Andreas Osiander had been forced into exile by the Interim, and he had died in Königsberg in 1552. Although we cannot be certain, it is possible that the Cranmers made their way to Strasbourg, like so many of the English Protestant exiles. In 1554 Edmund was formally deprived because he was married. His replacement as archdeacon of Canterbury was Nicholas Harpsfield.

From the cathedral chapter at Canterbury came the final series of crises that resulted in Cranmer's arrest and his ultimate destruction. Richard Thornden, the suffragan bishop of Dover, restored the Latin Mass in the cathedral without consulting Cranmer or obtaining his permission. We have already noted in Chapter 6 that Thornden was implicated in the Prebendaries' Plot of 1543, when he escaped serious punishment by begging for Cranmer's forgiveness. Rumours spread in London that Cranmer planned to say Mass at St Paul's for the repose of Edward's soul according to the Latin missal as a means to gain the queen's favour.

Cranmer was grievously offended to have his authority challenged, and he denounced Thornden as 'a false, flattering, and dissembling monk'. Cranmer devised a bold counterattack: he suggested that if Queen Mary granted permission, a panel five or six Protestant theologians of his own choice would engage in a formal disputation that would prove that Edward had replaced the Mass with 'Christ's holy supper' as the apostles had known it in the days of the Primitive Church. The *Book of Common Prayer* and the ministering of the sacraments in Edward's Church were 'more pure' than any that had been used in England in the previous thousand years, he suggested. Oxford's Regius Professor of Divinity, Peter Martyr Vermigli, who had just arrived at Lambeth after fleeing from implacable hostility, would be one of the disputants. Together they would expose 'the great abuses of the Latin Mass' for its 'manifold errors', which Cranmer attributed to 'Christ's ancient adversary', the devil.[17]

Probably Cranmer intended this disputation to take place when Convocation met in October, when the latest directions for the English Church would be defined. He intended to exert himself to the utmost so that in the next settlement, Mary's Church would remain Protestant. In the meantime, Cranmer intended to make a public disavowal of the rumours that he had set up the Latin Mass. In a tacit challenge to the queen's authority, he prepared a statement that he planned to post under his own seal at St Paul's and on the doors of parish churches across London. But before he was fully ready to release his salvo, John Scory, recently deprived of his bishopric of Chichester, saw a draft among his papers. Scory begged to have an advance copy. News this provocative could not be kept secret. Scory lent the draft to a friend. Soon copies poured from 'every scrivener's shop' in London. Cranmer's protest created a sensation that threatened to encourage widespread unrest. He was summoned to the Privy Council on 13 September 1553, the same day that Latimer was sent to the Tower, and he was ordered to appear before the Star Chamber the next day.[18]

Cranmer spent his final night of freedom at Lambeth Palace. The next day, 14 September, he dined with Vermigli and warned him to flee. Then he crossed the river to Westminster and presented himself before the Star Chamber. Facing him were some of his oldest enemies: Stephen Gardiner, now lord chancellor; Thomas Howard, duke of Norfolk; and Cuthbert Tunstall, the aged bishop of Durham. Old friends, some of whom had been members of Jane's Privy Council with him, now also turned to confront him. His offences were discussed by the 'whole board' at great length. They said he had committed treason by rising for Jane against Mary. The protest that was circulating throughout London was deemed seditious. Defiant, Cranmer admitted that he had written it, but he told them that he had intended to release it himself to achieve an even greater effect. Immediately he was committed to the Tower.[19]

The traitor

Cranmer was given the same prison chamber that had been vacated by Northumberland, who was beheaded on 22 August. Perhaps Cranmer was able to observe a portion of the celebrations that marked Mary's coronation. The queen with her sister Elizabeth arrived at the Tower on 27 September 1553, and she was saluted with a round of gunfire. Elizabeth and Anne of Cleves rode after the queen from the Tower on the way to the coronation.

At Westminster Abbey on 1 October, Bishop Stephen Gardiner placed the crown on Mary's head.[20] A general pardon was issued in her name, from which Cranmer and the other prisoners in the Tower were exempted.

In the unlikely event that Cranmer had been able to maintain his liberty into the autumn, he might have been able to embarrass Mary's government in the session of Convocation that opened in mid-October. On its first day, his *Catechism* of 1548 was denounced as 'full of heresies', and the 1552 *Book of Common Prayer* was mocked as 'very abominable'. The next day, as a prelude to re-establishing the Mass, a bill was presented that endorsed the real presence in the sacrament of the altar. But in the debates that followed, a small group of Protestants among the archdeacons, including John Philpot (1516–1555), archdeacon of Winchester under Ponet, defended Cranmer's achievements, and they asked that Ridley and John Rogers could be allowed out of prison to take part. One after another the Protestants denied transubstantiation. Speaking for Mary's government was John Harpsfield (1516–1578). The debates became so heated that members of the House of Lords came into the Convocation House to observe, and in December the queen dissolved the session.[21] Within a year, Edward's Reformation was undone by Parliament.

By the time that Convocation was dissolved at the end of 1553, the see of Canterbury was declared vacant because Cranmer was condemned to death for treason. On 13 November, he was led out of the Tower on foot, where he and Lady Jane, with her husband and his brothers, were paraded in a humiliating spectacle through the streets of London to their trial at the Guildhall. Heavily guarded, Cranmer came first, attended by his jailors, and then Guilford Dudley and his guards, followed by Lady Jane with her gentlewomen and keepers. She carried an open book, probably a Bible, from which she read as she walked. At the Guildhall they appeared before the duke of Norfolk and they were charged with high treason. Cranmer was accused of proclaiming Jane queen when her Privy Council met at the Tower, and he was also accused of sending soldiers to Cambridge to oppose Mary. Initially he pleaded not guilty, but then he submitted to the charge. Cranmer was sentenced to be hanged, drawn, and quartered as a traitor.

They were all condemned. Then they were marched back the full mile to the Tower on foot.[22]

Cranmer was still in the Tower when Sir Thomas Wyatt (d. 1554) led an armed uprising early in 1554 that was triggered by the news that Mary intended to wed Philip (1527–1598) of Spain, the son of the Emperor Charles V. Mary's choice revived fresh fears against the Habsburgs and the papacy, because many people believed her marriage would threaten England's independence. Wyatt's revolt almost succeeded. He marched from Maidstone in Kent and reached Fleet Street in London before his rising failed. Mary's government remained deeply troubled by the spectre of further rebellion. Preaching at court on 11 February 1554, Gardiner asked that the 'rotten members' who endangered the health of the commonwealth be cut off. The next day Guilford Dudley and the Lady Jane were beheaded at the Tower.

The heretic

In the aftermath of the Wyatt uprising, Cranmer briefly shared the same cell in the Tower with Ridley and Latimer. Then the queen and the Privy Council decided to move them away from London. In early March 1554 they were sent together to Oxford, where in the following month they engaged in fresh rounds of disputations with theologians from both universities, ostensibly to take up some of the problems that had been initiated in Convocation in the previous autumn. Once more, the debates were meant to establish unity in faith for the entire realm, but now through realignment with the papacy. The questions that were considered again centred on the nature of Christ's presence in the Eucharist, and whether the Mass was a sacrifice that could propitiate for the sins of the dead as well as the living. However, the Oxford disputations were also meant to expose the opinions of Cranmer, Ridley, and Latimer as heretical. Richard Smyth had returned from exile in Louvain to resume his chair in divinity, and as the university's vice-chancellor he played a prominent role in their trials.

The Protestant bishops understood that their lives were forfeit. Cranmer was already legally dead as a convicted traitor. But they represented the legitimacy of Edward's Church and the cause of Protestantism even in defeat, and therefore they took every opportunity to make dramatic spectacles that bore witness to their faith, even though they knew the outcome was already determined against them. They were assisted by John Jewel (1522–1571), the future bishop of Salisbury, who as a student at Oxford had served as Vermigli's notary during Oxford's debates on the Eucharist in 1549.

The Oxford disputations were humiliating ordeals that were shams of impartial inquires. Cranmer, Ridley, and Latimer were required to debate separately. Latimer was ill, and he was unwilling to engage beyond saying that he believed as Cranmer had taught in his 1551 *Answer* against Gardiner.

Jewel noted that every time Cranmer spoke, the chamber erupted in 'a clapping of hands, and stamping of feet'.[23] He was introduced as a heretic who had cut himself off from the one true Church, and set forth erroneous doctrine, making every year a new faith. Although Cranmer was frequently interrupted, he responded so modestly, and so wittily, that some of his opponents wept as they listened to him. In one of the surreal moments of the proceedings, Cranmer served as an examiner when John Harpsfield was examined for his doctorate, and he was thanked for his participation.

On 20 April 1554, in the university's church, the outcome of their debates was announced. Everything Cranmer, Ridley, and Latimer had said was judged to be false. Then they were condemned as heretics. Immediately Cranmer wrote the Privy Council (in a letter that was probably not delivered) to protest that the purpose of the disputation was to 'condemn us in post haste'.[24]

Now they entered a period of almost complete eclipse that lasted more than a year. They were separated. Cranmer was kept in close confinement, usually in the Bocardo, the prison in Oxford's northern gatehouse. Most of the letters he wrote then have not been recovered, but he was able to revise the Latin version of his *Defence of the True and Catholic Doctrine*.

On 20 November 1554, Reginald Cardinal Pole arrived in Dover. Ten days later, at the Palace of Westminster, he completed England's reconciliation with the papacy. In December, Parliament restored the old medieval laws against heresy.

Gardiner and the Privy Council conducted the first trials under the revived heresy laws in early 1555, and in a coordinated display of power, executions began across the country. John Rogers, who had helped William Tyndale translate the Bible, was burnt at Smithfield on 4 February. On 9 February, some of the most outspoken members of Edward's church were executed. Hooper was burnt near his cathedral in Gloucester, and Rowland Taylor, one of Cranmer's chaplains and a Six Preacher of Canterbury, suffered at Hadleigh in Suffolk. Bishop Robert Ferrar of St David's was burnt in March. Their deaths marked the beginning of a campaign that by late 1558 resulted in the burnings of nearly three hundred men, women, and young people, many of whom were of humble backgrounds. There was no precedence in Europe at the time for persecutions on this scale, and the number of executions that were conducted during the last three years of Mary's reign are unparalleled in English history.

In early 1555, Cranmer's farewell letter to Vermigli was smuggled out of his close confinement, and it reached him in Strasbourg. Later still it was shared with Bullinger in Zürich. Cranmer wrote that he was under close watch, and he referred to the persecutions that were taking place as the paradoxical sign of God's nearness and his consolation.[25]

The burning of Latimer and Ridley, October 1555

Although Pole resided at Lambeth Palace, the archbishopric had entered into a curious state of limbo at Cranmer's attainder. Because he had received the pallium and papal approval at his elevation in 1533, the queen wanted to be certain that his deprivation was done correctly, which meant that permission had to arrive from Rome before he could be executed. The Oxford disputations in April 1554 were conducted before the medieval heresy laws were revived. Therefore his condemnation for heresy was not truly valid. Nor could he be executed, even as a traitor, without papal approval. Paul IV (Gian Pietro Carafa, r. 1555–1559) was elected pope in May 1555, and in June permission was granted to call Cranmer to Rome for trial. He was supposed to appear within eighty days.[26]

In September 1555, the papal summons reached Oxford, and preparations began for Latimer and Ridley's execution, which involved fresh rounds of examinations and debates leading to new death sentences. On 12 September, Cranmer was once again called to account before James Brooks, the new bishop of Gloucester and papal legate. Brooks sat in the university church near the high altar, beneath a pix that contained the consecrated Host. With him were emissaries from King Philip and Queen Mary. Cranmer refused to recognize the pope's authority, but he knelt to the royal representatives and he declared his fidelity to the crown. Cranmer's entire career was scrutinized. Brooks accused Cranmer of falling into open heresy and treason and that he had been used as an instrument to despoil the Church. Among the witnesses who appeared against him were Richard Croke (with whom he worked for the divorce in Italy in 1530), the Six Preacher Robert Serles (who had been punished for his involvement in the Prebendaries Plot), and Vice-Chancellor Smyth himself.

At Lambeth Palace, Pole's subordinates consulted Cranmer's Register, and they were taken aback by its record of the protest he had made at his consecration against the traditional oath he was made to swear to the pope. Cranmer was asked to explain himself, and he declared he had had the best legal advice in 1533 that permitted him to spare his conscience, for he refused to consent to the bishop of Rome any more than he would give himself to the devil. His answers stimulated a long discussion about the nature of authority and to whom it was due. His opponents asked him who was supreme head of the Church, and Cranmer responded that Christ was, though every king was supreme head over the Church in his own realm. Was this always so, he was asked, even under the Emperor Nero (d. 68)? Cranmer responded that Nero was indeed the temporal head of the Church and responsible for beheading Peter and the other apostles, just as in the present day Suleyman the Magnificent was head of the Church in Turkey. It is difficult to know what Cranmer meant by an assertion so outrageous that it shocked Foxe as well as recent historians, though it is possible that he wanted to show his accusers that he thought the papacy and Mary's government belonged in the same category with the most notorious persecutors of the early Christian Church and of many Christians in their own day.[27]

At the end of this set of proceedings, Cranmer sent a long letter to the queen to explain why he refused papal authority in England, and to warn her of the possible consequences should the pope infringe upon her prerogatives and English law. Cranmer believed that England 'should ever continue accursed' if the power and authority of 'the crown, laws, and customs' of her realm should be successfully challenged by the papacy. He could not see how he could declare his obedience to two powers who were locked in competition for ascendancy over England. Therefore he continued to refuse to acknowledge the jurisdiction of the bishop of Rome.[28]

Latimer and Ridley were tried, excommunicated, degraded, and sentenced to death in October 1555. Heretics had been burnt in Oxford before, most recently in 1538, when William Cowbridge (a few weeks after the burning of Friar Forest) died for his eccentric denial of Christ as the redeemer of the world. Foxe had attended his death when he was a student at Oxford.[29]

On 16 October 1555, Latimer and Ridley were brought to the same place Cowbridge died, an open place in Broad Street below the walls of Balliol College, around the corner from the Bocardo. The scene of their execution was immortalized by Foxe as the most important episode in his Book of Martyrs. They were chained to one stake, and after they bid the world farewell with words of mutual encouragement, the fire was lit. Cranmer was brought up on the leads of the Bocardo and made to watch. Latimer was one of his oldest friends. Ridley had led him to his mature understanding of the Eucharist. Latimer died quickly, without seeming to suffer pain, but Ridley suffered grievously for a long time. Cranmer wept in great distress, and he mourned his friends in the full knowledge that the same fate waited for him.

The recantations

Shortly after Ridley and Latimer's execution, Stephen Gardiner died after a long illness. Pole answered the letter Cranmer had sent the queen, and reproached him in the strongest terms for his disobedience and his perjury when he accepted the archbishopric. He warned Cranmer that his opinion towards the sacrament of the altar was plainly mistaken, and his soul was in danger of eternal damnation unless he repented his sins and errors.[30] Pole also sent the Spanish Dominican friars Pedro de Soto and Juan de Villagracia to Oxford to speak with him. Cranmer's deprivation and condemnation was completed in Rome before the end of 1555. The verdict arrived in England before the end of January 1556.

What followed are some of the most difficult episodes to understand in Cranmer's life. At Christmas 1555, he was moved from the Bocardo to friendlier accommodations, and he may have heard Mass at Christ Church Cathedral in Oxford. He was also asked to take up fresh theological questions by the friars, which caused him to examine his opinions in a new light.

Early in the new year, pressed very hard, Cranmer made a recantation: because the king and queen, with the consent of Parliament, 'have received the pope's authority within this realm, I am content to submit myself to their laws' and also 'to take the pope for chief head of this Church of England'. But a caveat at the end, 'so far as God's law and the laws and customs of this realm will permit' rendered his first recantation valueless, because privately he still believed that God's law did not permit the supremacy of the pope.[31]

Once Cranmer began to capitulate, he was pressured further. His next recantation declared that he submitted himself 'to the catholic church of Christ', to the pope as its supreme head, and to the king and queen and their laws. This too was considered inadequate. A third recantation followed, in which he promised 'to live in quietness and obedience unto their majesties', and to submit his latest book to judgement by the Catholic Church and the next general council. Nor was the third recantation accepted.

On 14 February 1556, in Christ Church Cathedral, Cranmer was degraded from all his orders in the Church. His high promotion as archbishop was symbolically undone, all the way down through the lowest of holy orders. Bishop Edmund Bonner of London, who was acting as metropolitan in Cranmer's absence, and Thomas Thirlby, now bishop of Ely, were sent to conduct the ceremony. The pope's commission was read, and Cranmer was dressed in a parody of an archbishop's garments so that he could be divested of them.[32]

But when they reached to take the crozier out of his hand, Cranmer surprised everyone when he suddenly pulled a legal document out of his sleeve (in imitation of Martin Luther, who had made a similar protest early in his career). Cranmer made a formal appeal to the next General Council. His document had been prepared even while he recanted three times. Because he had been cited to come to Rome, he insisted that he be heard because he had not been treated fairly during his imprisonment in Oxford.[33]

Thirlby had been Cranmer's friend for most of their lives, and, deeply upset, he promised to plead for him to the king and queen, and he wept through the ceremony. Bonner and Thirlby now reached for the simulated pallium, and Cranmer asked them: 'Which of you hath a pall, to take off my pall?' As they continued to strip him, Cranmer said 'I had myself done with this gear long ago'. At the end, he was given a second-hand garment to wear, a cast-off that had once belonged to some humble layman, and a townsman's cap to cover his bald head.

Two days later, Bonner came to visit him, and Cranmer recanted again for the fourth time. Now he confessed, 'concerning the sacraments of the Church, I believe unfeignedly in all points' as the Catholic Church taught, 'and hath believed from the beginning of Christian religion'.

Cranmer's seeming willingness to submit as the time for his execution approached placed the queen and Pole in a quandary. Mary had no intention of reprieving Cranmer, even though there were some, like Thirlby, who would have been glad if he were spared. Bonner carried the fourth recantation back to London, where it was released, and it caused a sensation that disturbed the Privy Council.[34]

Historians still disagree how effectual Mary's government was in seizing the opportunities that the printing press offered to enhance its rule. If Cranmer could have been made to recant openly, before a large audience, he would have been discredited forever, along with the Protestant Church in England that he symbolized as its architect. But could they have trusted him to make a clear and unequivocal submission? This seems unlikely, especially after his theatrical appeal at his degradation. Other Protestants turned rather than burn. Immediately after Latimer and Ridley's execution, Edward Crome submitted to Cardinal Pole. He recanted before witnesses, if not at Paul's Cross, and he was pardoned.

Little was made by the government of Crome's capitulation. Probably the authorities judged correctly (based on the record of his recantations in Henry's reign) that they could not count on what he would say or do if he spoke before a sizeable audience.

Crome and Cranmer (like Smyth) reached maturity before John Calvin established the concept of the 'Nicodemite' from the story in John's Gospel. Nicodemus was the Pharisee who came to consult Jesus secretly by night, who believed in his teaching but would not confess it openly. From the mid-1540s, at about the same time that Anne Askew was executed, Calvin argued that compromise or backsliding was unacceptable among Protestants. Insincerity was a sign of imperfect faith. Foxe and others were persuaded by Calvin that dissimulation or equivocation was unworthy of Christians under persecution. Their duty was to die as witnesses to their faith in Christ if there was no other recourse. Ridley and Latimer, like Askew, willingly sacrificed their lives.[35]

Meanwhile, Cranmer indulged in the hope that he would be allowed to live, and the last weeks of his life were full of distress. On 26 February 1556, Villagracia persuaded him to make a more complete recantation. He prepared a document which Cranmer signed that repudiated the teaching of Martin Luther and Huldrych Zwingli.[36]

Now Cranmer made a full capitulation. Penitent, he asked for absolution and to be allowed to return to the Roman Church. He attended Mass again. Still, the fifth recantation was deemed inadequate for the salvation of his soul, and on 18 March Cranmer signed an abject submission that repudiated his role in ending the marriage of the queen's parents. It ended with a reference to the thief who was crucified with Christ, who was promised entrance into paradise.

Why Cranmer was willing to recant is difficult to explain. He knew that the documents he was signing were being collected to discredit him, and that his reputation would be destroyed once they were released. Perhaps he believed that once he was brought back into the Roman Church he would be allowed to live, fully repentant and fully reconciled, though it is difficult to believe, from his own words at his execution, that he was sincere in his submissions.

However, Mary had no desire to allow him to escape punishment as a reconciled penitent, even though she was reminded that he had interceded with Henry for her life in 1536. His execution was briefly postponed, but then he was warned that he must die. Now another comprehensive statement was prepared for him to read at his execution, which he was asked to write out in advance, again and again, for distribution after his death. He was to declare that he was a sinner, ashamed, and in need of prayer. Now was the moment when all of his past life hung in the balance: would he spend eternity with Christ forever in joy, or be in pain forever with the wicked devils in hell? The faith he confessed at his end would determine his future. The statement that was prepared for him concluded with a repudiation of all the books he had written against the sacrament of the altar since the death of Henry VIII. Cranmer's last utterance before he died was supposed to be: 'I say and believe that our Saviour Christ Jesu is really and substantially contained in the blessed sacrament of the altar under the forms of bread and wine'. Had Cranmer read these words as his final statement at his death, everything he had built for Edward's Church would have been discredited.[37]

The execution

On 21 March 1556, through rainy streets, Cranmer was brought again to the University Church of St Mary the Virgin, where the marks of the platform on which he was stood can still be seen on a pillar today. He stood weeping as Henry Cole (d. 1580) denounced him in a sermon that suggested that Sir Thomas More's death in 1535 had been avenged by the execution of Northumberland. But how could the loss of the incomparable Bishop John Fisher be made good? The burnings of bishops Ridley, Hooper, and Ferrar were insufficient, Cole announced, and now Cranmer was to be added to make the balance even.[38]

It may be that this outrageous suggestion caused Cranmer to make a decision that he had agonized over in the last hours of his life. He had written out the prepared text that he was supposed to read, but he had also made ready an alternative ending that now, perhaps at the instigation of Cole's sermon, he decided to read instead. His statement was almost unchanged until the end, when Cranmer announced that he renounced 'things written with my hand, contrary to the truth which I thought in my heart, and written for fear of death, and to save my life if it might be'. Everything he had written since his degradation he repudiated. 'I have written many things untrue. And forasmuch as my hand offended, writing contrary to my heart, my hand shall first be punished'. Cranmer said he would hold his hand in the flames and let it burn first. Then he cried out that he refused the pope as Christ's enemy, and he believed as he taught in the book he had written against Gardiner.[39]

Before Cranmer finished reading, he was pulled from the platform, and he was brought to the walls of Balliol College, to the same place where Ridley and Latimer had died. As he ran towards the stake, Cranmer explained to Villagarcia that he had made his recantations merely 'to save my life'.[40]

If the scene of Latimer and Ridley's burning was the great centrepiece of Foxe's *Actes and Monuments*, then Cranmer's execution was the next most important, and it was essential in vindicating English Protestantism. As promised, once the fire was kindled, Cranmer held his hand steadily in the flames, moving only once or twice to wipe his head, each time, placing his hand back into the fire. He was heard to murmur 'my unworthy right hand'. He also repeated the words of St Stephen, the first martyr of the Church, 'lord Jesus receive my spirit' until he died.[41]

Cranmer knew St John Chrysostom's and St Basil's homilies that recalled how St Barlaam of Antioch (d. 304) went to a martyr's death. After a long period of imprisonment and torture, Barlaam was brought out of prison to offer a sacrifice, and he was given incense with live coals to scatter on a pagan altar. But rather than drop the burning incense to honour a pagan god, he held it and sacrificed his own hand instead.[42] We cannot know if Cranmer thought of emulating Barlaam in his last hour, but certainly his enemies saw the association. Within a few years, as Harpsfield denounced English heresies, he warned his readers not to think of Cranmer as 'our Barlaam'.[43] The power of Cranmer's final gesture in testifying to his own faith, and in affirming the legitimacy of the English Church, counteracted the impression that was made when his recantations were printed in their original form. His final statement corrected the version of the recantations that were released by Bonner. The manner of Cranmer's death meant that Protestants could claim him as a martyr. This was a claim that had first been made on his behalf as long ago as 1537, when Osiander wrote in the dedication of his *Harmony* that Cranmer's love for the Gospel and true religion was so great, that he was willing to work only for the glory of Christ. Cranmer had 'a spirit equal to martyrdom'.[44]

Notes

1 Cranmer's collect for the first Sunday in Lent from the 1549 Prayer Book: *The booke of the common prayer and administracion of the sacramentes and other rites and ceremonies of the Churche: after the vse of the Churche of England* (London: Edward Whitchurch, March 1549, *RSTC* 16267), 32v.

2 O. O'Donovan, *On the Thirty-Nine Articles: A Conversation with Tudor Christianity*, 2nd. ed. (London, 2011); S. M. Holmes, 'The Title of Article 27 (26): Cranmer, Durandus and Pope Innocent III', *JEH*, 64 (2013), 357–64.

3 *Articles agreed on by the Bishoppes, and other learned menne in the Synode at London, in the yere of our Lorde Godde, M.D.LII.* (London: Richard Grafton, June 1553, *RSTC* 10034.2); MacCulloch, Cranmer, 503, 536–7.

4 G. Bray, ed., *Tudor Church Reform: The Henrician Canons of 1535 and the Reformatio Legum Ecclesiasticarum*, Church of England Record Society, 8 (2000), xxvi–xxix, xxxviii–xliv, lxiv, lxxiii–lxxvi. Also, *The Reformation of the Ecclesiastical Laws of England, 1552*, ed. J. C. Spalding, vol. 19, Sixteenth Century Essays and Studies (1992).

5 Cranmer, *Miscellaneous*, no. 310.

6 See Dale Hoak's entry for the king in the *ODNB*.

7 Wriothesley, *Chronicle*, 2, 81; E. Ives, *Lady Jane Grey: A Tudor Mystery* (Oxford, 2009).

8 [John Ponet], *A Short Catechisme, or playne instruction, conteynynge the summe of Christian learninge* (London: John Day, May 1553, *RSTC* 4812). fols. 69r–86r; *Articles agreed on by the Bishoppes, and other learned menne in the Synode at London, in the yere of our Lorde Godde, M.D.LII.* (London: Richard Grafton, June 1553, RSTC 10034.2), MacCulloch, Cranmer, 536–7.

9 35 Henry VIII (1544), c. 1; S. E. Lehmberg, *The Later Parliaments of Henry VIII 1536–1547* (Cambridge, 1977) 193–4.

10 Cranmer, *Miscellaneous*, letter to Queen Mary, no. 310; MacCulloch, *Cranmer*, 540–1; Ives, *Lady Jane Grey*, 165.

11 Foxe, *AM*, 6, 385–6.

12 Wriothesley, *Chronicle*, 2, 88.

13 *The Chronicle of Queen Jane*, ed. J. G. Nichols, CS, 48 (1850), 1–11; MacCulloch, *Cranmer*, pp. 543–4; 'The Vita Mariae Angliae Reginae of Robert Wingfield of Brantham', ed. D. MacCulloch, *Camden Miscellany*, 28, CS, 4th series, 29 (1984), 181–301; Ives, *Lady Jane Grey*, 192–224.

14 Cranmer's letter to Queen Mary: Miles Coverdale [and Henry Bull], *Certain most godly, fruitful, and comfortable letters of such true saintes and holy martyrs of God* . . . . (London: John Day, 1564, RSTC 5886), 1–3; and *Miscellaneous*, no. 310.

15 Foxe, *AM*, 8, 19–20, 44.

16 The will of Edmund Cartwright of Ossington, Notts., made 8 September 1553 and proved 30 August 1554, TNA: PRO, PROB 11/37, 56r–57r; Cranmer, *Miscellaneous*, letter to Mistress Wilkinson, no. 311.

17 Cranmer's letter setting out his response to the rumours that he would set up the Mass again: CCCC, MS 105, 321–2. It was printed in Latin as an appendix to the *Vera expositio disputationis institutae mandato D. Mariae Reginae* ([Cologne, 1554, RSTC 19891); Cranmer, *Lord's Supper*, 428–30; Foxe, *AM*, 6, 589–90.

18 Foxe, *AM*, 8, 37–8; MacCulloch, *Cranmer*, 547–51.

19 *APC*, 4, 345–7.

20 Wriothesley, *Chronicle*, 2, 103.

21 [John Philpot], *The trew report of the dysputacyon had and begonne in the conuocacyon hows* (Basel [Emden], 1554, RSTC 19890), a translation of the *Vera expositio disputationis*; Foxe, *AM*, 6, 395–411.

22 *Chronicle of Queen Jane*, 26–59; Ives, *Lady Jane Grey*, 249–52; Ridley, *Cranmer*, 367–8.

23 *The Trve Copies of the Letters between . . . John [Jewel] and D. Cole* . . . (London: John Day, 1560, RSTC 14613) 46r, 63r.

24 Cranmer, *Miscellaneous*, letter no. 312.

25 Cranmer, *Miscellaneous*, no. 317; reproduced in MacCulloch, *Cranmer*, 574.

26 MacCulloch, *Cranmer*, 561–4.

27 Foxe, *AM*, 8, 44–7; Cranmer, *Miscellaneous*, 212–24; MacCulloch, *Cranmer*, 575–9.

28 Cranmer, *Miscellanous*, no. 314.

29 T. S. Freeman and S. Royal, 'Stranger than Fiction in the Archives: The Controversial Death of William Cowbridge in 1538', *British Catholic History*, 32 (2015), 451–72.

30 Cranmer, *Miscellaneous*, 534–41.

31 *All the submyssyons, and recantations of Thomas Cranmer, late Archebyshop of Canterburye truely set forth both in Latyn and Englysh, agreable to the originalles, wrytten and subscribed with his owne hande*, ed. Edmund Bonner (London: John Cawood [1556], RSTC 5990); Cranmer, *Miscellaneous*, 563–5.

32 Foxe, *AM*, 8, 71–82; Ridley, *Cranmer*, 391–3.

33 Foxe, *AM*, 8, 71–82; Cranmer, *Miscellaneous*, 224–8.

34 MacCulloch, *Cranmer*, 595–6.

35 John 3:1; and see A. Overell's forthcoming *Nicodemites between Italy and Tudor England*.

36 Ridley, *Cranmer*, 394–5; MacCulloch, *Cranmer*, 594–7.

37 *Recantations of Thomas Cranmer*, B2r.

38 Foxe, *AM*, 8, 85.

39 Cranmer, *Miscellanous*, 563–6.

40 Foxe, *AM*, 8, 89.

41 Foxe 1563, 1502–3.

42 Basil's homily 17 on St Barlaam: *Patrologia Graeca*, 31, cols. 484–90; Chrysostom's 'Laudatio Sancti Martyris Barlaam', *Patrologia Graeca*, 50, cols. 675–82.

43 In the original: 'nostrum Barlaam': Nicholas Harpsfield [pseud. Alan Cope] *Sex Dialogi contra Summi Pontificatus . . . .* (Antwerp: Christopher Plantin, 1566), 743–4.

44 See Osiander's dedication in his *Harmoniae Evangelicae*; Osiander to Cranmer, 24 January 1538: BL, Harley MS 6989, 80 (*LP*, 13 (1), no. 140 and also no. 648); MacCulloch, *Cranmer*, 70–1, 74–5; Ridley, *Cranmer*, 40–2; G. Cuming, *The Godly Order: Texts and Studies Relating to the Book of Common Prayer*, Alcuin Club, 65 (1983), 72.

10   Thomas Cranmer's legacy for the English Church

'O God, the king of glory, which hath exalted thine only son Jesus Christ, with great triumph into thy kingdom of heaven: we beseech thee, leave us not comfortless, but send to us thine holy ghost to comfort us, and exalt us unto the same place, whither our saviour Christ is gone before: who liveth and reigneth with thee and the Holy Spirit, one God, now and forever.'[1]

Cranmer's family

Thomas Cranmer's dramatic gesture at his execution was widely accepted as a definitive statement of his faith as well as a proclamation of the legitimacy of the Protestant Church. In 1557, the English exiles released a new edition of his *Defence of the True and Catholic Doctrine*, in which Edmund Cranmer was distinguished as the brother of the martyr.[2] John Parkhurst (d. 1575) praised Cranmer in verse for his courage, and spoke of his mind rising to the stars when his body was burnt.[3] In 1559 John Bale described Cranmer as another Polycarp, the second-century bishop of Smryna, who was burnt for refusing to make a sacrifice to the emperor of Rome.[4]

While they were still in exile at the end of 1556, Margaret Cranmer married Edward Whitchurch, the printer of the Great Bible of 1539–1540. Edmund Cranmer died abroad, probably shortly before the unexpected occurred: Mary and Cardinal Pole both died on 17 November 1558. Immediately upon Elizabeth's accession, John Jewel travelled back to England from Strasbourg, bringing with him the archbishop's son, the young

Thomas Cranmer, and the surviving members of the archbishop's family. Lands and revenues, including the former monastery of Kirkstall in Yorkshire that had been confiscated at his attainder, eventually were restored to his widow and their son.[5] When Sir John Markham died late in 1559, he left the young Cranmer the money he had borrowed from his father, even though the archbishop had forgiven the debt shortly before his arrest.[6]

Whitchurch arranged a marriage between the archbishop's daughter Margaret to the lawyer and man of letters Thomas Norton (d. 1584). There were no children from this marriage. Since the archbishop's son remained childless, Cranmer's direct line of descent came to an end late in the sixteenth century. But Norton married as his second wife Edmund Cranmer's daughter Alice, with whom he established a large and flourishing posterity. Although the younger Thomas Cranmer led a troubled life, he and Norton remained close, and when Norton died in 1584, 'brother' Thomas Cranmer became the executor of his will. Norton trusted him to dispose of his goods on behalf of his wife Alice and their children.[7]

Many people had competing claims as Cranmer's heirs. Matthew Parker, who succeeded Pole to the archbishopric of Canterbury, was an eager collector of books and manuscripts, and he wanted all of Cranmer's writings that could be recovered. As we have already seen, Ralph Morice's reminiscences were written for Parker's history of the archbishops of Canterbury.[8] They are preserved in the Parker Library of Corpus Christi College, Cambridge. Facsimiles of its manuscripts are available on the Internet.

Cranmer's large and varied library was partially broken up upon his arrest, and an untold number of his Protestant books were destroyed. Many of his manuscripts were lost, and despite Parker's best efforts, they could not be found again. A substantial portion of Cranmer's printed books went first to Queen Mary's lord high steward and then to his son-in-law John, first Lord Lumley (d. 1609). After his death they passed to Henry, prince of Wales (d. 1612), and then they entered the Royal Library. The Royal Library was incorporated into the British Library, where Cranmer's books can be consulted today.[9]

Parker discovered that some manuscripts in Cranmer's own hand were kept by his physician, Dr John Herd (1511–1584), who attended him in Oxford. Many of Cranmer's belongings remained in the hands of his widow and children, and ultimately some of them, like Cranmer's drafts of canon law, passed to Norton. Whitchurch died in 1562.[10] Then Margaret made an unfortunate third marriage to Bartholomew Scott, from whose unkindness she was forced to flee. She took refuge with Reyner Wolfe, who also held on to many of Cranmer's manuscripts. Margaret's last years were probably passed in difficult circumstances, and we do not know when or where she died. Late in her life, she still had among her meagre possessions some rings that probably belonged to Cranmer.[11]

The Elizabethan Church

As archbishop of Canterbury from late 1559, Parker played a substantial role in preserving Cranmer's legacy in the Elizabethan Church. The new queen needed her Protestant subjects to secure her succession. When her Privy Council was constituted, Mary's councillors were excluded. The task of making Elizabeth's Church Protestant was eased by Cardinal Pole's death, for it is likely that he would have exerted enormous influence against the new queen's government had he survived Mary. In December 1558, Parker was summoned to wait upon the queen, and despite the reluctance he felt (which he attributed to his own sense of inadequacy), at length he was nominated, confirmed, and consecrated archbishop of Canterbury by the end of 1559.

Fresh compromises were necessary at the establishment of Elizabeth's Church in 1559. The 1552 *Book of Common Prayer* was restored but with conservative alterations that brought back the phrasing from the 1549 communion service. The 'black rubric' was omitted. Clergymen were again required to wear surplices. Some of the changes created lasting controversies.

Dangerous disagreements had erupted on the continent among the English exiles about the Prayer Book. At Frankfort, most of the exiles wanted to follow the 1552 Prayer Book, and they had strong links with other English churches in Zürich, Strasbourg, and Emden. John Knox arrived as a minister in Frankfort in 1554, and at Christmas he provoked a crisis when he refused to administer the Lord's Supper in accordance with the Prayer Book, because he wanted to bring worship services closer to the practices that were followed in southern Germany and Switzerland. He appealed to John Calvin for support. When, on 17 March 1555, Knox openly criticized the 1552 Prayer Book in a sermon that compared the Emperor Charles V to Nero, the safety of the exiles was jeopardized. Knox was banished in a move that was orchestrated by Richard Cox at Strasbourg, who wished to defend Cranmer's achievement against Knox's repeated criticisms. He spent the next few months with Calvin in Geneva before he returned to Scotland.[12]

Like Knox, there were many returning exiles who wished Elizabeth's Church would accommodate greater changes than were allowed under the Act of Uniformity of 1559 and the 1559 Prayer Book. Problems that began during Cranmer's archiepiscopate continued to have important long-term consequences in the late sixteenth and seventeenth centuries that go beyond the scope of this study. They helped to create a dynamic tension inside the English Church between those who were willing to conform, and those who were dissatisfied or openly nonconformist, who later became known under the useful label 'Puritans'. Elizabeth's settlement represented another new start as a Reformed Protestant Church.

A second book of homilies was released in 1563 to accompany the 1547 book. Although it has been described as less distinguished than its predecessor, Elizabeth valued it for the conformity it encouraged.[13] The queen preferred that homilies be read rather than sermons preached in parishes, because she thought the homilies as set texts provided a better encouragement to obedience. The story of Archbishop Edmund Grindal, Nicholas Ridley's former chaplain and Parker's successor, whose career was destroyed in 1576 by his temerity in defending continental styles of preaching known as 'exercises of prophesying', is familiar through the work of the late Patrick Collinson. Grindal spent the final years of his life in exclusion, all but deprived of the office of archbishop of Canterbury. The disaster that overtook Grindal is another symbol of the extent to which the office of archbishop was demoted by the royal supremacy over the English Church.[14]

In 1571 the *Forty-Two Articles* were revised as the *Thirty-Nine Articles*, and they became definitive for the English Church.

They were printed in the Prayer Book, and they were restored with it when the English Church was re-established at the Restoration in 1662. They have been periodically endorsed and frequently invoked to the present day.

Cranmer's revision of English canon law was consigned to oblivion by Queen Mary, but Cardinal Pole was hardly more successful in revising canon law for England. He had the additional challenge of incorporating changes in the laws of the Roman Church that were being developed by the Council of Trent (1545–1563). The new canons were passed by Parliament in early 1556, shortly before Cranmer's execution, and they were in force less than three years when Mary and Pole died. How effective they were in that brief time is still not understood.[15]

Cranmer's canon law project was revived in the next reign by Norton, John Foxe, and Foxe's printer John Day as one of the responses that was made to defend Elizabeth after she was excommunicated by Pope Pius V (Antonio Ghislieri, r. 1566–1572) in 1571. Norton was in the House of Commons. Working from Cranmer's paperwork, he introduced the *Reformatio Legum Ecclesiasticarum* for adoption. An edition of the proposed code was printed by Day with a plea from Foxe that at long last, the new laws should be adopted for the realm. But once again, the measure did not succeed. Elizabeth also had her misgivings about the advisability of allowing the Church to make its own policies without parliamentary supervision, and Cranmer's law code lost a last real chance to succeed.[16]

John Foxe and the reluctant martyr

In terms of Cranmer himself, as a man and an archbishop, John Foxe in the *Actes and Monuments* addressed the complexities and contradictions that his career presented by comparing his life against the daunting standard for bishops established by St Paul in his epistles to Timothy and Titus: 'A bishop must be blameless'.[17] Verse by verse, Foxe measured Cranmer's actions and achievements against Paul's exemplars. Foxe could no more reconcile every contradiction he observed in the decisions Cranmer made than have his later biographers. Cranmer's treatment of John Lambert at his trial in 1539 especially made Foxe uneasy.

Within a decade Cranmer believed the same tenets for which he was willing to condemn Lambert to the stake. Was Cranmer truly a martyr? Foxe seemed to have doubts that he was hard-pressed to reconcile, for in his 1570 and subsequent editions of the *Actes and monuments* he suggested that by 'evil subscribing' to his recantations, Cranmer should have perished' for ever. Instead, 'by well recanting', he was preserved by God. Lest Cranmer 'should have lived longer with shame and rebuke, it pleased God to take him away'. God had fortified the Church 'with the testimony and blood of such a martyr'. His burning was 'a cross of tribulation' that God used to 'purge his offences in this world', 'not only of his recantation' but also of his standing against Lambert and any others with whose blood or burning Cranmer's hand had been polluted. Instead, by dying as he did with the utmost courage, Foxe thought Cranmer could be numbered among the martyrs of Christ.[18]

Notes

1 Cranmer's collect for Ascension from the 1549 Prayer Book: *The booke of the common prayer and administracion of the sacramentes and other rites and ceremonies of the Churche: after the vse of the Churche of England* (London: Edward Whitchurch, March 1549, RSTC 16267), 68r.

2 Thomas Cranmer, *Defensio verae et catholicae doctrinae de sacramento corporis et sanguinis Christi* (Emden [Egidius van der Erve], 1557, RSTC 6005), A8v.

3 John Parkhurst, *Ludicra siue Epigrammata iuuenilia* (London: John Daye, 1573, *RSTC* 19299), 183.

4 John Bale, *Scriptorvm Illustrium maioris Brytanniae, quam nunc Angliam et Scotiam uocant: Catalogus.* (Basle: Joannis Oporium, 1557, 1559), 691.

5 P. M. Black, 'Matthew Parker's Search for Cranmer's "great notable written books"', *The Library*, fifth series, 29 (1974), 312–22.

6 C. H. Garrett, *The Marian Exiles* (Cambridge, 1938), p. 136; *Zurich Letters*, 1, 8; the will of Sir John Markham, made 1 April 1559 and proved 28 October 1559, TNA:PRO, PROB 11/42B, 397v–398v.

7 The will of Thomas Norton, TNA:PRO, PROB 11/66, 276v.

8 Black, 'Matthew Parker's Search', 312–22.

9 D. Selwyn, *The Library of Thomas Cranmer*, Oxford Bibliographical Society, third series, 1 (1996).

10 The will of Edward Whitchurch, made 26 November 1562 and proved 3 December 1562, TNA:PRO, PROB 11/45, 227r–227v.

11 See Mary Prior's account of Margaret Cranmer's life in the *ODNB*.

12 Jane Dawson, *John Knox* (New Haven, 2015), 90–108.

13 *The seconde tome of homelyes of such matters as were promysed and intituled in the former part of homelyes, set out by the aucthoritie of the Quenes Maiestie: and to be read in euery paryshe churche agreablye* (London: Richard Jugge and John Cawood, 1563, RSTC 13663), R. Bond, ed., Certain Sermons or Homilies (1547) (Toronto, 1987), 9.

14 P. Grindal, *Archbishop Grindal, 1519–1583: The Struggle for a Reformed Church* (London, 1979).

15 G. Bray, ed., *The Anglican Canons 1529–1947*, Church of England Record Society, 6 (1998), xliii–liv.

16 *Reformatio legum ecclesiasticarum ex authoritate primum Regis Henrici. 8. inchoata: deinde per Regem Edouardum 6. Prouecta* (London: John Day, 1571, RSTC 6006); G. Bray, ed., *Tudor Church Reform: The Henrician Canons of 1535 and the Reformatio Legum Ecclesiasticarum*, Church of England Record Society, 8 (2000), lxxxvii–cv.

17 1 Timothy 3:1–7; Titus 1:7–9.

18 Foxe 1570, 2, 1888.

Suggestions for further reading

We are living in a golden age for scholarship on the Tudor dynasty and on the Reformation. The following is only a brief list of recommendations from a much larger array of books, articles, and Internet materials that will interest the general reader as well as the student.

General reading on the Tudors

Over the last five decades, Henry VIII and his reign have been the subject of many perceptive studies of lasting value. As a starting place, readers might like to consult entries for individual members of the Tudor court through *The Oxford Dictionary of National Biography (ODNB)*, which is available in bound volumes in research libraries and on the Internet through local and university libraries.

J. J. Scarisbrick's *Henry VIII* (Yale, 1997), which was first published in 1968, remains unequalled for its examination of the king's 'Divorce' from Katherine of Aragon, the royal supremacy, and the diplomatic conundrums that the king confronted in setting policy for the realm. In the Routledge Historical Biography series, *Henry VIII* by L. Wooding (second edition, London, 2015) is unusually helpful. D. Starkey's *Six Wives: The Queens of Henry VIII* (New York, 2003) is a valuable guide to all of Henry's marriages. E. Ives produced an important biography: *The Life and Death of Anne Boleyn: 'The Most Happy'* (Oxford, 2005). For her religion, see E. Ives, 'Anne Boleyn on Trial Again', *JEH*, vol. 62 (2011), pp. 766–8. His last book, *Lady Jane Grey: A Tudor Mystery* (Oxford, 2009), unpacks the confusing events that brought Mary Tudor to the throne, and it provides a sensitive account of the brief life of 'the nine days' queen'. In addition to his award-winning biography of Thomas Cranmer, D. MacCulloch has also written extensively for the sixteenth century and the Reformation, including *The Boy King: Edward VI and the Protestant Reformation* (London, 2001). For the Routledge Historical Biography series, J. R. Richards has written *Mary Tudor* (London, 2008) and *Elizabeth I* (London, 2011).

As an introduction to the factional struggles inside the Tudor court, many people now start with H. Mantel's award-winning trilogy on the career of Thomas Cromwell, beginning with *Wolf Hall*, and *Bring Up the Bodies*. Non-fiction studies of Cromwell's career include *Policy and Police: The Enforcement of the Reformation in the Age of Thomas Cromwell* (Cambridge, 1985) by G. R. Elton; *The Rise of Thomas Cromwell: Power and Politics in the Reign of Henry VIII, 1485–1534* (New Haven, 2015) by M. Everett; and *Thomas Cromwell: Servant to Henry VIII* by D. Loades (2015). Further work on Cromwell is expected by D. MacCulloch.

General reading on the Reformation

Martin Luther continues to command attention for his instrumental role in challenging the power of the Roman Catholic Church. In addition to many other valuable studies, readers who want to understand Luther from the perspective of a successful author would do well to read A. Pettegree's *Brand Luther: How an Unheralded Monk Turned His Small Town into a Center of Publishing, Made Himself the Most Famous Man in Europe – and Started the Protestant Reformation* (Penguin, 2015). Professor Pettegree has also written *Reformation and the Culture of Persuasion* (Cambridge, 2005). In the Routledge Historical Biography series, M. A. Mullitt has written a comprehensive introduction in *Martin Luther* (London, 2014).

For other important Reformation figures, see M. Greschat's *Martin Bucer: A Reformer and His Times* (2004), J. Dawson's *John Knox* (New Haven, 2015), T. Kirby's *The Zurich Connection and*

Tudor Political Theology (Leiden, 2007), as well as many other valuable studies. Amongst recent biographies of Sir Thomas More is Peter Ackroyd's *The Life of Thomas More* (London, 1998). Also recommended is A. Dillon's *Michelangelo and the English Martyrs* (Aldershot, 2012).

For parish life in England before the Reformation, E. Duffy's *The Stripping of the Altars: Traditional Life in England 1400–1580* (New Haven, 2005) is unsurpassed except by his *Fires of Faith: Catholic England under Mary Tudor* (New Haven, 2010).

Readers will also want to consult P. Marshall's *The Oxford Illustrated History of the Reformation* (Oxford, 2015) and A. Ryrie's *Being Protestant in Reformation Britain* (Oxford, 2013).

Index

Abell, Thomas 151
adiaphora 208
Agrippa, Henricus Cornelius 54
Aldington, Kent 57, 78
Alesius, Alexander 102, 110,
    113–14, 118, 121,
    145–6, 225
Anabaptism 9, 134, 140–2, 206–7
Anne Boleyn, queen 39, 43, 55–6,
    58, 61–2, 67, 71–8, 82–3, 85,
    89, 98–9, 105–20, 133, 147,
    151, 159
Anne of Cleves, queen 148–51,
    162, 177, 227–8
Aristotle 6, 25
Arthur, prince of Wales 40–4
Aske, Robert 124–5
Askew, Anne 157, 171–7, 187–8,
    207, 236
Askew, Edward 173
Aslockton, Notts. 13–15, 42, 197
Audley, Thomas 74, 79, 82–5,
    89–90, 114–16, 140, 143,
    150, 156
Augsburg Confession 103,
    137, 143

Bale, John 27, 32, 69, 175,
    187–8, 242
baptism 121, 141, 198, 204
Barbarossa 101

Barnes, Robert 19, 101, 138, 141,
    149–51, 173, 177
Barton, Elizabeth 10, 78–84, 136
Basel 30, 49, 99, 133, 203, 207
Battle of Mühlberg 187
Beaufort, Lady Margaret 15,
    20, 26
Becon, Thomas 167
Bekesbourne, Kent 171
Benson, William (*alias* Boston),
    abbot and dean of
    Westminster 16–17, 22, 33,
    69, 84–5, 120, 158, 193, 202
Berthelet, Thomas 48
Bible 101, 123, 125, 139–40,
    165–6, 187–94, 197; English
    (New Testament) 3, 67, 71–2,
    88, 132–3, 165; Great Bible
    (1539, 1540) 142, 149, 163
Bigod, Sir Francis 124
Bilney, Robert 19, 34, 50–1, 72,
    86, 91
Bingham, Jane (Cranmer)
    (sister) 168
Bland, John 167
Bocher, Joan 10, 206–7, 209
Bocking, Edmund 78–9, 81, 83
Boleyn, George, Lord Rochford
    44, 77, 114, 116
Boleyn, Jane, Lady Rochford
    161–2

Boleyn, Thomas, earl of Wiltshire 43–5, 47, 91, 120; *see also* Anne Boleyn, queen; Carey, Mary (Boleyn)

Bonner, Edmund, bishop of London 163, 172, 192, 206, 225, 234–8

Book of Common Prayer 1, 3, 170; first (1549) 137, 186–212; second (1552) 192, 209–10, 225, 228; third (1559) 244–5

Book of Homilies: first (1547) 3, 188–94, 218; second (1563) 245

Boston, Lincs. 13

Boxley, Kent 80, 135–6

Brandon, Charles, duke of Suffolk 74–5, 83, 91, 111, 124, 146–7, 149, 156

Brandon, Katherine, duchess of Suffolk 198

Bray, Gerald 219–20

Bray, Lady Katherine 26

Bredon, Worc. 46–7

Brenz, Johann 52

Bristol 102

Brooks, James, bishop of Gloucester 232

Brooks, Peter Newman 8

Bucer, Martin 1, 8, 50, 55, 99, 133, 140, 146, 148, 175, 192, 203–6, 208–11

Bullinger, Heinrich 1, 7, 99, 133, 174, 181, 203–4, 208, 222, 231

Bullock, Henry 25, 28

Burchard, Franz 137–40, 142, 148

Butler, John 134–5

Butts, Dr William 42, 157, 169–70, 197

Calais 66, 134–5, 143

Calvin, John 1, 8, 49, 99, 174, 181, 211, 236, 245

Cambridge: Buckingham College (Magdalene) 23; Corpus Christi College 167, 243; Jesus College 22–7, 32–5, 39–40, 69, 76; King's College 39; University of Cambridge 19–35, 42, 46, 204, 209–10

Campeggio, Lorenzo Cardinal 34–5

Canterbury: Cathedral 70, 78–80, 103, 136, 158–60, 166–70, 207, 225–6; Christ Church priory 70, 78, 80, 158; diocese of 3; Palace 168; province of 3; Six Preachers 158–60, 166–70; town of 104, 148

Capito, Wolfgang 119, 203

Capon, John (*alias* Salcot) 69, 79–80, 163

Capon, William 33–5, 76

Carey, Mary (Boleyn) 44, 117

Carey, William 44

Cartwright, Agnes (Cranmer) (sister) 225

Cartwright, Edmund (brother-in-law) 225

Cecil, William 23, 219

Champion, Richard 134–5, 159–60

Chapuys, Eustace 57–9, 109, 111

Charles V, Holy Roman Emperor 4, 7, 31, 40, 45, 51–2, 56, 76, 85, 101, 109, 111, 113, 115–16, 120, 149, 164, 176–7, 187, 196, 229, 245

Cheke, Sir John 23, 211, 219

Church: English 1–2, 9–10, 71–3, 98–100, 103, 121, 136–7, 170, 187–94, 209, 226, 229–30, 238, 242–6; Roman Catholic 8–9, 104, 136–8; *see also* Council of Trent; *Forty-Two Articles*; *Institution of a Christian Man*; *A Necessary Doctrine*; papacy; *Ten Articles*

Church Councils 77, 79, 101, 112, 120, 133, 136, 211–12, 234; *see also* Council of Trent

Clement VII 40, 45–7, 60, 76–8, 83, 117–18

Cochleus, John 54

Colchester, Essex 25, 141

Cole, Henry 237

Collinson, Patrick 22, 28, 245

Cologne 55, 211

Consensus of Zürich 174–5, 204, 211

Constable, Sir Robert 124–5

Constantine the Great 136

Convocation: Canterbury Province 44–5, 47–8, 60, 66, 68–70, 73, 83, 87–8, 104–5, 110–11, 116–22, 124–5, 141, 143–6, 162–5, 171, 219–21, 226, 228; York Province 69, 120–2, 124–5, 141, 143–6, 219–21, 226, 228; *see also* Parliament

Cornwall 201–3

Council of Trent 2, 176, 178, 211–12

Coverdale, Miles 33, 72

Cowbridge, William 140, 233

Cox, Richard 33, 172, 245

Cranmer, Agnes (Hatfield) (mother) 15, 19–20, 23

Cranmer, Alice (sister) 15, 81, 108, 225

Cranmer, Edmund (brother) 4, 19–20, 23, 25–6, 81, 107–9, 136, 225–6, 242–3

Cranmer, John (brother) 16, 19

Cranmer, Margaret (Preu) (second wife) 54–5, 134, 145, 167–9, 196–7, 212, 225–6, 242–4

Cranmer, Thomas (father) 8, 13, 15–16, 18–20

Cranmer, Thomas (nephew) 19

Cranmer, Thomas, 68th arch-bishop of Canterbury 1, 56–61, 66–93, 106–9, 116–17, 126–7, 136–7, 225; as archdeacon of Taunton 44–5; arrest 2, 224–7; beginning of career 34–5, 39–44; birth 13; canon law reforms 72, 104–5, 219–20 246; *Catechism* 195–6, 221, 228; coat of arms 8, 13–15; consecration of 57–60, 71, 232; in debate against the Six Articles 142–4, 194–5; *Defence of the True and Catholic Doctrine* 205–6, 230, 242; as diplomat 45–7, 51–7, 67–8; enthronement 77, 79–80; as evangelical 27–35; execution 2, 10, 152, 237–8; first marriage 22–5, 70; as heretic 2, 27, 103, 160, 167–70, 229–38; and homi-lies 163, 188–94; hospitality of 108, 171; iconoclasm 80, 135–6, 160, 193, 200; imprisonment 2, 227–38; income 67; in Italy 45–7; as lecturer 26–35; library 3–4, 30, 243–4; and liturgies 52–3, 72, 134, 170, 186–212; as Lutheran 51–7, 135, 143–6, 171–6, 195–6; as martyr 2, 10, 238, 242, 246–7; ordina-tion 5, 25–7; and the pallium 57–9, 231–5; as preacher 31, 71, 85–6, 103–4, 107, 111; properties 67, 76, 107–8, 122, 177, 197–8; recanta-tions 2, 10, 233–8; as rector of Bredon, 46–7; schooling 16–18; second marriage 54–5; titles as archbishop 66, 69, 86–8; as traitor 2, 227–38; as undergraduate 19–25; visitations 80–1, 85–7, 102, 123; *see also Book of Common Prayer*; *Book of Homilies*

Cranmer, Thomas (son) 197, 212, 225–6, 242–3
Croke, Richard 28, 46, 232
Crome, Edward 32, 50, 106, 141, 146, 151, 159, 171–6, 235
Cromwell, Gregory 85
Cromwell, Thomas 4, 15, 34–5, 39, 50–1, 69, 73, 79, 82–5, 87–92, 98–122, 132–52, 156, 160, 163
Croydon, Surrey 67, 70, 74, 84, 180, 204
Culpeper, Thomas 161–2
Cummings, Brian 198

Damplip, Adam 135, 147
Dantiscus, Johannes, bishop of Warmia 54–5, 151–2
Darcy, Thomas 124
Davington, Kent 107–8
Day, John 246
Daye, George 69, 138, 163, 166
Denny, Joan 173–6
Denny, Sir Anthony 157–8, 173–6, 178–81, 202
Dereham, Francis 161–2
Devon 201–3
Douglas, Lady Mary 162
Drum, Michael 159
Dudley, Guilford 222, 228–9
Dudley, John, earl of Warwick and duke of Northumberland 176, 202, 220, 227

Eck, Johannes 203
Edward III, king of England 59
Edward VI, king of England 1, 69, 125–7, 133, 156, 164, 178–82, 186–212, 220–4, 226
Elizabeth I, queen of England 2, 4, 77, 82–3, 109–10, 118–19, 169–70, 177, 180, 221, 224, 227–8, 244–6

Elton, G. R. 147
Elyot, Sir Thomas 51–4
Emden 207, 209, 344
Erasmus, Desiderius 5, 18, 25, 28–30, 33, 35, 49, 57, 78, 193, 207
Eucharist 3, 6, 74–5, 121, 134, 139, 143–6, 172–6, 194–212, 229–30; *see also* Lord's Supper; Mass
evangelicalism 5, 114–15
Exeter, Devon 201

Faculty Office 82, 87
Fagius, Paul 203–4
faith 2, 5–6, 71, 165–6, 188–94, 209–10
Ferdinand II, king of Hungary 51, 56, 164
Ferrar, Robert, bishop of St David's 231, 237
Fetherstone, Richard 151
First Helvetic Confession 203
Fisher, John, bishop of Rochester 20, 30–1, 74, 79, 81–2, 84–6, 89–93, 98, 102–3, 166, 237
Fletcher, John 169–70
Forest, John 136–8, 140–1, 233
Forty-Two Articles (Thirty-Nine Articles) 3, 211, 218–19, 221, 235–6
Fox, Edward, bishop of Hereford 39–42, 44, 47–9, 69, 102–3, 120–1, 124–5, 133, 138–9, 142
Foxe, John 4, 10, 22–4, 30, 33, 42, 74, 146–7, 157, 169–70, 177–8, 187, 219–20, 233–8, 246–7
Francis I, king of France 43, 45–6, 51, 56, 77, 91, 101, 164, 177–8, 186–7
Frankfort 209, 244
Frith, John 10, 33–5, 74–6, 91, 173, 175

Gardiner, Stephen, bishop of Winchester, lord chancellor 4, 35, 39–42, 61, 68, 73, 87–8, 93, 100, 113–14, 117, 141–2, 149–52, 156, 160, 163, 164–70, 172–82, 186–212, 221, 223, 225, 227–8, 230–8
Garrard, Thomas 149–52
Geneva 1, 99
Ghinucci, Girolamo, bishop of Worcester 46–7, 86
Gloucester Cathedral 231
Gold, Henry 78–9, 81, 83
Goldwell, Thomas 80
Gonell, William 33
Goodrich, Thomas, bishop of Ely and lord chancellor 15–16, 22, 69, 121, 143–4, 210, 222–3
Grantham, Lincs. 15–16
Greenwich 77, 109, 149, 223
Gregory the Great, pope 66
Grey, Frances (Brandon), duchess of Suffolk 221
Grey, Lady Jane, queen of England 222–4, 227–9
Grindal, Edmund, archbishop of Canterbury 219, 245
Gryneaus, Simon 49, 99, 133, 146, 203
Gwent, Richard 59, 70, 104–5

Habsburg dynasty 4, 42, 101, 111, 228; *see also* Charles V; Ferdinand II; Philip II
Hadleigh, Suff. 67, 134, 173, 231
Hampton Court Palace 42, 126, 162, 177–8, 202
Harpsfield, John 190, 228, 230
Harpsfield, Nicholas, archdeacon of Canterbury 87–8, 168–9, 226, 238
Hatfield, Laurence (grandfather) 15–16
Hawkins, Nicholas 33, 48, 56, 6, 75–6, 79

Heath, Nicholas 69, 77, 80, 138, 141, 163, 172
Henry II, king of England 80
Henry II, king of France 202
Henry VII, king of England 14–15
Henry VIII, king of England 1, 8, 14, 18, 31, 34–5, 39–50, 54–5, 57–61, 67, 73–6, 78, 80, 82–3, 85, 88–9, 98–104, 107–27, 132–52, 156–82, 186–9, 202, 205, 219, 223–4, 236–7
Herbert, Anne (Parr) 158, 173–6
Herbert, Sir William 158, 173–6, 178–81
Herd, Dr John 243–4
heresy 79, 140–2, 230–8
Hermann V von Wied, archbishop of Cologne 55–6, 67, 198, 203–4, 211
Hewet, Andrew 75–6
Hilsey, John 102, 135, 145, 148
Holbeach, Henry (*alias* Rands), bishop of Lincoln 17, 33, 134, 187, 197
Holbeach, Joan 197
Hooper, John, bishop of Gloucester 208–9, 211, 226, 231, 237
Houghton, John 90–1
Howard, Henry, earl of Surrey 178–81
Howard, Thomas, third duke of Norfolk 44, 52–4, 82–3, 90, 111, 124, 146–7, 149, 152, 156, 160, 164, 172, 176, 178–81, 211, 225, 227
Hull, Yorks. 124
humanism 27–35
Hungary 51, 164

Institution of a Christian Man (Bishops' Book) 125–6, 139, 143, 157, 163
Interim 187, 196, 206–7
Ipswich, Suffolk 34–5, 44

Italian Wars 56, 164
Ives, Eric 224

James V, king of Scotland 160, 162, 164
Jane Seymour, queen 110, 118, 120, 125–7, 181
Jerome, William 149–52
Jewel, John 230, 242–3
John, Elector of Saxony 41, 49
John Frederick I, Elector of Saxony 53, 77, 100–3, 137–40, 146, 186
Jonas, Justin 195
Joye, George 72–3
justification 6, 29–30, 85, 100, 121, 126, 138, 149, 165, 190–1, 193, 209, 211, 218; *see also* faith; works

Katherine of Aragon, queen 34–5, 39–43, 45–6, 50–1, 54, 58–60, 77, 82–3, 85, 87, 101, 109–15, 118–19, 133, 151, 223–4
Katherine Howard, queen 149–51, 160–2
Katherine Parr, queen 157–8, 167, 173–6, 178
Kelly, Henry Ansgar 117
Kenninghall, Suffolk 223–4
Kent 3, 67, 70, 74, 81, 103, 105, 107–9, 113, 160, 166–72, 207, 225, 228
Kett, Robert 201–2
King Henry VIII (All is True) 169–70
Kirkstall Abbey 197–8
Knole 67, 113, 177
Knox, John 209–11, 219, 244–5

Lambert, John 10, 140–3, 246–7
Lambeth Palace 3, 14, 67, 84, 92, 102, 114, 116, 118, 124, 136–9, 146–7, 167, 173, 197, 201, 204, 207–9, 227, 231–2

Lascelles, John 160–1, 173–6
Lasco, John à (alias Jan Laski) 207–11
Latimer, Hugh, bishop of Worcester 15, 19, 22, 25, 34–5, 50, 69, 72–3, 75, 79, 99, 102, 106–7, 112, 116, 120–1, 125, 133, 136–8, 141–5, 163, 173–6, 207, 221, 229–35
Lawrence, Robert 90–1
Lee, Edward, archbishop of York 42, 69, 117, 120–2, 124–5, 187
Lefèvre, Jacques 5, 28–30, 33, 35, 43, 191–2, 207
Legh, Lee 168–70
Lehmberg, S. E. 112
Leicestershire 15
Leland, John 19
Leo X, pope 30–1, 52
Lincolnshire 13, 160; Rebellion (1536–7) 122–5, 133, 160, 201
Lollardy 9, 207
Lombard, Peter 19, 27
London 84–5, 90–1, 125, 180, 222–4; Paul's Cross 31, 79, 110–12, 135–6, 146, 149–51, 167, 171–6, 194, 207; Smithfield 136–8, 141, 151, 207, 209, 230; St Paul's Cathedral 61, 87, 122, 187, 207, 210, 226; Stranger churches 207–9; The Tower 85, 90–1, 114, 116, 118–19, 150–1, 167, 169, 180, 194, 202, 205, 223, 227–9
Longland, John, bishop of Lincoln 46–7, 58, 61
Lord's Supper 7–8, 74–5, 121, 171–6, 197–201, 203–4, 209–10, 244–5; *see also Book of Common Prayer*; Eucharist; Mass; sacraments
Louis II, king of Hungary 51

Louth, Lincs. 123
Luther, Katharina (von Bora)
    54, 197
Luther, Martin 5–7, 9, 27–8, 30–1,
    33, 41, 49–50, 52, 54, 57,
    74, 101, 106, 113, 120, 133,
    152, 165, 174–5, 195, 203–4,
    234, 238
Lutherans 8–9, 133, 187, 195–6,
    211; *see also* Schmalkalden,
    League of

MacCulloch, Diarmaid 4, 22–4,
    27, 163, 181
Margaret (Tudor), queen of
    Scotland 162
Marguerite, queen of Navarre 43
Markham, Sir John 15, 26, 34,
    124, 193, 225, 243
marriage of clergy 24, 138–9,
    143–6, 151, 168–9, 197–8
Marshall, Peter 100, 136–7
Mary I, queen of England 2, 40,
    58, 71, 83, 109, 113, 116,
    119–20, 177, 220–38, 242,
    244, 246
Mary (Tudor), queen of
    France 221
Mary of Hungary 51, 111
Mary, Queen of Scots 164
Mass 6, 72, 120–2, 138–9, 143,
    157, 176–7, 187, 203, 206,
    225, 238; in English 134; in
    German 52–3; *see also* Lord's
    Supper
McEntegart, Rory 99, 142
Melanchthon, Philip 27, 31,
    49–50, 54–5, 99, 101–2, 113,
    137, 146, 148, 174, 188,
    207, 211
Mirk, John 189
Mohás, Battle of 51
More, Sir Thomas, lord chancellor
    33, 42, 44, 47, 49–50, 57, 68,
    74–5, 78–9, 81, 84–5, 89–93,
    98, 103–4, 111, 135, 237

Morice, James 26
Morice, Ralph 4, 14, 18–19,
    22–6, 33, 40–2, 70, 77, 88,
    120, 144, 146–7, 150, 161,
    165–70, 177–8, 193
Morice, William 173
Mortlake, Surrey 67, 122
Moyle, Sir Thomas 164–70
Myconius, Friedrich 137–9, 142

A Necessary Doctrine (the King's
    Book) 163, 165–6, 193
Nero, emperor of Rome 232, 245
Nevinson, Anne (Bingham)
    (niece) 168
Nevinson, Christopher 167–8,
    193, 207
Nicodemites 236
Nix, Richard 50, 86
Norton, Alice (Cranmer)
    (niece) 243
Norton, Margaret (Cranmer)
    (daughter) 197, 212,
    225–6, 243
Norton, Thomas (son-in-law)
    243–4, 246
Norwich, Norfolk 202–3
Nottinghamshire 13, 113, 225
Nun of Kent: *see* Barton, Elizabeth
Nuremberg 5, 28, 51–6, 106, 134,
    197; Diet of 52

Ochino, Bernardino 196
Oecolampadius 74–5, 135, 205
Order of the Communion 195,
    199–200
Osiander, Andreas 52–6, 99,
    195–7, 211, 226, 238
Osiander, Katharina (Preu) 54
Otford 67, 113, 140, 177
Oxford 2, 60, 229–38; Balliol
    College 233; Cardinal College
    33–5, 44; Christ Church
    Cathedral 234; University of
    Oxford 33–5, 46, 165–70,
    188, 196, 201, 226, 237–8

Paget, Sir William 156, 176–7, 202
papacy 8, 58, 61, 67, 77, 81, 83, 87, 91–3, 100, 103, 111–12, 119–20, 134
Paris 49; University of 28, 46, 207
Parker, Margaret 197
Parker, Matthew, archbishop of Canterbury 22–4, 33–4, 114, 197, 209, 243–5
Parkhurst, John 242
Parliament 44–6, 47–8, 57, 60, 81–3, 98, 104–5, 110–13, 116–22, 143–6, 151, 157, 166–7, 171, 178, 194–6, 206, 210, 219–20, 222, 228; *see also* Convocation
Parris, George van 209
Parsons, Robert 168
Paul III, pope 91, 101, 103, 120, 133, 141
Paul IV, pope 231
Percy, Henry, earl of Northumberland 43, 117
Perne, Andrew 209–10
Peterborough Abbey 109
Philip, Landgrave of Hesse 41, 49, 77, 100–3, 134, 140, 148, 178, 187
Philip II, king of Spain and England 228, 232
Philips, Rowland 70, 84
Philpot, John, archdeacon of Winchester 228
Pilgrimage of Grace, Yorks. (1536–7) 122–5, 133, 160, 201
Pius V, pope 246
Plantagenet, Arthur, viscount Lisle 135–6
Poland 51, 151, 207
Pole, Reginald Cardinal, archbishop of Canterbury 2, 46, 48–9, 60, 137, 147, 169, 230, 232–8, 242–4, 246
Pollard, A. F. 4

Polycarp, bishop of Smyrna 242
Ponet, John, bishop of Winchester 69, 206, 221
Powell, Edward 151
praemunire 44, 57, 68, 86, 119, 132, 137–8
Prayer Book risings of 1549 200–3
Prebendaries' Plot: *see* Canterbury Cathedral
predestination 166
Privy Council 156–82, 188–212, 219, 222–5, 227, 244
Protestantism 1, 41, 72; *see also* Lutherans, Swiss Reform

Ratramnus of Corbie 174–6, 196
Regensburg (Ratisbon), Diet of 51, 178
Reynolds, Richard 90–1
Richard III, king of England 14
Ridley, Jasper 4, 27, 146
Ridley, Lancelot 159
Ridley, Nicholas, bishop of London 8, 15, 159, 172–6, 186, 193–6, 206–11, 224, 228, 229–35, 237
Ridley, Robert 22
Rochester, Kent 82, 84, 85, 148
Rogers, John 228, 230–1
Rome, city of 34, 39–40, 45–7, 51, 231
Roper, William 104
rosary 72
Rosell, Dorothy (Cranmer) (sister) 77
Rosell, Harold (brother-in-law) 16, 77, 113
Russell, Lord John 201
Ryrie, Alec 100, 146, 176, 206

sacraments 121; *see also* baptism; Eucharist; Lord's Supper
Salcot, John: *see* Capon, John
Sampson, Richard 116, 138, 140–1
Sander, Nicholas 168

Scarisbrick, J. J. 178
Schmalkalden, League of 49–50, 52, 73, 98, 100–3, 113, 133–4, 137–9, 143, 178, 187; *see also* Lutherans
scholasticism 20, 27
Scory, John, bishop of Chichester 159, 168–70, 227
Selwyn, David 27
Serles, Robert 159–60, 232
Servetus, Michael 9
Seymour, Edward, earl of Hertford and duke of Somerset 110, 126, 149, 156, 176, 178–81, 186–212
Seymour, Thomas 108; *see also* Jane Seymour, queen
Shakespeare, William 3, 10, 170
Shaxton, Nicholas, bishop of Salisbury 69, 121, 144–5, 163, 173–6
Sibylle of Cleves 139
Skyp, John 117
Smyth, Richard 188, 196, 206, 229, 232
Soto, Pedro de 233–8
Southwell, Notts. 14–15
Speyer 52; Diet of 7, 41
St Ambrose 121
St Augustine of Canterbury 57
St Augustine of Hippo 20, 34
St Barlaam of Antioch 238
St Basil 189, 238
St Gregory Nazianzine 149
St Jerome 28, 123
St John of Beverley 14
St John Chrysostom 149, 189–90, 196, 238
St Mary, the Blessed Virgin 7, 80, 121, 136, 141, 200
St Mary Magdalene 156
St Paul 5, 29–30, 71, 188, 190–1, 246
St Peter 232
St Stephen 238
St Thomas the Apostle 13
St Thomas Aquinas 6, 20

St Thomas Becket 78, 80, 122, 136, 141–2
Standish, Henry 59
Stokesley, John 4, 46, 48, 61, 73, 75, 86–8, 93, 100, 110, 116, 121, 132, 136–8, 141, 145, 148, 163
Strasbourg 1, 99, 106, 119, 133, 196, 203, 208, 226, 231, 244–5
Strype, John 4, 181–2
Submission of the Clergy 68, 104–5, 219
Suleyman the Magnificent, sultan of the Ottoman Empire 51, 56, 164, 232
Sutterton, Lincs. 13
Swiss Reform 8–9, 49–50, 99, 135, 176, 203–4, 211, 245

Taunton, Devon 44
Taylor, Rowland 134, 193, 231
Ten Articles 120–3, 125–6, 143
Thirlby, Thomas, bishop of Westminster, and Ely 163–4, 179, 234–5
Thirty-Nine Articles: see Forty-Two Articles
Thornden, Richard, suffragan bishop of Dover 168–70, 226
transubstantiation 7–8, 27, 55, 122, 126, 135, 143–4, 200, 204–5, 218; *see also* Eucharist, Mass
Tudor dynasty 3, 14
Tunstall, Cuthbert, bishop of Durham 111, 138–9, 141–2, 149, 172, 182, 207, 211, 225, 227
Tyndale, William 50, 68, 71–2, 74, 91, 98, 111, 125, 173, 231

Vadian, Joachim 135
Vermigli, Peter Martyr 1, 196, 201, 204–6, 208–10, 226–7, 231

vestments controversy 176, 208–10, 235
Villagracia, Juan de 233–8

Walkenden, Humphrey 25, 28
Walsingham, Norfolk 135
Waltham 39–42
Warham, William, archbishop 9, 44–5, 50, 56–7, 59, 67–8, 70, 72, 76, 78, 105, 117, 141, 219
Warham, William, archdeacon 70, 79, 81, 168–9
Webster, Augustine 90–1
Welbeck Abbey 14, 16, 26
Westminster Abbey 61, 69, 158, 181–2, 225, 228
Whatton, Notts. 14–16, 18–19, 197
Whitchurch, Edward 242, 244
Whitehall Palace 118, 169, 180
Whitwell, John 17
Wilkinson, Thomas 16
William the Conqueror 13
Wilson, Nicholas 84, 138
Winchester Cathedral 102
Windsor 102
Windsor Castle 102, 124–5, 167, 181, 202, 210
Wisdom, Robert 167

Wittenberg 102–3, 113, 139, 152
Wittenberg Concord 203
Wolfe, Rayner 225–6, 244
Wolsey, Thomas Cardinal, archbishop of York 25, 31, 33–5, 40, 43–4, 47, 58, 69, 78, 82, 133, 145
Woolf, Virginia 10
Wootton, Nicholas 159
works, good 6, 188–94; *see also* faith; justification
Worms 52; Diet of 31
Wriothesley, Charles 148
Wriothesley, Thomas, lord chancellor 113–14, 152, 173, 180–1, 186
Wyatt, Sir Thomas 43, 117
Wyatt, Sir Thomas the younger 229
Wycliffe, John 9, 101

York 25
Young, John 209–10

Zürich 1, 7, 99, 133, 196, 208, 222, 231, 244
Zwingli, Huldrych 7, 9, 30, 49–50, 52, 74, 99, 135, 174, 203–5, 209, 238